COLORADO

CABINS LODGES & COUNTRY B&Bs

by

Hilton and Jenny Fitt-Peaster

Rocky Mountain Vacation Publishing, Inc.

Boulder, Colorado

5101 Pennsylvania Avenue, Boulder, Colorado 80303-2799

Photo Credits:
Front cover: a cabin at Rockmount, one of the many around Estes Park, Colorado, with the Continental Divide in the background © Hilton Fitt-Peaster, Boulder, Colorado.
Front cover inset: The Homestead cabin at T Lazy 7 Guest Ranch, near Aspen, Colorado.
Back cover (top to bottom):
Horseback riding in Rocky Mountain National Park, Colorado, © Jim Osterberg, Photostock, Estes Park, Colorado.
Mountain biking at Snow Mountain Ranch®, YMCA of the Rockies, Winter Park, Colorado, © Carl Scofield Photography, Breckenridge, Colorado.
Hiking in autumn above Bear Lake, Rocky Mountain National Park, Colorado, © Osterberg.
Cross country skiing at Bear Lake, Rocky Mountain National Park, Colorado, © Osterberg.
Fishing in front of Circle H Lodge on Lake Granby, a 39", 31 pound lake trout caught May 20, 1996 by Paul Navarre owner of Circle H Lodge, Granby, Colorado

Cover design: Robert L. Schram, BookEnds, Boulder, Colorado.

Library of Congress Catalog Card Number: 97-91551

Publisher's Cataloging-in-Publication
(Prepared by Quality Books, Inc.)

Fitt-Peaster, Hilton.
Colorado cabins, lodges & country B&Bs: scenic getaways for every season / by Hilton and Jenny Fitt-Peaster. -- 3rd ed.
p. cm.
Includes index.
ISBN: 1-883087-03-1
3rd ed. of: Colorado cabins, cottages & lodges.

1. Vacation homes--Colorado--Guidebooks. 2. Colorado--Guidebooks. I. Fitt-Peaster, Jenny. II. Title. III. Title: Colorado cabins, lodges and country B&Bs. IV. Title Colorado cabins, cottages and lodges.

TX907.3.C5F588 1997 647'.94788
QBI97-40199

Printed in the United States of America by Victor Graphics, Inc., Baltimore, MD

5 4 3 2

Contents

Colorado

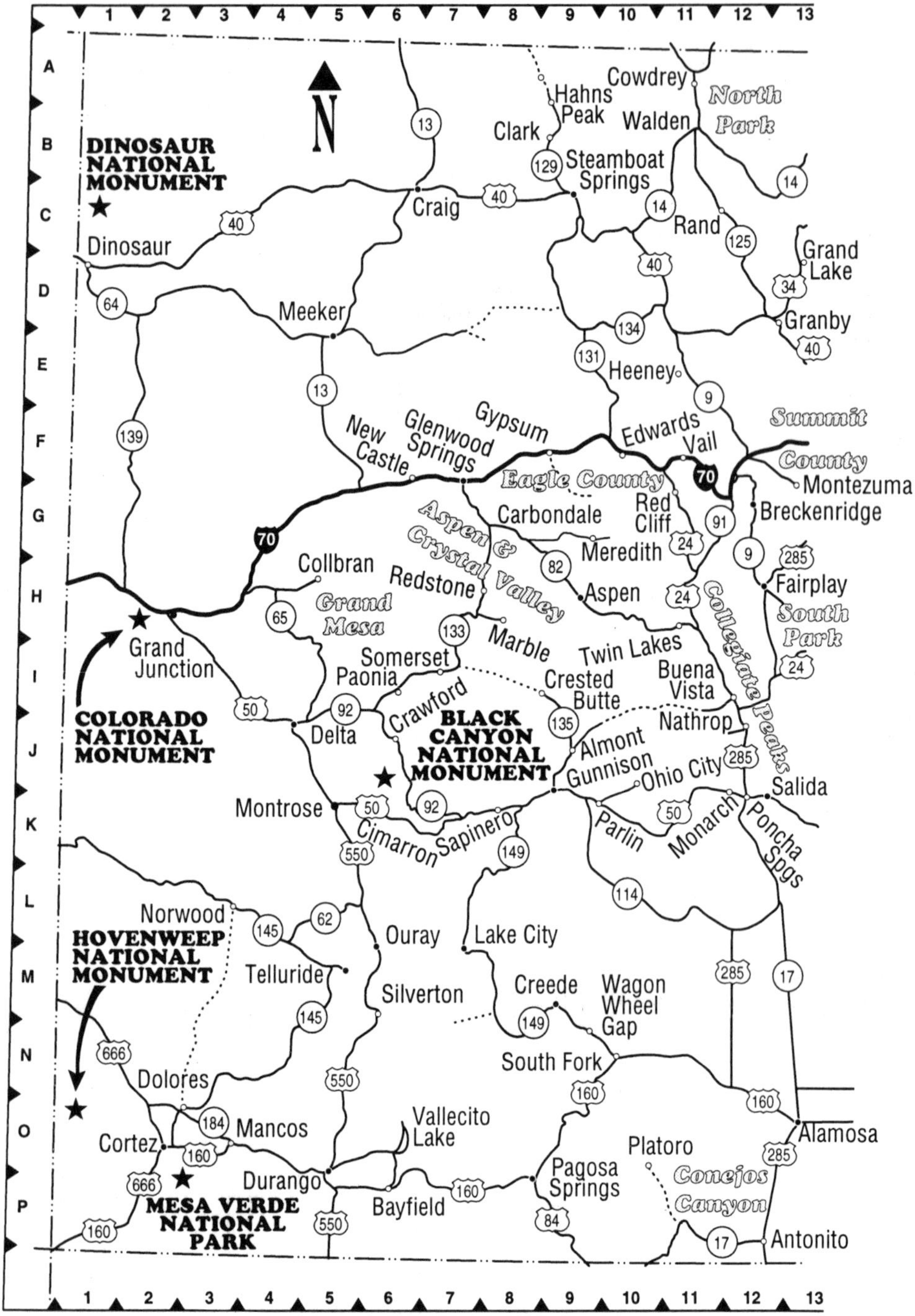
1 2 3 4 5 6 7 8 9 10 11 12 13
A B C D E F G H I J K L M N O P
N
DINOSAUR NATIONAL MONUMENT
Dinosaur
Craig
Clark
Hahns Peak
Cowdrey
Walden
North Park
Steamboat Springs
Rand
Grand Lake
Granby
Meeker
Heeney
New Castle
Glenwood Springs
Gypsum
Edwards
Vail
Summit County
Eagle County
Montezuma
Breckenridge
Carbondale
Red Cliff
Meredith
Aspen & Crystal Valley
Collbran
Redstone
Grand Mesa
Aspen
Fairplay
South Park
Collegiate Peaks
Grand Junction
Marble
Somerset
Paonia
Twin Lakes
Buena Vista
Crested Butte
COLORADO NATIONAL MONUMENT
Delta
Crawford
BLACK CANYON NATIONAL MONUMENT
Nathrop
Almont
Gunnison
Ohio City
Salida
Montrose
Cimarron
Sapinero
Parlin
Monarch
Poncha Spgs
Norwood
HOVENWEEP NATIONAL MONUMENT
Telluride
Ouray
Lake City
Silverton
Creede
Wagon Wheel Gap
South Fork
Dolores
Mancos
Cortez
Vallecito Lake
Alamosa
Platoro
Conejos Canyon
Durango
Pagosa Springs
MESA VERDE NATIONAL PARK
Bayfield
Antonito
13 40 129 14 125 34 64 134 131 9 139 70 91 24 82 285 65 133 50 92 135 550 149 114 62 145 666 184 160 84 17

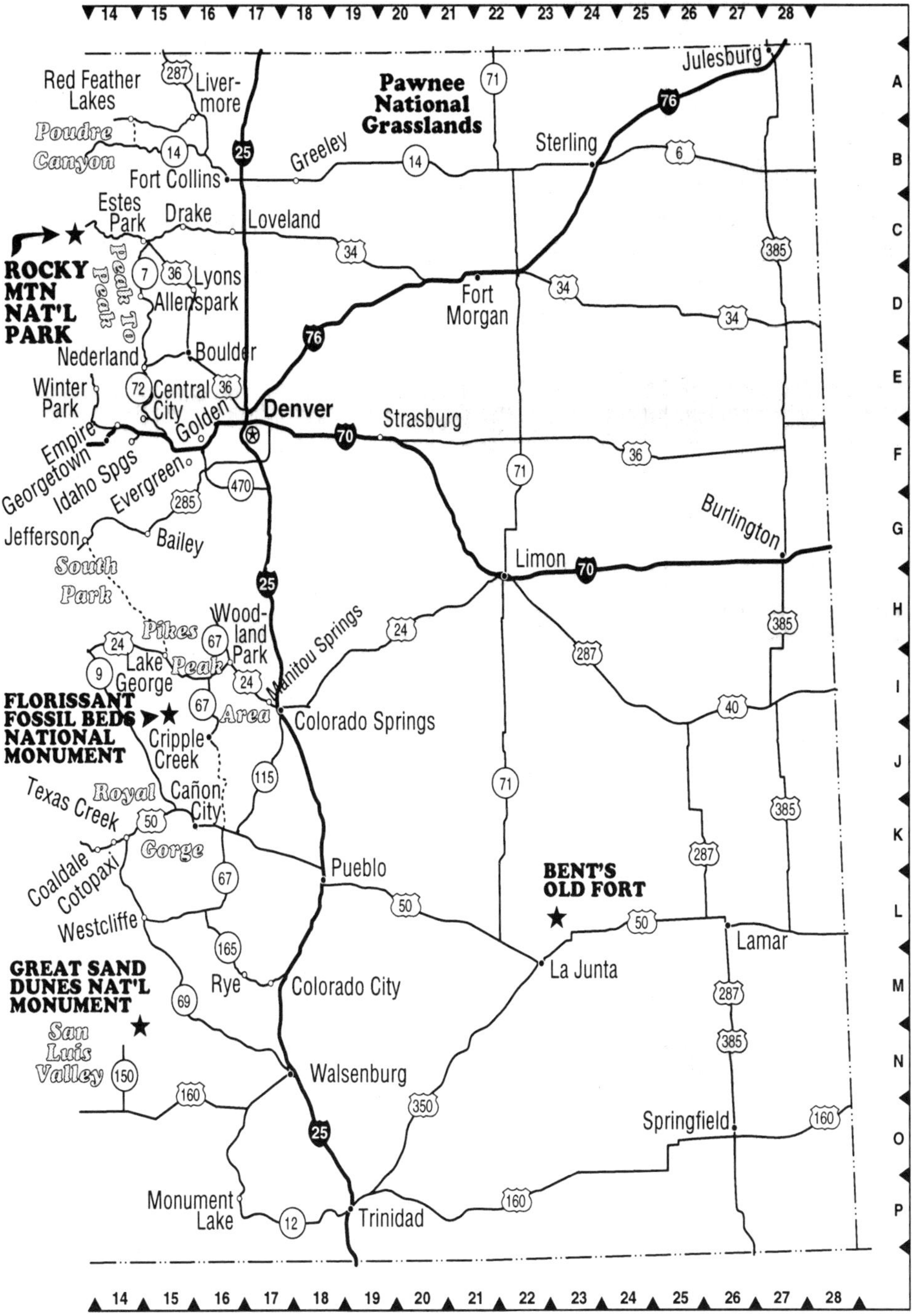

Note: not all highways, roads and towns appear on map

List of Towns & Areas

Foreword

This one-of-a-kind book offers answers to your questions about Colorado's abundant cabins, cottages, lodges and country B&Bs. In its pages, you'll find that romantic cabin getaway, the perfect family reunion cottage, remote trout stream lodge or winter recreation getaway.

I've known the authors, Hilton and Jenny Fitt-Peaster, for 15 years, and can assure you that no two people have traveled as many miles in this state seeking these sometimes hidden treasures. Hilton and Jenny have done all the work for you!

You'll find activities such as hiking, mountain biking, cross-country skiing, whitewater rafting, fly fishing, canoeing and more in fabulous locations throughout our state — many available right on the premises. The accommodations in this guidebook range from rustic to opulent, timberline to trailhead, historic to modern, in-town to remote wilderness. Your dining options range from cozy kitchenettes to hearty family-style ranch fare to spectacular gourmet meals. The possibilities are endless!

I invite you to select a cabin, cottage, lodge or country bed and breakfast and discover all Colorado and its friendly hosts has to offer. Let your adventure begin!

Rich Meredith
President
Colorado Travel & Tourism Authority
March 1997

Preface

Colorado — an outdoor recreation paradise. **But where do you stay to escape the ordinary and truly live the Colorado experience?** Surely there are places off the beaten path which offer diverse, memorable and unique adventures — places which are extremely enjoyable to visit and explore, yet close enough so you can enjoy vacation activities.

We know where they are. We drive 6-8,000 miles each summer (since 1988) on Colorado's highways and byways searching out and visiting Colorado's wonderful cabins, cottages, lodges and country B&Bs, even some hidden away in remote places.

To share our discoveries, we wrote the first definitive guide to Colorado's cabins, cottages and lodges in 1993. Here now is our third edition — expanded, rewritten and improved. We hope you like our index (beginning on page 271). Its arranged so you can easily find a vacation spot that suits your special interests.

Consider a fall, winter or spring vacation/getaway, when rates can be lower, reservations easier, things are quieter and the scenery even more spectacular.

Feel free to give us any feedback or comments about this book — and be sure to tell your cabin, cottage, lodge and B&B hosts that you read about them in this book.

We wish to acknowledge the invaluable services of the following people, without whom this book would have never been published: Rebekah Fitt-Peaster (our daughter) our Associate Publisher since 1992, Kathe Conti for expert and creative editing, Cindy Fedor for proofreading, Rodney Sauer of RDD Consultants for computer layout design, Arthur Fitt of FittWare Consultants (our son) for making our computer database (he designed) talk with our word processing program, Bob Schram of BookEnds for cover design, Bob Quam for his computer support, and to all the cabin, lodge and country B&B owner/operator-hosts in this book who double checked the accuracy of their listings and supplied artwork.

There's something special about staying in a cabin. We hope our book helps you find the right resorts for your fun and recreation. Enjoy Colorful Colorado!

Hilton and Jenny Fitt-Peaster
Authors
March 1997

How to Use This Book

This book describes a variety of cabins, lodges, country B&Bs and fun things to do. The book is organized into chapters. Each chapter covers a town or area. Chapters are arranged A–Z by town or area name. Within each chapter, the properties are arranged A–Z. This makes it easy for you to find these accommodations in Colorado.

Use the List of Towns & Areas to locate the town or area which interests you. Most towns are grouped together into a common geographic area. The first page of each chapter details information about the area plus nearby fun things to do. Map coordinates are also shown. Use these to help locate the town on the map at the front of this book. These map coordinates are the same ones used on the official State of Colorado highway map.

Definitions—Types of Accommodations

We realize you may not be familiar with the terms we use in this book, so here are definitions for you.

Resort means any "cabin resort" or accommodation listed in this book. We are talking about "Mom-and-Pop" resorts. To some people, the word "resort" only means a world-class, all-inclusive, expensive place. We use the term "resort" more broadly.

Cabin, Cottage, Chalet or Guest House — what you call them oft' depends on where you're from. Cabins are usually log or log-sided; cottages are frequently frame construction. Here, we use "cabin" to mean all of these.

Vacation/Mountain Home generally describes an accommodation unit with three or more bedrooms, separate living areas (kitchen, living room, dining room) and more modern amenities than a cabin. This is truly a "home away from home". Often these homes are used for multi family getaways or small retreats.

Housekeeping means equipped with a kitchenette or kitchen, cooking and eating utensils so *you* can keep house, and the hosts do *not* provide daily maid service. Accommodations with kitchens are not supplied with food, so remember to bring your own as it is seldom sold at the resort.

Modern means a bathroom (toilet and hot shower or tub) are inside the cabin.

Rustic either describes atmosphere or style, *or* means a bathroom is *not* inside the cabin, but usually in another building.

Primitive means no electricity.

Camper Cabin usually located at a campground, means an inexpensive, non-housekeeping, rustic and sometimes primitive cabin. Bring your own sleeping bags or blankets. Camper cabins are usually not heated — think of them as a "wooden tent." A brand of camper cabin is a Kamping Kabin™, which is a trademark of Kampgrounds of America, Inc.

Lodge Room, often called a historic hotel room, includes linens, a bathroom in the room or a shared bath down the hall. Rooms in a lodge are usually entered from inside the building. Some lodge rooms are more akin to a small apartment or suite of rooms, which may include a kitchen.

Bed and Breakfast room may be in a lodge, inn or owner's home, and always includes breakfast.

Rates

Cabin and room prices constantly change, both seasonally and annually, therefore we provide a price range. The 1997 rates for *two* people per night are indicated. Please note the rates listed are the best available information at time of publication. As we cannot guarantee the rates, be sure to verify them and other important items and features when making your reservations.

Abbreviations

After Credit Cards:

V means **V**isa
M means **M**asterCard
A means **A**merican Express
D means **D**iscover

Glyphs Used in Book

At the Resort:

 Hot Tub/Spa

 Snacks served

 Some Meals served (inquire if Breakfast, Lunch, or Dinner)

 Well behaved Pets are okay on leash

 Well behaved Pets are okay on leash for a fee or security deposit

 Group Meeting area either indoor or outdoor.
In the index **i** indicates indoor and **o** outdoor

 Guest's Horses Permitted

 RV Sites

 Tent Sites

On Resort or within a 15 minute drive:

Swimming Pool

Fishing

Horseback Riding (guided)

Golf Course (not mini golf)

Rafting (guided)

Recreational Lake or Reservoir for Boating or Fishing

Mountain Bike Trails

4-Wheel Drive Tours/Rentals

Downhill (Alpine) Skiing

Cross Country (XC, Nordic) Skiing

Snowmobile Trails

Hunting

Hiking—we did not include a glyph for hiking as it is generally available for all ages and abilities throughout colorful Colorado.

Index

An alphabetical index to all the accommodations in this book begins on page 271. In the index, under each of the 20 special interest glyphs defined on page 2 and 3, you will find a • if that activity is located at the resort, or a number which is the driving time in minutes if that activity is located near the resort. If the resort allows pets there will be either a • to indicate pets permitted or a $ if there is a fee or security deposit required for a pet. (*If* that activity is located *more* than 15 minutes drive from the resort, it is *not* shown.)

So, for example, if you want to find a resort that has a hot tub *and* is near cross country skiing, simply look down those two glyph columns until you find a place that has a • under the hot tub glyph and either a • or a number under the cross country skiing glyph. If you want to take your dog with you on the ski trip, also look under the pets permitted glyph until you find a place marked under all three of these items you desire.

Reservations, Facilities, and Fun Things To Do

Be aware that reservations are recommended, sometimes months in advance for holiday weekends and during the peak summer and winter seasons of June 15th to August 20th, and the week between Christmas and New Years. Depending on location, other busy times include the fall hunting seasons of mid-September to mid-November. In winter, properties near a ski area, President's Day weekend and Easter weekend and spring vacation should also be reserved well in advance.

Consider a fall, winter or spring vacation when rates can be lower, reservations easier, fewer people are around and the scenery even more spectacular.

When selecting accommodations for your vacation, phone the owner/operator to check what they have to offer: price, facilities, reservation deposit/refund policy, non-smoking units available, pet policy, and so on. Season opening dates may change, depending on the weather.

Facilities at commercial campgrounds, cabin resorts and lodges often include a store with some groceries, ice, firewood, and camping and fishing supplies. They may also offer a game room, recreation hall, gifts and souvenirs, pool, hot tub, playground, basketball, volleyball, miniature golf and a snack bar or restaurant. Best of all, the owner/operator lives on site — they should care about you and can serve as your personal hosts providing for your safety and security.

Activities in which you can participate may include fishing, guides and outfitters, nature walks, hiking, climbing, hay rides, water sports, barbecue cookouts, potluck dinners, ice cream socials, campfire programs, movies, slide shows, whitewater raft trips and kayaking, four wheeling, square dancing, sightseeing, tours, gold panning, rockhounding and horseback riding. In the fall, viewing the aspen colors and small and big game hunting are popular pursuits. Winter brings snowmobiling, cross-country and downhill skiing, ice fishing, sleigh and snow-cat rides and snuggling up by a cozy fire. Inquire about rental equipment and instructions for activities when you talk with the owner/operator.

Altitude Awareness

In Colorado's high country, skies are bluer and stars are brighter because of our altitude. Our air is thinner, with less oxygen, than at sea level, especially above 8,000 feet. Until your body adjusts, go easy on physical activity; drink more water than usual; minimize your intake of alcohol, caffeine and salty foods; and eat high-carbohydrate foods, such as grains, fruits and vegetables. There is less atmosphere to screen out ultraviolet rays, so remember to use sunscreen, sunglasses and a hat with a brim for shade. If you adopt the proper *attitude* toward Colorado's *altitude*, you and your family will have the most enjoyable vacation experience possible.

Aspen & Crystal River Valley

Including Carbondale, Marble, Meredith & Redstone — Map: G-8, H-8 & G-10

Aspen is a renown ski resort, an historic mining town, a relaxing mountain retreat and a cultural hot spot with its art galleries and glittering stars who vacation here. The town began as a remote mining camp in 1879 and became one of the richest silver producing areas in the world until the silver market crashed in 1893. In the Roaring Fork Valley, Aspen offers a winter wonderland for all outdoor enthusiasts and in summer hosts a music festival, theater, ballets and other entertaining events. Fishing spots, hiking and mountain biking trails abound on public forest lands near this mountain town. The Maroon Bells is said to be one of the most photographed peaks in North America and is a must-see. Down the road in the Crystal River Valley is towering Mount Sopris. Its peak reaches 12,953', and dominates the vista of the charming town of **Carbondale**. Formerly the only stagecoach stop on the 40-mile run to Aspen, Carbondale takes pride in its specialty shops, local arts and crafts and fine restaurants. Pick from one of many nearby mountain bike trails, fish the Roaring Fork River for its large trout or enjoy the scenery on the Crystal River. Thirty miles from Aspen and 12 miles from Glenwood Springs, this valley, surrounded by the White River National Forest, offers unique charm and secluded, untouched beauty. For a retreat even further off the beaten path, try the Redstone-Marble area with its mining past, ghost towns and dramatic mountain scenery. **Redstone** was founded by John Cleveland Osgood at the turn of the century as a model community to house employees of his coal mines. Although the workers and their families lived in simple cabins, Osgood built the luxurious Cleveholm Castle for himself, furnished with Tiffany chandeliers and Italian paintings. **Marble** was best known for its quarries, which produced a pure marble that rivaled Italy's Carrerra marble. Some of it was used in the Lincoln Memorial monument and the Tomb of the Unknown Soldier. The difficulties of mountain transportation closed down the quarries, but you can still visit them.

Fun Things to Do

- Aspen Art Museum (970) 925-8050
- Aspen Golf Course (970) 925-2145
- Crystal Glass Studio, Carbondale (970) 963-3227
- Main Street Gallery, Carbondale (970) 963-3775
- Redstone Art Center (970) 963-3790
- Redstone Castle Cleveholm Museum (970) 963-3463
- Redstone Historical Museum (summer only open 10 a.m. - 5 p.m.)
- Roaring Forge, Carbondale (970) 963-1930
- Snowmass Golf Club & Cross-Country Center (970) 923-3148
- T Lazy 7 Ranch stables and snowmobiling, Aspen (970)925-4614
- Wheeler Opera House, Aspen (970) 920-5770

Alpine Lodge

Snuggle under a cozy, goosedown comforter with your own Teddy Bear at the 100-year-old Alpine Lodge in Aspen. Stay in a charming cabin with a kitchenette or in the main lodge. Like the lodge, all cabins have those cuddly comforters and Teddy Bears, as well as full baths, queen beds, color cable television and telephones. Every lodge room is graced with fresh flowers and most boast views of Aspen Mountain. Four of the rooms have private baths while three other rooms share two baths. A continental breakfast is included in the summer and full breakfasts and dinners are available in the winter for a small additional charge.

Enjoy European hospitality, gourmet meals and a cozy Bavarian setting within walking distance from the center of town when you stay at Alpine Lodge. It almost goes without saying that the downhill skiing here is memorable, but so is the cross-country skiing. In the summer, take a hike to majestic Maroon Bells or mountain bike any of the numerous forest trails. Explore the shops and galleries of Aspen and relax in the lodge's outdoor hot tub afterwards. This is truly one of the most comfortable and affordable vacation spots in Aspen.

The rooms at Alpine Lodge are non-smoking.

Location: West on I-70 to Glenwood Springs. South on Hwy 82 into Aspen.

4 Cabins with Kitchens
7 Lodging Rooms
Central Woodstove

Room Phones
Bed & Breakfast Available
All Non-Smoking in Units
Recreation Room
Elevation: 8000
Credit Cards: VMAD
2 people a night: $50 - $128
Open: All Year

Jim & Christina Martin, Owners
1240 E Cooper
Aspen CO 81611
970/925-7351
970/925/5796 Fax

At the resort:

At resort or within 15 minutes:

Avalanche Ranch Cabins and B&B

Avalanche Ranch offers 45 acres of lush countryside overlooking the Crystal River, surrounded by the Elk Mountain Range and the White River National Forest. The original 1913 farmhouse, featured in several national publications, has been restored to a country bed and breakfast inn, romantically decorated with antiques. The cozy log cabins, offering abundant views, have full kitchens, sleeping lofts, porches, private yards, picnic tables and barbecues. All rooms are non-smoking and televisions are only available upon request.

The ranch restaurant serves breakfast to those staying at the inn while cabin guests may join in for $7.95. This is an excellent place for children — they can play in the tree house and the kid's cabin, or with the ranch animals. Take a mini-cruise with the canoe on the ranch's pond. Explore trails that skirt the valley on foot, by mountain bike, on horseback, on snowshoes or on cross-country skis. Horseback riding is within 5 miles. The historic towns of Redstone and Marble are nearby, while five major downhill ski resorts, including Aspen/Snowmass, are within an hour's drive. The famous Glenwood Springs Hot Springs pool is less than an hour away. Local trout fishing is world-renowned in the Crystal, Roaring Fork and Frying Pan rivers.

Avalanche Ranch provides an ideal setting for romantic getaways, family reunions and weddings. There are no TV's in the cabins or rooms, but available upon request. Smoking is not permitted in the ranch buildings and pets are allowed only with cabin guests.

Location: On Highway 133, near milepost 56.

12 Cabins with Kitchens
4 Lodging Rooms
5 Woodstoves
Central Fireplace
Central Campfire Area

Lobby Phone
Bed & Breakfast Available
All Non-Smoking in Units
Recreation Room
Elevation: 7000
Credit Cards: VMD
2 people a night: $75 - $135
Open: All Year

Sharon Boucher, Owner
12863 Hwy 133
Redstone CO 81623
970/963-2846
970/963-3141 Fax

At the resort:

At resort or within 15 minutes:

BRB Crystal River Resort

Rocky Mountain splendor at its finest! B-R-B is located at the base of spectacular, 13,000-foot Mount Sopris on the lively Crystal River which has some of the best fishing in Colorado. The resort has recently updated its modern log cabins with new carpet, stoves, ovens and heating systems. Each has a kitchen, linens, a fire pit, a picnic table and a barbecue grill; some have fireplaces. The cabins can accommodate up to 10 people. All cabins face the scenic river and some are a few steps from its banks. Come for the tranquil mountain scenery, stay for all the outdoor recreation. Numerous trees surround the resort and you'll be lulled to sleep at night by the steady, soothing sounds of the Crystal River.

On-site, play horseshoes, basketball, volleyball, badminton, ping pong, tether ball and at the playground. Fish along the half-mile of accessible river frontage or try the gold medal fishing in nearby Frying Pan River. The main lodge has a small grocery store and gift shop. Local hunting is some of the best in the country. Horseback riding trails, four-wheel driving roads, mountain biking trails and river rafting trips are nearby. The open-air hot tub and swimming pool are a welcome retreat after a day of adventuring. Glenwood Springs natural hot springs pool is only 18 miles away. History buffs will want to tour the historic towns of Marble and Redstone just up the road as well as the hand-hewn log school built in the late 1800s and open till 1946 right on the resort.

RV sites and indoor/outdoor group meeting areas are also available.

Location: On Highway 133 (West Elk Scenic Byway), near milepost 62, 6 miles south of Carbondale.

13 Cabins with Kitchens
2 Fireplaces

Pay Phone(s)
Elevation: 6600
Credit Cards: VMD
2 people a night: $60 - $90
Open: All Year

Umar and Ruth Sultan & Parveen Riaz, Owners
7202 Hwy 133
Carbondale CO 81623
970/963-2341 & Fax
800/963-2341

At the resort:

At resort or within 15 minutes:

Chair Mountain Ranch

At the base of Chair Mountain, secluded among the pine trees along the beautiful Crystal River, this 8-acre ranch is a peaceful mountain retreat, with fully equipped, two bedroom housekeeping cabins with full bathrooms. Kitchens with all the utensils you require and plenty of bedding and linens are supplied. Sit on the cabin's porch and read a book or just watch nature unfold before you on the pond. A newly renovated 1,200-square foot upstairs, two bedroom apartment with a full kitchen and bathroom is also available. Relax in front of the fireplace in the spacious living room with a spectacular view of the mountains. For those who like to rough it, try the rustic camping cabin with no water and a bath house close by.

Romp with the whole family on the large grassy area in the summer, perfect for football, baseball, volleyball, horseshoes and basketball. Picnic in the covered picnic area with its marble barbecue pit. Fish for gold-medal trout on ranch grounds along the Crystal River. Take a brave dip in medicinal hot springs pouring out of the mountainside into the river a few miles down the road. Visit historic Redstone with its quaint shops. Add a splash of excitement by whitewater rafting on the Roaring Fork or Colorado rivers. Check out the local riding stables that offer everything from breakfast rides to several-day pack trips. Your hosts can arrange horse or four-wheel drive vehicles to excellent deer and elk hunting in the area. Hike or bike on the abundant, scenic trails; you can rent mountain bikes in Redstone.

Groups, family reunions, weddings and seminars are welcomed here. Pets are allowed for an additional fee.

Location: Take Marble turnoff from Highway 133, near milepost 46.

5 Cabins with Kitchens
1 Lodging Rooms
2 Camper Cabins
1 Fireplace
Central Campfire Area

Lobby Phone
Recreation Room
Elevation: 7640
Credit Cards: VMD
2 people a night: $35 - $100
Open: All Year

Dave & Linda Adams, Owners
0178 CR 3
Marble CO 81623
970/963-9522 & Fax

At the resort:

At resort or within 15 minutes:

T Lazy 7 Ranch

Family owned and operated since 1938, T Lazy 7 Ranch is only five minutes from Aspen and is spread over 500 private acres. It's seclusion is enhanced by a quarter of a million acres of surrounding national forest and wilderness. Not to be confused with neighboring Colorado dude ranches, T Lazy 7 operates on a unique, informal level. The lack of structure allows you to enjoy your vacation at your own pace in recently renovated rustic cabins. Six lodges contain three or four cabin like apartments, each with modern kitchens, baths, and fireplaces. The unique decor emphasizes quality, rustic furnishings and original handmade hardware throughout.

The ranch is located near the base of beautiful Maroon Bells, the most photographed peaks in North America! Three miles of private fishing streams, stocked beaver ponds, rolling pastures, thick stands of aspen and pine, waterfalls, horses, and animals grace this exquisite valley. Ranch activities include horseback riding, fishing, and partaking in western chuckwagon parties. Pick among any number of guided horseback rides from breakfast rides, to Maroon Bells lunch rides, to Tennessee Walker day rides. In the winter snowmobile to historic mining sites or frolic on the world-class downhill slopes in Aspen. At the resort, enjoy a year-round heated swimming pool and jacuzzi.

Guest are welcomed to stay from two nights to a relaxing month. Pets are permitted in selected cabins.

Location: On Maroon Creek Road, 5 minutes from downtown Aspen.

T-LAZY-7
THE RANCH
ASPEN·COLORADO

19 Cabins with Kitchens
9 Fireplaces
9 Woodstoves

Pay Phone(s)
Non-Smoking Units Available
Elevation: 8400
Credit Cards: VMD
2 people a night: Call for Rates
Open: 5/1 to 9/30 and
11/24 to 4/14

Landon & Rick Deane & Bill McEnteer
PO Box TT
3129 Maroon Ck Rd
Aspen CO 81612-0240
970/925-7254
970/925-4614 Activities
888/T7-LODGE (8756343)
E mail: aspen.com/tlazy7

At the resort:

At resort or within 15 minutes:

Yolande Placer Cabins

Located on Fryingpan River, just 2 miles past Ruedi Reservoir, Yolande Placer cabins are rustic yet modernized. The six housekeeping units have bathrooms and double beds. One new, large cabin has beautiful views and sleeps up to six. Another cabin, which has a fireplace, can accommodate up to eight.

Anglers will appreciate the convenience of fishing the river right outside their door or the nearby reservoir. Other fishing spots include the Chapman Dam and Lake and the Little Hoover Dam. Famous Glenwood Springs Hot Pool, once a favored place among the Ute Indians to relax, is just a scenic hour drive away. Open May to October, Yolande Placer is in the midst of great hunting, hiking, horseback riding and mountain biking country. A restaurant is conveniently located minutes away for those evenings when you don't want to cook your own meals.

Two full service RV sites are also available. Your horse is welcomed to accompany you here.

Location: From Highway 82, in Basalt take Fryingpan River past Ruedi Reservoir, about two miles.

6 Cabins with Kitchens
1 Fireplace

Lobby Phone
Non-Smoking Units Available
Elevation: 8000
No credit cards
2 people a night: $60 - $125
Open: 5/1 to 11/1

Dennis, Monika & Carl, Betty South, Owners
24635 Frying Pan Rd
Meredith CO 81642
970/927-3296
970/241-8645 Winter

At the resort:

At resort or within 15 minutes:

Black Canyon Area

Including Cimarron, Crawford, Hotchkiss & Montrose — Map: K-6, J-6, I-6, K-5

Bordered by Gunnison National Forest, **Cimarron** is known for its old narrow-gauge railroad, with a part of the original trestle crossing the creek. The 469-foot Morrow Point Dam and Cimarron Canal supply water for the arid Uncompahgre Valley. Cimarron River yields a variety of trout. Just west is the Curecanti National Recreation Area where breathtaking scenery emphasizes the series of dams created to alter the Gunnison River's course. Nearby Marrow Point Reservoir is a mixture of jagged rock jutting out over calm water. Named for the former Ute Chief Curecata, the area also boasts 20-mile long Blue Mesa Reservoir. The lake is ideal for sailing and windsurfing. Its 96 miles of shoreline offer up rainbow, brook and brown trout, mackinaw, and kokanee salmon. **Crawford** is a town where cowboys still wear Stetson hats and spurs, and cattle drives take place down Main Street. An adventurer's paradise, Crawford offers outstanding big game hunting, excellent fishing, four-wheel drive tours and hiking in Gunnison National Forest. Crawford Reservoir, good for rainbow trout and perch, also has swimming and boating. **Montrose** is the gateway to the San Juan Skyway and the Ridgway State Recreation Area. Take a scenic day trip to Telluride, Grand Mesa, Blue Mesa, Owl Creek Pass and Silver Jack Reservoir. The Black Canyon to the west is the most stunning day trip of all: as deep as 2,700' and as narrow as 1,300', the canyon was shaped by the churning waters of the Gunnison River. A 50-mile long chasm, the Black Canyon's sheer, shadowy rock walls drop more than a half mile to the river creating a somber and memorable site. Ute Indians did not enter the canyon, preferring to stay on the rim and hunt and when you visit, you'll see why — there are difficult trails down. Take raft trips through the steep canyon to see otherwise inaccessible sites. The Montrose area offers some of the best fishing in Colorado on the Gunnison, San Miguel and Dolores rivers. Keep an eye out for the many golden eagles, red-tailed hawks, prairie falcons and great horned owls that live here. The Ridgway State Recreation Area provides boating, fishing, and swimming opportunities. Visit the Ute Indian Museum, dedicated entirely to one tribe, to understand a bit of the region's rich history.

Fun Things To Do

- Black Canyon of the Gunnison National Monument (970)240-5430
- Crawford Reservoir & State Park (970) 921-5721
- Curecanti National Recreation Area, Gunnison (970) 641-2337
- District Forest Service Office, Gunnison (970) 641-0471
- Montrose Golf Course (970) 249-8551
- Ute Indian Museum, Montrose (970) 249-3098

Becker Ranch Bed & Breakfast

Becker Ranch is a spacious, stone country home on 40 acres in one of Colorado's most picturesque valleys. The Becker's non-smoking home becomes yours during your family getaway. Each room is uniquely furnished and decorated such as Joni's with its queen size brass bed and royal blue accessories. Jeff's is a family room with a queen bed and a bunk bed, Kris' features a queen bed, a small child's bed, and baby bed for the small family, and oak furnishings give Bret's room a masculine touch. Becker Ranch serve breakfasts made with their own homemade sausages, too!

Amenities include satellite television, a swimming pool, a soon to be fenced-in children's playground and lots of room to play. Nearby, go hunting, fishing, hiking, river rafting, water-skiing, snowmobiling and downhill and cross-country skiing. Becker Ranch is near the spectacular north rim of the Black Canyon of the Gunnison. Enjoy several local, summertime festivals, such as the Delta County Fair, Crawford Pioneer Days and the Little Britches Rodeo.

Children are always welcome.

Location:
Approximately 8 miles south of Hotchkiss on Highway 92, near milepost 29.

4 Lodging Rooms
Central Woodstove

Lobby Phone
Bed & Breakfast Available
All Non-Smoking in Units
Recreation Room
Elevation: 6800
Credit Cards: VMD
2 people a night: $45
Open: All Year

Myron E. & Joan Becker, Owners
3798 Hwy 92
Crawford CO 81415
970/921-6877
800/392-3765

At the resort:

At resort or within 15 minutes:

Last Frontier Lodge

Vacation in a lodge on a lake, far from shopping malls, highways and condos. This rustic lodge, with modern conveniences is in a part of Colorado where the "Old West" is still a natural and daily way of life.

Relax and enjoy the good, hearty meals served family style included with your room. The lodge specializes in fabulous, locally grown premium beef and seasonal fruits and vegetables. Last Frontier Lodge has an outdoor hot tub, paddle and row boats, and horseshoes. In winter enjoy their sledding hill, for a faster pace snowmobile, or to slow down cross country ski in this area. Explore the best of Colorado's lakes, rivers and wilderness on foot. The North Rim (the quiet side) of the Black Canyon of the Gunnison National Monument is only a 30 minute drive. Rent horses or bring your own for a trip into the West Elk Wilderness (no motorized vehicles are permitted), with its undisturbed lakes, sparkling streams, mountain peaks and canyons.

Your hosts work with local cattle ranchers and outfitters for special vacation activities. Ask about the special cattle drives. Kids under 6 stay free; ask about their special rates for kids between 6 and 12 years of age.

Location: One-quarter mile South of Crawford, off Highway 92, near milepost 32.

8 Lodging Rooms
Central Fireplace
Central Campfire Area

Lobby Phone
Bed & Breakfast Available
Recreation Room
Elevation: 6800
No credit cards
2 people a night: $90 - $90
Open: All Year

Greg & Sharon Caldwell, Owners
PO Box 248
4020 C Hwy 92
Crawford CO 81415-0248
970/921-6363

At the resort:

At resort or within 15 minutes:

Pleasant Valley Cabins & Campground

A good place to vacation and relax, Pleasant Valley has seven cabins along Little Cimarron River on the western slopes of the Colorado Rockies. All cabins are heated with modern gas and have private bathrooms. One cabin features a fireplace and most have kitchenettes. Bedding and linen are provided and a limited supply of cooking utensils is in each kitchenette. A coin laundromat is available. A clean, quiet, friendly haven, this is a great retreat for families.

The convenience store, in addition to groceries, hunting and fishing licenses, has a wide selection of antiques and collectibles. Pleasant Valley is close to major attractions such as the Black Canyon of the Gunnison National Monument and Blue Mesa Reservoir. Try your hand at the excellent trout fishing on the property or nearby. Hunt in some of the best deer and elk areas in the state, explore a four-wheel drive roads or browse among the antiques. Horseback riding is minutes away and guest horses are welcomed.

RV and tent sites are also available. Reservations are accepted with a one-day deposit. Children and controlled pets are welcomed.

Location: 3 miles east of Cimarron on Highway 50, near milepost 115.

5 Cabins with Kitchens
2 cabins without Kitchens
1 Fireplace

Pay Phone(s)
Elevation: 7500
Credit Cards: VMD
2 people a night: $32 - $45
Open: 5/1 to 11/23

Larry & Linda Griffin, Owners
Box 127
84100 E Hwy 50
Cimarron CO 81220-0127
970/249-8330

At the resort:

At resort or within 15 minutes:

Stewart Homestead Cabin

In the picturesque Onion Valley, 9 miles southeast of Crawford, Stewart Homestead Cabin offers a quiet, peaceful rest with no phone or television to distract you from relaxing. The cabin features a full kitchen and bath, glass door wood stove for cozy winter days and can sleep up to nine. This homestead cabin offers you a chance to see what life was like 100 years ago will all the conveniences of today.

Nearby are the Blue Mesa, Black Mesa, Gould and Crawford Reservoirs for fishing and water sports. A visit to the stunning Black Canyon of the Gunnison will prove to be unforgettable. Activities in this area include horseback riding, mountain biking, hiking, fishing, cross-country skiing and snowmobiling. Your hosts encourage you to bring your family and share the adventure!

Location: Nine miles southeast of Crawford on Highway 92, between milepost 40-41 on the Westhoop Scenic Byway.

1 Cabin with Kitchen
1 Woodstove
Central Campfire Area

No Phones Available
Elevation: 7800
No credit cards
2 people a night: $75
Open: All Year

Jim & Susan Ayer
4156 B Rd
Crawford CO 81415
970/921-6751

At the resort:

At resort or within 15 minutes:

Western Recreation Ranch

The new housekeeping cabins at Western Recreation Ranch overlook Smith Fork Stream. The four cabins sleep two to six. The working cattle ranch is on 300 acres. Be sure to ask about the occasional cattle drives when making your reservations.

Fish at the stocked trout ponds here or at the stream. Horses are welcomed to accompany you and there is a roping arena available to guests. Dine at the steak house located on the ranch that features a dance pavilion for special events. The ranch is also close to a hunting outfitters, perfect for your backcountry treks in the fall hunting seasons. The Crawford area is great for hiking, mountain biking or horseback riding — yours or theirs. Take the whole family on a hay ride and experience the real West.

Rustic tent and RV sites are also available only 100 yards from the stream. Pets are also welcomed here.

Location: Off Highway 92 on the north side of Crawford on Dogwood Ave. 1 mi down Smith Fork Creek.

4 Cabins with Kitchens
1 Fireplace
3 Woodstoves
Central Campfire Area

Lobby Phone
Bed & Breakfast Available
Elevation: 6500
Credit Cards: VM
2 people a night: $80
Open: 5/25 to 11/15

Clair & Nola Hicks, Owners
PO Box 162
276 3850 Drive
Crawford CO 81415-0162
970/921-Horse (4677)
888/921-Horse (4677)
970/921-4FUN (4386)

At the resort:

At resort or within 15 minutes:

Central City to Georgetown

Including Black Hawk, Empire, Golden & Idaho Springs — Map: F-14 & F-16

Once known as the richest square mile on earth, **Central City** is again enjoying a boom. A historic mining town where fortunes were made and lost, this mountain city now has legal gambling mixed in with Victorian houses, the fanciest opera house in the west and abandoned mines. The entire city, just a mile up the road from **Black Hawk**, is part of a National Historic District. Because Central City attracted more than 20,000 people in the 1860s, it became a cultural center for Colorado. The Central City Opera House, which opened in 1878, still runs a nationally renown summer season. Gambling has brought people back in droves and the city is once again filled with dance hall music and the clink of coins. Hiking around Central City and Black Hawk is not recommended because the hillsides are dotted with abandoned mine shafts. Take a tour instead at the Lost Gold Mine and see how early settlers lived at the Thomas House. The first major gold strike in Colorado on Jan. 7, 1859, was in **Idaho Springs** by George Jackson. Today would-be miners should check out the Argo Mine & Mill where they can pan for gold and gemstones or tour the still operating Phoenix Gold Mine. south of town, on Flirtation Peak is the Bridal Veil Falls where the largest water wheel in the state was built in 1893. Idaho Springs was named for the geothermal pool and baths fed by waters considered scared to the Utes who once relaxed here. Drive the Mt. Evans Scenic and Historic Byway 14 miles to the summit of the 14,264' peak. Along the highest paved highway in America look for bighorn sheep, elk and goats among alpine tundra and bristlecone pines. The "Oh My God Road" links Central City to Idaho Springs and passes by hundreds of abandoned mines and mills. St. Mary's Glacier, only 15 minutes away, is a popular, year-round ski and snowboard area for those who don't mind hiking in with their equipment so they can ski a snow bowl in August. Encompassing the town, Arapaho National Forest offers endless alpine hikes which turn into great cross-country skiing trails in the winter.

Fun Things To Do

- Arapaho National Forest (970) 887-4100
- Argo Mine & Mill, Idaho Springs (303) 567-2421
- Central City Opera House (303) 292-6700
- Clear Creek Ranger District Office (303) 567-2901
- Echo Lake Lodge, Idaho Springs (303) 567-2138
- Edgar Mines, Idaho Springs (303) 567-2911
- Georgetown Loop Railroad (800) 691-4FUN
- Gilpin County Historical Museum, Central City (303) 582-5283
- Phoenix Gold Mine, Idaho Springs (303) 567-0422
- Teller House & Tours, Central City (303) 582-3200

A Royal Scot Bed & Breakfast

This bed and breakfast is on nine acres snuggled up against a mountain with breathtaking views. This mountain retreat is a contemporary home with all the conveniences of modern living with a taste of Scotland. Choose among five rooms, all of which have bathrooms, fans and televisions. The Tartan Room is an elegant corner room with a cherrywood, four poster queen bed and magnificent views of nearby mountains. The Heather Room is done in alpine blues accented with light oak furniture and a queen bed. Named after the traditional flower of Scotland, the Thistle Room has a cozy ambiance of light oak furniture with a thistle purple color scheme and mountain views. The Highland Rose Room, on the first floor, has an antique dark oak bed complemented by a Balmoral tartan and a blush carpet. The Scottish word for family, the Clan Room, has an elegant queen brass bed and a spacious area for children. A full, home-cooked breakfast is served daily in the downstairs breakfast room or out on the redwood deck.

Spend time on the decks to watch the eagles soar far above and the elk graze in the meadow below. The Golden area offers fishing, hiking, mountain biking, horseback riding, cross-country skiing and golfing. Numerous ski resorts and Central City's historic gambling are within a reasonable drive. The Denver area, with its big city attractions, is also a short drive away. After a day spent exploring, come back to relax in the outdoor hot tub, read a book in front of the fire, or chat with other guests in the sitting room while sipping wine or hot mulled cider. The Royal Scot also offers its guests a pool table, library, VCR and videos, and massage and/or body work with reservations.

No smoking or pets allowed.

Location: From I-70, exit 252 to Highway 40 west, then 1.3 miles (Will cross back over I-70).

5 Lodging Rooms
Central Fireplace

Lobby Phone
Bed & Breakfast Available
All Non-Smoking in Units
Recreation Room
Elevation: 7000
Credit Cards: VMA
2 people a night: $69 - $89
Open: All Year

Susan Casper, Proprietor
30500 Hwy 40
Golden CO 80401
303/526-2411

At the resort:

At resort or within 15 minutes:

Call of the Canyon

Enjoy elegance in the rough at Call of the Canyon's luxury cabins at the base of 14,258-foot Mount Evans. The knotty pine cabins, built in the 1930s, have full kitchens, fireplaces and other amenities. Surrounded by Arapaho National Forest, the cabins are only 25 feet from a mountain creek. Settle under a down comforter on the queen-sized bed at night and listen to the rushing sound of West Chicago Creek right outside your window. In the early morning, if you're quiet and lucky, you might meet Hal, the giant rainbow trout who lounges about in the pool under the bridge.

Activities include mountain biking, hiking and fishing — but don't touch Hal! Take an excursion to the ice fields of St. Mary's Glacier in the summer where some hikers go for back country, downhill skiing in July. Go whitewater rafting nearby and then relax in Idaho Springs' hot springs afterwards. Winter is great for cross-country skiing here and the resort is a short drive from the ski resorts at Winter Park, Loveland and Keystone. Be sure to drive up Mount Evans — the highest road in America — where you might spot herds of bighorn sheep and mountain goats grazing above timberline. Other wildlife you might spot are deer, hawks, ravens, marmots, bear, elk and if you're really lucky, cougars. One critter you'll be sure to met is Pinhead, the resident cat at Call of the Canyon.

Location: 6.3miles from Idaho Springs, turn right off Highway 103, between milepost 6-7 onto County Road 114, on West Chicago Creek.

3 Cabins with Kitchens
4 Fireplaces

Lobby Phone
All Non-Smoking in Units
Elevation: 9000
Credit Cards: VM
2 people a night: $75 - $80
Open: All Year

Richard Eakins, Owner
104 CR 114
Idaho Springs CO 80452
303/567-0170
800/257-4783

At the resort:

At resort or within 15 minutes:

Conestoga Wagon Cabins & RV Campground

Just five miles west of historic Empire, Conestoga Wagon Stop sits in the tall pines of the Arapaho National Forest. The newly remodeled, five cabins are available all year. Each fully furnished cabin has a kitchenette with cookware and utensils. You'll enjoy the beautiful view of Clear Creek River near your cabin, and the peaceful sound of rushing water will lull you to sleep every night. RV camping and tent sights are also available.

Both your horse and pet are welcome at Conestoga Wagon Stop. Area activities include fishing right at the resort, river rafting, horseback riding, golfing, boating on lakes and mountain biking — all within a short drive. In the winter, you can enjoy downhill and cross-country skiing, snowmobiling, ice fishing and hunting.

RV sites are also available.

Location: Off I-70, 5 miles from Empire on Highway 40 near milepost 250.

5 Cabins with Kitchens
Central Campfire Area

Lobby Phone
Elevation: 9650
Credit Cards: VM
2 people a night: $40
Open: All Year

Dale & Pam Holzer, Owners
PO Box 334
7364 US Hwy 40
Empire CO 80438-0344
303/569-3066 & Fax

At the resort:

At resort or within 15 minutes:

Gingerbread Estate Cottages

The cottages at Gingerbread Estate were built at the turn of the century and have been lovingly renovated. Overlooking charming downtown Central City, the private, single-storied Victorian cottages feature high ceilings as well as the original moldings and trim that recall the period in which they were built. All cottages have private parking and entrances, furnished parlors with cable television, a dining room with a local phone, one and two bedrooms and either a three-quarters or full bath. Each has a full kitchen with microwave, range, refrigerator and coffee maker.

The main lure of Central City and Black Hawk was once gold and it is the same today. The limited-stakes gambling casinos in both these quaint mountain towns have brought them roaring back to life, much like they must have been in the 1800s. In addition to the casinos, Central City offers a glimpse of the past with its summer opera season and tiny museums. Take the opportunity to explore this town's past while vacationing here while discovering the lure of striking it rich today!

Reservations are highly recommended. With special advance notice, your host will arrange for limo service, made-to-order cakes and personal touches. Ask about the senior discount when you call.

Location: In Central City, about 4 blocks from center of town, on East Fourth High.

3 Cabins with Kitchens

Room Phones
Non-Smoking Units Available
Elevation: 8496
Credit Cards: AD
2 people a night: Call for Rates
Open: All Year

Paulette Russell, Owner
PO Box 392
Central City CO 80427-0392
800/582-3226
303/582-3227

At the resort:

At resort or within 15 minutes:

Van Eden Ranch Retreat, B&B and Mountain Cabin

The motto at Van Eden is: "Big enough to serve you, small enough to care." The ten bedroom moss rock lodge features private baths, wall-to-wall carpeting and fireplaces. One room has a jetted tub and Primestar TV. This romantic, bed and breakfast lodge also has some non-smoking rooms. Plus there is a log vacation home that sleeps up to 16 people and has a kitchen.

Imagine waking up to a delicious breakfast before relaxing by a mountain stream, hiking the forest and meadow or horseback riding along a picturesque trail. The first floor of the lodge has a large outdoor deck and cozy lounge with a moss rock, sunken fireplace for relaxing and catching up on some reading. Western horseback rides with either steak or vegetarian cuisine (homemade by prior arrangement) box lunches are also available. Gambling at nearby Central City and Blackhawk is only 30 minutes away. Surrounded by the Arapahoe-Roosevelt National Forest, the ranch is secluded and quiet, up two and a half miles of private road. For a relaxing vacation, soak in the seasonal hot tub before getting a refreshing, professional massage.

Van Eden is ideal for small groups and reunions. Your horse is welcome to vacation with you.

Location: 35 miles west of Denver and 4.5 miles South of Idaho Springs off I-70, exit 241A.

1 Vacation Home
10 Lodging Rooms
16 Beds in Bunk House or Dorm
2 Fireplaces
1 Woodstove
Central Fireplace
Central Campfire Area

Lobby Phone
Bed & Breakfast Available
Non-Smoking Units Available
Recreation Room
Elevation: 9000
Credit Cards: VM
2 people a night: $40 - $100
Open: All Year

Pat & James Fleming, Owners
PO Box 1169
3001 Van Eden Rd
Idaho Springs CO 80452-1169
303/567-2566
303/914-3590 Denver local

At the resort:

At resort or within 15 minutes:

Collegiate Peaks Area

Including Buena Vista, Granite, Monarch, Nathrop, Poncha Springs, Salida & Twin Lakes — Map: I-12, J-12, K-12, J-13 & H-11

The small town of **Buena Vista**, nestled at the base of the Collegiate and Sawatch Mountain Ranges, is named for its "good view." In the Upper Arkansas River Valley, Buena Vista and its surroundings were once home to the Ute Indians. Lt. Zebulon Pike, who passed through in 1806, found evidence of some 3,000 Utes. Like other Colorado towns, miners came when they learned of gold strikes in the area and ranchers eventually followed. The city has a rowdy past, once hosting 36 bars and a hanging judge. Now Buena Vista is the jumping off point for some of the best river rafting in Colorado. Brown's Canyon, 8 miles south, is often called the whitewater capital. The impressive Collegiate Range, lies to the west has the most concentrated number of peaks above 14,000' in Colorado, abounds with hiking trails, mountain bike trails and riddled with ghost towns. Another feature of the Buena Vista area are the natural hot springs where you can soothe your body while gazing up at majestic, snowcapped peaks. **Salida** grew quickly in the 1880s when the railroad made it a rail hub. A rip-roaring town, Salida had a famous madam, Laura Evans, who ran a bordello in town from 1896 to 1950! Today, it's still a roaring town, roaring with rapids, that is. Salida boasts the headquarters for the Arkansas River Valley State Park. The town has one of the largest, indoor, hot springs. The Arkansas River is a launching point for some of the best whitewater rafting and is the most boated in the country with rapids ranging from easy to challenging. Accessible from Salida are the Rainbow and Colorado trails for mountain bikers and hikers can enjoy. In the winter try skiing at the much-praised, less-visited Monarch Ski Resort whose basin traps 300 inches annually fluffy powder. **Twin Lakes**, at the base of Independence Pass, are natural, glacier-made lakes, measuring 90' deep, almost 2 miles wide and 6 miles long. You can fish from the shoreline or a boat. The majestic mountain backdrop makes this a photographer's dream.

Fun Things to Do

- American Adventure Expeditions (800)288-0675
- Buffalo Joe River Trips, Buena Vista (800) 356-7984, (719) 395-8757
- Collegiate Peaks Golf Course, Buena Vista (719) 395-8189
- Independent Whitewater Raft Trips (800)428-1479, (719)395-2642
- Monarch Ski Area (719) 539-3573
- Monarch Tours Guided Snowmobiling (800)539-2573, (719)539-2572
- Pa & Ma's Guest Ranch (719)486-3900
- River Runners Ltd., Salida (800) 525-2081
- Salida Hot Springs (719) 539-6738
- Twin Lakes Mountain Bike Rentals (800)626-7812

Forest Creek Cabins

The cabins at Forest Creek are located in a quiet, secluded area away from traffic about a half mile west of Buena Vista. The fully self-contained, all non-smoking cabins have full-size kitchens for your cooking convenience. The rough cut pine exteriors, knotty pine interiors and vaulted ceilings are tastefully decorated for the'90s. Some of the furniture is custom made of aspen logs for a full Colorado mountain experience. The whole family will appreciate the board games left in each cabin for your enjoyment. Forest Creek Cabins offers a vacation off the beaten path on Cottonwood Pass.

Surrounded by the Collegiate Peaks, Forest Creek has a small creek running through the property. Try your luck catching some of the tasty trout at Cottonwood Lake nearby. The cabin resort is close to all area attractions, including hiking, biking, downhill and cross country skiing, and snowmobiling in the Collegiate Peaks mountain ranges and rafting the Arkansas River.

Multiple night and weekly rentals are available. A deposit is required with your reservation. Reservations are advised.

Location: Once in town, drive exactly 2 miles west of the only traffic light toward Cottonwood Pass. On Country Road 306.

3 Cabins with Kitchens
1 Woodstove

No Phones Available
All Non-Smoking in Units
Recreation Room
Elevation: 8000
Credit Cards: VM
2 people a night: $85 - $95
Open: All Year

Polly Thomas-Hopple & Brian Hopple, Owners
16115 CR 306
Buena Vista CO 81211
719/395-4819
800/603-7690

At the resort:

At resort or within 15 minutes:

Love Ranch

The Love Ranch was named during the 1930s when Mark and Josephine Love purchased a ranch in Chalk Creek Canyon, a mountain paradise located between Mount Antero and Mount Princeton. Now a guest ranch, this resort is a friendly, family kind of place with both modern and rustic cabins with names like Hermit, Honeymoon, Woodsy, Knotty Pine and Ship Ahoy. All of the cabins are adjacent to numerous streams.

On-site, you and your family can play badminton, volley ball and horseshoes. Anglers will enjoy the plentiful fishing for rainbow and brook trout in the ranch stream and in the two lakes just a mile from the cabins. Nearby activities include horseback riding, hiking to mountain lakes, swimming in the Princeton Hot Springs pools, exploring ghost towns, whitewater rafting and kayaking. Visit the town of Buena Vista for golfing and dining.

Location: 6 miles south of Buena Vista on Highway 285, near milepost 142, then 8 miles west on County Road 162.

8 Cabins with Kitchens
1 Fireplace
6 Woodstoves
Central Campfire Area

Lobby Phone
Elevation: 8500
Credit Cards: VM
2 people a night: $25 - $65
Open: 5/1 to 9/30

Georgia & Richard Zoll, Managers
18670 CR 162
Nathrop CO 81236
719/395-2366

At the resort:

At resort or within 15 minutes:

Mount Elbert Lodge & Cabins

Step out of today's often hectic world into an earlier time at Mount Elbert Lodge for year-round fun in the Colorado Rockies. On Lake Creek at the base of Mt. Elbert, this former, turn-of-the-century stage stop lodge is easily accessible, yet remotely private. The comfortable, log housekeeping cabins feature separate kitchen and living spaces, private bathrooms, and porches that encourage relaxing in the sun. The bed and breakfast lodge has five rooms, including the "Mount Elbert" room, with a southern exposure and a private balcony; and the "Twin Peaks" room, with a view of the valley from its east and south windows. The lodge's common area offers a woodstove for cozy winter retreats. There are no televisions, radios or phones so you can truly get away from hectic city life.

The lodge serves healthy and wholesome complimentary breakfasts. Step out your cabin door and choose a hike to the peaks (trailhead to Mount Elbert begins at the lodge), wander the mountain meadows, mountain bike rides though San Isabel National Forest or sit on the porch and soak up the glorious Colorado sun and sky. Aspen and Leadville offer shopping, dining and exploring in old mining towns. Climb several other "fourteeners" nearby in the summer. Enjoy excellent lake, reservoirs and stream fishing and some of the country's best whitewater rafting. In winter the landscape changes from green to white so you can cross-county ski or snowshoe from your back door. Alpine skiing is only a 45 minutes drive. Other winter activities include ice skating and ice fishing.

Visit their Web site at www.colorado-bnb.com/mtelbert/.

Location: Off Highway 82. About 4.5 miles west of Twin Lakes village.

6 Cabins with Kitchens
5 Lodging Rooms
Central Woodstove

Lobby Phone
Bed & Breakfast Available
All Non-Smoking in Units
Recreation Room
Elevation: 9800
Credit Cards: VMAD
2 people a night: $44 - $85
Open: All Year

Scott Boyd & Laura Downing, Owners
PO Box 40
W of Twin Lakes on Hwy 82
Twin Lakes CO 81251-0040
719/486-0594 & Fax call 1st
800/381-4433
E-mail: mtelbert@rmi.net

At the resort:

At resort or within 15 minutes:

Mountain Cabin Rentals

Surrounded by majestic snow-capped mountain peaks, Mountain Cabin Rentals offers completely furnished cabins and vacation homes. The Snowshoe Inn and the Hidden Arrow are perfect for families of four to ten with two bedrooms and a sleeping loft, two bathrooms, a laundry room and deck with a charcoal grill for evening BBQs. The Amen Chalet built in the 1800s, was a one-room school house. It sleeps 12 to 20 with six bedrooms, four bathrooms, a large living room with an electric log fireplace, and a river deck with picnic area for family reunion gatherings. Amen River House, which sleeps six to ten, has three bedrooms, two bathrooms, a fireplace with electric logs, coin laundry, a deck overlooking a mountain stream and two covered porches to enjoy your morning coffee and the clean mountain air. Amen Cabin sleeps two to six and has two bedrooms, one bathroom, a deck overlooking a stream and access to a river deck for casting your line. The Bear's Den has three bedrooms, a loft bedroom, two bathrooms and a porch with a grill.

The rentals are located in the historic mining town of Garfield. Fish on the South Arkansas River on the property. Mountain bike trails begin at the rentals. Area summer activities include river rafting, horseback riding, hiking including the nearby Colorado Trail, tennis and four-wheel driving. Swim and soak in natural hot springs pools, explore ghost towns and enjoy the beauty of San Isabel National Forests. In the fall view the spectacular changing colors and hunt deer and elk in season. In the winter there's plenty to do, from downhill skiing at nearby Monarch Ski Area to cross-country skiing through the woods. If you've never tried snowmobiling, take one of Bill's guided tours to experience this fun winter sport.

Location: On Highway 50, 4 miles east of Monarch Ski Area, in Garfield/Monarch.

3 Cabins with Kitchens
4 Vacation Homes
2 Fireplace

Phones in some units
Elevation: 9500
No credit cards
2 people a night: $65 - $125
Open: All Year

Diane & Bill Block, Owner/Agents
PO Box B
Monarch CO 81227
719/539-4057

At the resort:

At resort or within 15 minutes:

Piñon Valley Ranch

Encircled by lovely mountain views and located on a 73-acre spread, off the highway and peaceful, Piñon Valley Ranch has quiet country cabins equipped with either a kitchenette or full kitchen. A television and VCR are provided in the cabins for in-room movie viewing. Broadcast channels are not available. The kitchenette cabin sleeps four while the full kitchen cabin can accommodate up to six comfortably (more if you want to be cozy). With only 2 cabins on 73-acres there are few people and an abundance of nature and tranquility. A continental breakfast is provided for all guests.

The Ranch is a mere 20 minutes from Monarch Ski Resort and 15 minutes from Salida's soothing hot springs pool. Restaurants, jeep tours, a bowling alley and golf course are all nearby. Area activities include whitewater rafting, mountain biking, horseback riding, fishing and hunting.

No pets are allowed at the ranch. Cots are available for an extra fee.

Location: Off Highway 50, about 2 miles west of junction 50 & 285, then north on County Road 250 (first county road after junction) a quarter mile beyond County Road 140. Not as far west as Maysville.

2 Cabins with Kitchens
1 Fireplace

No Phones Available
Bed & Breakfast Available
All Non-Smoking in Units
Elevation: 7500
No credit cards
2 people a night: $48 - $58
Open: All Year

Paul & Cheri Jensen, Owners
8309 CR 250
Salida CO 81201
719/539-6729

At the resort:

At resort or within 15 minutes:

River Run Inn Bed & Breakfast

At this inn, majestic mountains rise in the distance and the Arkansas River flows past. Walk along the gracious front porch of this turn-of-the-century country home and into a large sitting room featuring 12-foot ceilings and a library. Wake daily to great coffee and a full breakfast of fresh fruit, homemade coffeecakes and hearty entrees. Choose among the seven bedrooms on the first two floors, three with private baths and four which share two baths. All bedrooms are furnished with antique poster beds, comfortable mattresses and most have mountain views. For larger groups, ask about the third floor dormitory with 13 beds, a large bathroom, table and chairs.

River Run Inn also has a back porch to relax on and, down the hill, a stocked trout pond by the river. Enjoy the homemade cookies and other afternoon snacks. Salida and the surrounding area is rich in numerous activities for outdoor enthusiasts, no matter the season. Sightseeing offers many natural wonders, old mining towns, local galleries and gift shops. Among the many things to do in this area are whitewater rafting, mountain biking, hiking, golfing, downhill and cross-country skiing, snowmobiling, horseback riding and gambling at Cripple Creek. Fish in the stocked pond or on the Arkansas river. In season hunt elk, big horn sheep, mule deer and bear. Within a scenic hour or two drive are the Royal Gorge, the Sand Dunes and many historic mining towns.

This is a non-smoking inn and no pets are allowed. Children over 12 are welcomed. Ideal for reunions and weddings.

Location: South of Highway 291, on County Road 160, 3 miles east of US 285, 3 miles west of Salida.

7 Lodging Rooms
13 Beds in Bunk House or Dorm

Lobby Phone
Bed & Breakfast Available
All Non-Smoking in Units
Recreation Room
Elevation: 7000
Credit Cards: VM
2 people a night: $60 - $70
Open: All Year

Virginia Nemmers, Owner
8495 CR 160
Salida CO 81201
719/539-3818
800/385-6925

At the resort:

At resort or within 15 minutes:

Sagewood Cabins

High in the heart of the Collegiate Peaks Range, at the foot of Mt. Harvard (14,000+ feet) Sagewood offers quaint, quiet, country log cabins located on a small family ranch. A true Colorado getaway, the cabins, adjacent to the San Isabel National Forest, have no televisions or telephones (the office phone is available if you need it). These country style cabins are full of antiques. Some cabins have fireplaces; all have private baths and lofts. Each is set up for basic housekeeping with dishes, cooking utensils and linens.

Area activities include hiking, biking, fishing, horseback riding, four-wheel driving trails and exploring ghost towns. In the winter, come for snowmobiling and skiing. Year-round, enjoy shopping or resting and relaxing away from it all. Stay for a night, a week or a month.

Reservations are recommended. Sagewood is normally open from May through November; however, the season may begin earlier or later due to weather conditions. Call ahead for open dates.

Location: 11.5 miles north of Buena Vista on Highway 24, near milepost 199/200, a quarter mile west of the highway.

3 Cabins with Kitchens
2 Fireplaces

Lobby Phone
Elevation: 9000
No credit cards
2 people a night: $65
Open: 5/1 to 11/15

Kristen Ahlstedt-Killinen & Steve Killinen, Managers
38951-B N Hwy 24
Buena Vista CO 81211
719/395-2582

At the resort:

At resort or within 15 minutes:

Thunder Lodge

Vacation at "your home away from home" at Thunder Lodge, on the tree lined banks of Cottonwood Creek. Eight roomy family-size log cabins are nestled along the shady, tree-lined banks of Cottonwood Creek. Clean and quiet, the cabins surround a nice grassy lawn in a relaxing atmosphere. All cabins come with modern conveniences, such as fully equipped kitchenettes and color cable television, while featuring a western Indian motif of pine and oak interiors and furnishings. Each cabin has two double beds including a hide-a-bed in the living room, accommodating large families comfortably. Enjoy a summer evening cooking outside your cabin on the BBQ grill and eating at your picnic table as the sun sets over the mountain peaks.

After a day exploring, play a game of shuffle board on the Lodges' large lawn. A wide range of year-round activities are available, including sightseeing, arrowhead hunting, trout fishing, hiking, biking, downhill and cross-country skiing, snowmobiling on groomed trails, hunting and just plain taking it easy. The area offer elk, deer, bear and lion hunting. Both Ski Cooper and Monarch Ski area are within an hours drive.

The lodge is open all year, with off-season rates. Cribs are available; children three and under stay free. The lodge requires a deposit with reservations. If you stay ten nights or longer ask about discounted rates. From June through August there is a two night minimum stay for advance reservations.

Location: 2 blocks north of stoplight and one block west of Highway 24, near milepost 210 in Buena Vista.

8 Cabins with Kitchens
Central Campfire Area

Pay phone
Elevation: 8000
Credit Cards: VMD
2 people a night: $40 - $68
Open: All Year

Robert Reichert, Manager
PO Box 504
207 Brookdale Ave
Buena Vista CO 81211-0504
719/395-2245
800/330-9194

At the resort:

At resort or within 15 minutes:

Twin Lakes Nordic Inn & Mountain Bike Rentals

An authentic century-old stagecoach stop and former brothel, the Twin Lakes Nordic Inn has been romantically restored with imported Austrian featherbeds and antiques. All of the rooms offer different styles, views and architecture. Some have their own baths; others have shared baths.

The inn's restaurant, open all day, specializes in authentic German cuisine, beers and wines and fireside dining. A video room with a film library is available for those evenings when you want to relax indoors. Ask your host to arrange river rafting trips on the Arkansas in the summer. Explore the ghost town of Interlaken on the south side of the larger twin lake and accessible only by horseback, mountain bike, skis or on foot. In the heart of the Pike-San Isabel National Forest on the shore of Twin Lakes, the Nordic Inn is an ideal base camp for cross-country and alpine skiing, fishing, hiking, hunting and windsurfing. You can rent mountain bikes and canoes at the Inn. Twice a year, be sure to attend the "Hookers Ball" — but only with an appropriate costume!

Location: In Twin Lakes, off of Highway 82, near milepost 79.

17 Lodging Rooms
Central Fireplace

Pay Phone(s)
Bed & Breakfast Available
All Non-Smoking in Units
Recreation Room
Elevation: 9227
Credit Cards: VM
2 people a night: $47 - $65
Open: All Year

Leo Kniebel, Owner
PO Box 410
6435 Hwy 82
Twin Lakes CO 81251-0410
719/486-1830 & Fax
800/626-7812

At the resort:

At resort or within 15 minutes:

Twin Peaks Cabins

Twin Peaks Cabins are at the edge of the forest and offer a lovely view of the south side of upper Twin Lakes. These modern, fully equipped, log-sided housekeeping cabins have the mountain peaks of the Sawatch Range looming at their door step. The large cabin has 4 bedrooms with queen-size beds, 2 baths, a deck and can sleep up to 10 persons. The small cabin is ideal for a couple, with a double bed, small refrigerator toaster oven and double hot plate for cooking. The medium size cabin has two rooms: a kitchen/living room and bedroom with two double beds. None of the cabins have televisions or telephones; however, there are books, magazines, and games to pass the time.

The gift shop on-site features leather and fur items including sheepskins, steer hides and alpaca; and southwestern gifts. For the sports enthusiasts there is a basketball court, volleyball/badminton net, and horseshoe pit. The kids will love the sandbox complete with shovels and play toys. Bring your boat to take advantage of the good fishing in lakes, boat ramps within minutes. Fish for brook, lake, and brown trout in the many streams, some within walking distance. Hiking trails begin near the cabins and offer enough scenery to keep photographers busy for years! The cabins are a quarter mile west of Twin Lakes on the road to Independence Pass, the "high road" to Aspen.

Location: Off of Highway 82, near milepost 78. A quarter mile west of Twin Lakes.

2 Cabins with Kitchens
Central Campfire Area

Lobby Phone
Elevation: 9200
Credit Cards: VM
2 people a night: $40 - $70
Open: 5/15 to 11/15

Fred & Judy Woodcock, Owners
PO Box 86
6889 Hwy 82
Twin Lakes CO 81251-0086
719/486-2667 & Fax

At the resort:

At resort or within 15 minutes:

Win-Mar Cabins

In an excellent, central location, Win-Mar has 11 log cabins with fantastic views of the highest peaks in Colorado — Mount Elbert – 14,433' and Mount Massive – 14,418'. In addition, they are cozy, modern and clean, with fully equipped kitchens; however, the atmosphere is rustic. Cabins range a single room to 3 bedrooms in size, with 4 one-bed cabins, 6 two-bed cabins and 1 three-bedroom, two bath cabin.

Fish for weeks on nearby Twin Lakes and Clear Creek Reservoirs. Anglers will enjoy fly fishing along the Arkansas River. Ask your hosts about other mountain adventures, such as hiking, hunting, mountain biking, whitewater raft trips, rock climbing and panning for gold. Just a few miles down the road, you'll see the historic town of Leadville, with its famous Opera House and other historic buildings.

Nightly and weekly rates are available. Reservations are recommended. A one night deposit is required in advance with all reservations.

Location: At the intersection of Highways 24 and 82, near milepost 191. Just 15 miles south of Leadville or 17 miles north of Buena Vista.

11 Cabins with Kitchens
1 Woodstove

Lobby Phone
Elevation: 9000
Credit Cards: VMD
2 people a night: $50 - $60
Open: 5/30 to 9/2

Rod & Dolores Rodaway, Managers
Twin Lakes Star Route
Granite CO 81228
719/486-0785
800/6-Win Mar (694-6627)

At the resort:

At resort or within 15 minutes:

Conejos River Canyon

Including Antonito & Platoro — Map: P-13 & O-11

The southern San Luis Valley city of **Antonito** is rich in culture and history from the Ute Indians and the Spanish who called the valley home. Antonito lies between the Conejos and the San Antonio rivers at an elevation of 7,888' and is the gateway to the beautiful, 40-mile Conejos River Canyon where outdoor enthusiasts can fish, hunt and hike. The upper Conejos River offers excellent trout fishing and the lower part is good for rainbows, browns and the occasional northern pike. The Platoro Reservoir has wonderful fishing for browns, rainbows and some kokanee soon after the spring thaw and is stocked with rainbow trout in the summer. No matter the river or lake, fishermen will always have something biting their line in Conejos River Canyon area. Antonito was once the "mainline" of the infant Denver and Rio Grande railroads. Today, Antonito is the main station for the Cumbres & Toltec Scenic Railroad — the highest and longest narrow-gauge railroad in the North American continent — an authentic railroad trip to Chama, New Mexico, that brings Colorado history to the present day. Nearby the town of Conejos boasts the oldest church in Colorado, Our Lady of Guadeloupe Church. The Rio Grand National Forest offers rolling hills, river canyons, and thick pine and aspen forests to explore.

Fun Things to Do

- Cumbres & Toltec Scenic Railroad (719) 376-5983
- Our Lady of Guadeloupe Church (719) 376-5985
- Rio Grande National Forest Headquarters (719) 852-5941

Conejos Cabins

Near the Continental Divide on an easily-traveled 23-mile gravel road, Conejos Cabins has ten riverside cabins. The large, family cabin can sleep up to 18 people. The two bedroom cabin can accommodate up to 8, while the small cabin with one bedroom sleeps 4. Cabins have dishes, cooking utensils and bedding while larger cabins have fireplaces furnished with wood. Cook your daily meals inside or outside on the handy grills. The resort is surrounded by mountains, on the Conejos River and an old gold mining town.

Plan to rent fishing boats to cruise the nearby Platoro Reservoir. Rent a horse nearby or bring your own for a ride to the high mountain lakes in the surrounding area where the fishing is pristine.

First night's deposit is required within 10 days of making a reservation. Also visit their Web site at http://www.conejoscabins.com.

Location: Take Highway 17 west from Antonito 23 miles, near milepost 17, to Horca. Go north 23 miles on gravel road #250, follow the river up to the cabins.

9 Cabins with Kitchens
1 Vacation Home
5 Fireplaces

Lobby Phone
Elevation: 9750
Credit Cards: VM
2 people a night: $55 - $90
Open: 5/25 to 10/15

Bob, Dixie & Troy Peterson, Owners
PO Box 519
FR 250 at Platoro
Antonito CO 81120-0519
719/376-2547
417/842-3279 Winter

At the resort:

At resort or within 15 minutes:

Conejos River Guest Ranch

With a mile of river frontage, Conejos River Guest Ranch is situated in the Rio Grande National Forest on twelve acres. Enjoy a bed & breakfast adventure in the 104 year-old lodge with a classy western decor and exterior wrap-around deck. The lodge rooms have private baths, and a choice of king, queen or double bed, and a hide-a-bed. A full, scrumptious breakfast is included as well. Or choose a comfortable housekeeping cabin featuring a fully-equipped kitchen sleeping from five to eleven people. Some of the cabins include a cozy woodburning stove. All guests can enjoy the common den area in the lodge with a fireplace, satellite television, game table, bar, and mini-library.

During your stay, be sure to take advantage of basketball, volleyball, horseshoes, hiking, relaxing by the river, and, of course, fishing—all on the premises. Children will enjoy the stocked children's fishing pond and wandering farm animals. Boxed lunches are available daily for your outdoor excursions. Browse through the gift shop for your perfect southwest sovenier. Take a tour of the Rio Grande Forest or the Great Sand Dunes National Monument. Ride on the Cumbres & Toltec Narrow Gauge Railroad; your hosts can make reservations for you. Big game hunting in season is especially popular. Rent a snowmobile or cross-country skis for winter sports. After a full day of activity, enjoy the "Best food in the Canyon" at the restaurant. Campfires and chuckwagon meals are spontaneously planned by your hosts. They would be delighted to help organize and customize your next party, meeting or family reunion.

Advance reservations are recommended. A 50% deposit is required.

Location: At 25390 Highway 17, near milepost 26, in Antonito.

6 Cabins with Kitchens
8 Lodging Rooms
4 Woodstoves
Central Woodstove
Central Campfire Area

Pay Phone(s)
Bed & Breakfast Available
Recreation Room
Elevation: 8700
Credit Cards: VMD
2 people a night: $69 - $95
Open: 5/12 to 1/2

Shorty Fry, Manager
PO Box 175
25390 Hwy 17
Conejos CO 81129-0175
719/376-2464

At the resort:

At resort or within 15 minutes:

Cottonwood Meadows Cabins & Fly Shop

The modern housekeeping cabins at Cottonwood Meadows are in the midst of San Luis Valley's prime fly-fishing country. The cabins are comfortably equipped with a kitchenette, cooking and eating utensils and baths with a tub or shower. The large cabin on the banks of the Conejos River sleeps up to 7 persons. Anglers will want to make this their base camp for catching tasty, trout suppers!

Take guided fishing trips into the Rio Grande National Forest, including the Conejos River and its many tributaries. If you crave solitude while casting, fish all day in backwoods streams. Most Cottonwood Meadow trips are limited to no more than two guests per guide. The completely stocked fly shop on-site has all you need, including rods, reels and waders. Buy your other vacation supplies at the on-site grocery store. In addition to guided fishing trips, take a horseback ride or go on an overnight trip into the wilderness. Other nearby attractions include the Cumbres & Toltec Scenic Railroad, the Great Sand Dunes National Monument and the Rio Grande Gorge.

Location: 5 miles west of Antonito on Highway 17, near milepost 35.

5 Cabins with Kitchens

Pay Phone(s)
Elevation: 7600
Credit Cards: VMAD
2 people a night: $45 - $100
Open: All Year

Randy & Naomi Keys, Owners
34591 Hwy 17
Antonito CO 81120
719/376-5660

At the resort:

At resort or within 15 minutes:

Josey's Mogote Meadow

Placed among seven acres of green grass and shady cottonwood trees, Josey's has modern housekeeping cabins fully equipped with kitchenettes, cooking and eating utensils and modern baths. In addition, there are on-site trailers for rent. Laundry facilities are available at this friendly, family atmosphere resort in a mountain meadow.

Beautiful and relaxing, Josey's offers fishing in the Conejos River and nearby lakes. Mountain bike trails and horseback riding are minutes away. Explore the sand dunes and beautiful scenery of this area. Join the nightly campfire and bring something for the Wednesday night pot luck dinners. On Sundays, the whole family will like the pancake breakfast. Josey's sits right by the Los Caminos Antiguos Scenic Byway which runs southwest over La Manga and Cumbres pass, both over 10,000' in elevation. Within an easy day trip are the Red River, Wolf Creek Pass, and Taos and Chama in New Mexico. For a trip into the past, take a ride on the Cumbres-Toltec Scenic Railroad.

RV sites with cement patios and an outdoor, group meeting area are also available. Reservations are necessary.

Location: 5 miles west of Antonito on Highway 17, near milepost 34.

2 Cabins with Kitchens
Central Campfire Area

Pay Phone(s)
Recreation Room
Elevation: 8066
No credit cards
2 people a night: $38
Open: 5/1 to 10/20

Bob & Anne Josey, Owners
34127 Hwy 17
Antonito CO 81120
719/376-5774

At the resort:

At resort or within 15 minutes:

Mountain Home Lodge

Located in southern Colorado in the scenic Conejos Canyon 22 miles west of Antonito, Mountain Home Lodge has breath-taking scenery year-round. Choose between one and two bedroom, modern, light housekeeping units. Both have full kitchens and separate living areas. The one bedroom units have a king bed and a queen hide-a-bed. The two bedroom units have a king bed, two single beds and a queen hide-a-bed.

Mountain Home Lodge has a restaurant, gift shop/convenience store, and laundry facilities on the premises for your convenience. In the winter, take a snowmobile tour or rent cross-country skis at the store. In the summer, take in the breathtaking scenery of the San Juan Mountains via horseback. This area offers excellent big game hunting and gold medal waters for trophy trout fishing. The Conejos River has been designated a Wild Trout River by the state of Colorado. The lodge is less than 30 minutes from the famous Cumbres Toltec Narrow Gauge Steam Railroad — a ride on this is a trip through the past as well as panoramic vistas. Be sure to take time out for a dip in the hot tub after your day's adventure.

Location: On Highway 17, milepost 17.

12 Lodging Rooms
Central Woodstove

Pay Phone(s)
Non-Smoking Units Available
Recreation Room
Elevation: 8650
Credit Cards: VMAD
2 people a night: $50 - $70
Open: All Year

Betty & Sherman Matthys, Owners
0047 FDR 250
Antonito CO 81120
719/376-5393
719/376-2245 Fax

At the resort:

At resort or within 15 minutes:

Ponderosa Cabins & Campground

The combination of pine trees, cottonwood trees and the Conejos River make this a beautiful vacation spot. Stay in newly remolded, housekeeping cabins surrounded by large cottonwoods, pines, firs and willows. Gather firewood in the area. A place for leisure with its clean, crisp mountain air, Ponderosa Cabins includes one mile of access along the rushing Conejos River and rests at the foot of the scenic Cumbres Pass. In the summertime, the climate is dry in the day and cool at night.

Hot showers, clean restrooms and a coin laundry are on-site for your convenience. A game room with board games, pool table and video games and a playground are on the property. With the river just steps away, fishing opportunities abound. Mountain biking and hiking trails are a short distance away. Kayaking and rafting is excellent here in June.

RV and tent sites and an indoor, group meeting area are also available.

Location: On Highway 17 at milepost 19.

6 Cabins with Kitchens
Central Fireplace

Lobby Phone
Recreation Room
Elevation: 8500
Credit Cards: VM
2 people a night: $38
Open: 5/26 to 10/1

Karl Casebeer, Owner
19600 W Hwy 17
Antonito CO 81120
719/376-5857

At the resort:

At resort or within 15 minutes:

Texan Court Cabins

Snug in the high mountains of southern Colorado Texan Court Cabins features housekeeping cabins and lodge rooms. Their cabins sleep from two to four people and are completely furnished with kitchens and private bathrooms. Each lodge room sleep two and has private bathrooms. The cabins are surrounded by the San Juan Mountains with breathtaking views and nestled near the Conejos River for your audio visual delight.

Texan Court has a lodge featuring a game room with a pool table, gift shop and coin laundry. There are ample mountain biking trails in the area and with the resorts bike rental facility its easy to plan a last minute excursion. The area offers some of the best hunting and fishing in the state. Bring your boat and enjoy Platoro Reservoir, the highest man made lake in North America, a short drive away. In addition to the reservoir there are over 100 lakes in the area, an anglers delight. Bird enthusiast will be delighted and photographers should bring extra film. There are guided fishing and horseback riding tours leaving right from your cabin. The resort is open through the first rifle season in October.

A deposit of one night is required with reservations. Stay seven nights and only pay for six. Children under 5 years old stay free. Pets are welcome to join you.

Location: Take Highway 17 west from Antonito 20 miles, near milepost 17, to Horca. Go north 23 miles on gravel road #250, follow the river up to the cabins.

10 Cabins with Kitchens
2 cabins without Kitchens
Central Fireplace
Central Campfire Area

Pay Phone(s)
Recreation Room
Elevation: 10000
Credit Cards: VMD
2 people a night: $25 - $75
Open: 5/30 to 10/16

Otto & Audrey Kuhlmann, Owners
FDR 250 at Platoro
Antonito CO 81120
719/376-2321
970/483-6394 Winter

At the resort:

At resort or within 15 minutes:

Twin Rivers Cabins & RV Park

Away from the hustle and bustle, at the mouth of the beautiful Conejos Canyon where the fishing and hunting are excellent, are Twin Rivers' country-decorated cabins. Choose from 8 rustic housekeeping cabins sprawled about Twin Rivers' 12 acres ranging in size from a studio to 2 bedrooms. Each is furnished with linens, dishes, cooking utensils and color television, plus an outdoor bar-b-que grill and picnic table.

Fly fish right at your doorstep in the park's two stocked streams. Or cast your line in nearby reservoirs, mountain lakes, rivers and streams. Play volleyball, badminton, or horsehoes while letting the kids romp in the playground. A tackle and gift shop are on the property for supplies, ice and souvenirs. Arrange for a catered chuckwagon dinner or a good old fashioned hay ride. The Rio Grande National Forest and San Juan Mountains are within 10 miles for outstanding hiking and mountain biking. Take a trip to Taos, New Mexico or the Great Sand Dunes National Monument, both just an hour away. Guest horses are allowed.

RV and tent sites in the shade, an indoor, group meeting area, group activities and catering are available. Ask about the family rates.

Location: 5 miles west of Antonito and the Cumbres & Toltec Scenic Railroad depot, on Highway 17, near milepost 34.

8 Cabins with Kitchens
Central Campfire Area

Pay Phone(s)
Recreation Room
Elevation: 8000
Credit Cards: VMD
2 people a night: $38 - $60
Open: 5/1 to 11/15

Jim & Linda Mcgee, Owners
34044 Hwy 17
Antonito CO 81120
719/376-5710 & Fax

At the resort:

At resort or within 15 minutes:

Creede

Map: M-9

Isolated and picturesque, **Creede**, at 8,854', is in Mineral County where 95 percent of the land is national forest or wilderness. Prospector Nicholas Creede discovered silver here in 1889 and one of his mines, the Amethyst, produced $2 million one year. What attracted hundreds of miners also brought crooks: "Soapy" Smith opened the Orleans Club to separate miners from their riches. He was eventually banned from Creede which was also home to other famous westerners, including Calamity Jane and Bob Ford, the man who shot Jesse James in the back. Today, the old mining town atmosphere still exists in restaurants, shops and the Creede Repertory Theater. The Wheeler Geologic Area, 24 miles northeast, is a photographer's dream: unusual volcanic rock formations have earned it the name City of Gnomes. From the Rio Grande Reservoir, 30 miles away, to Creede, people raft and fish for the plentiful German brown trout along the Rio Grande headwaters. The Bachelor Historic Loop, a 17-mile ride through the unique silver mining district and two ghost towns, and the Silver Thread Scenic Byway, which runs from South Fork through Creede east to Lake City, are two ways to enjoy the backcountry without crowds. Along the Silver Thread Scenic Byway, State Highway 149, are some of the most majestic valleys in all of Colorado — the distances between mountain peaks appears vast and mesmerizing.

Fun Things to Do

- Broadacres Stables (719) 658-2291
- Creede Ranger District (719) 658-2556
- Creede Repertory Theater (719) 658-2540
- Creede Underground Firehouse (719) 658-0811
- Rio Grande National Forest & Weminuche Wilderness (719) 658-2556
- Underground Mining Museum (719) 658-0811

Antlers Rio Grande Lodge

Homesteaded in 1896, Antlers Rio Grande Lodge is a picturesque mountain retreat nestled between the banks of the sparkling Rio Grande River and the Silver Thread Scenic Byway. Most of the secluded modern cabins and motel rooms have gas heat, two double or queen-sized beds, a bathroom with a shower and fully equipped kitchenettes. Enjoy a cup of coffee or a night cap on the porch swing outside your cabin door. If you want a more unique experience ask about their rustic cabins across the Rio Grande River. You'll have to carry your gear over the foot-bridge; but it's worth the effort. At night you'll feel a million miles from civilization with only the sound of the river to lull you to sleep.

For those days when you don't want to explore the outdoors, ranch facilities include a rec room with snack bar, children's playroom and television room with VCR and movies. Fly fish right from your front door or cross the foot-bridge to the quiet side of the ranch for your fishing. A fish fry/potluck dinner is a weekly event. You can purchase fishing licenses and supplies at the lodge store. The Lodge's 70 acres borders the Rio Grande National Forest, providing unlimited opportunities for spring, summer and fall enjoyment. Popular sports include hiking, whitewater river rafting, mountain biking and horseback riding.

Antlers Ranch offers group rates. Ideal for small groups and reunions. Pets and horses are welcomed for a fee and must be declared at registration.

Location: 5 miles southwest of Creede, just off Highway 149, near milepost 26.

13 Cabins with Kitchens
3 Woodstoves
Central Fireplace
Central Campfire Area

Pay Phone(s)
Non-Smoking Units Available
Recreation Room
Elevation: 8720
Credit Cards: VM
2 people a night: $50 - $77
Open: 5/1 to 10/30

Patty & Charles Powers, Owners
26222 Hwy 149
Creede CO 81130
719/658-2423 & Fax Call 1st
561/622-9797 Oct - April

At the resort:

At resort or within 15 minutes:

Broadacres Guest Ranch

A heavenly place to relax, Broadacres Ranch is a 600-acre working cattle ranch. With picture-perfect scenery, the cottages are quarter mile off the highway along the river in a high mountain valley. Some of the fully furnished, two- and three-bedroom modern cottages overlook the river. Broadacres office is close to the road; however, the cabins are set back from the road so you can look forward to quiet, cool nights away from it all.

Fish in the stocked Rio Grande River, in nearby streams or at a private lake for the abundant German brown trout. Take guided horseback rides right from the property along scenic mountain trails as the ranch borders National Forest lands. They own horses for trail rides and emphasize a ranch atmosphere at Broadacres. Four-wheel driving, mountain biking and whitewater river rafting are nearby. Take a drive on the Silver Thread Scenic Byway.

RV sites are also available.

Location: 4 miles southwest of Creede just off Highway 149, near milepost 25.

BROADACRES

12 Cabins with Kitchens
2 Fireplaces

Lobby Phone
Elevation: 8887
No credit cards
2 people a night: $37 - $67
Open: 5/26 to 10/31

Bea Collerette, Owner
PO Box 39
HCR 70
Creede CO 81130-0039
719/658-2291

At the resort:

At resort or within 15 minutes:

Broken Arrow Ranch

Stay at the Broken Arrow Ranch on the Silver Thread Scenic Byway and enjoy the spectacular views of Bristol Head and Red Mountains. Relax in either their modern or semi-modern cabins. Each rustic cabin is quaintly decorated and has either one or two bedrooms. The modern cabins have private baths and the semi-modern have a central bathhouse. Warm up on a cool morning by lighting the wood cook stove and putting on a pot of coffee. For the less adventuresome each cabin has a propane cook top and a propane heater. Bedding, linens, cooking and eating utensils are all furnished for your convenience.

The ranch is southwest of Creede in the breathtaking Upper Rio Grande Valley of the San Juan Mountains, A perfect family vacation spot. Encompassing 60 acres with unlimited access to the Rio Grande National Forest to the north and west, the Ranch provides you with some of the finest hunting and fishing in the area. Hike, mountain bike or fish from your cabin doorstep. A private stocked lake for fishing is available just a short walk or drive from the cabins. Team ropers beware, there are a few in the arena and an area nearby to practice. Take some time to travel into Creede to visit the historic underground mining museum and firehouse. Or, take a self guided tour around the Bachelor Loop and imagine 10,000 residents there at the height of the silver boom! Visit the many unique shops and galleries. Enjoy breakfast, lunch or dinner at any of the great restaurants in the area. Be sure to catch Creede Repertory Theater performances.

Ask about the group and off season rates. Great for family reunions. Guest horses are permitted with prior arrangement.

Location: 12 miles southwest of Creede on Highway 149 at milepost 33.

10 Cabins with Kitchens
Central Campfire Area

Lobby Phone
All Non-Smoking in Units
Elevation: 9000
Credit Cards: VMD
2 people a night: $39 - $49
Open: 5/15 to 9/30

Dale & Anne Pizel, Owners
32728 Hwy 149
HC 70
Creede CO 81130
719/658-2484 & Fax call1st
719/658-2533 Fax call 1st

At the resort:

At resort or within 15 minutes:

Soward Ranch

Off the beaten path in a scenic valley on the Rio Grande River, Soward Ranch has been in the same family for over 100 years — a true Colorado centennial farm. The ranch was homesteaded in 1886 before the time of Creede in what was originally known as Antelope Park. Surrounded by mountains, the large resort and cattle ranch has six lakes with outstanding views. Each cabin, located apart from the others to ensure privacy, are modernized with a full bath, gas heating for cooking and electricity. If you want to rough it, try the ranch's pioneer cabin. Dishes, silverware, utensils, bedding and linen are furnished in all cabins. A central shower and coin washer and dryer are available to all guests.

Fishing for trout on the property along several miles of creeks, on the Rio Grande and at three small private lakes is excellent. Soward Ranch is also close to many other state-stocked lakes, reservoirs and streams. Take a quiet hike along secluded trails and enjoy mountain serenity at its best.

Advance reservations are required.

Location: 14 miles southwest of Creede, off of Highway 149, near milepost 28.

11 Cabins with Kitchens
3 Fireplaces
1 Woodstove
Central Campfire Area

Lobby Phone
Recreation Room
Elevation: 9000
No credit cards
2 people a night: $40 - $65
Open: 5/26 to 10/7

Margaret M. Lamb, Owner
PO Box 130
SW of Creede Hwy 149
Creede CO 81130-0130
719/658-2295
719/658-2228 Winter

At the resort:

At resort or within 15 minutes:

Thirty Mile Resort

To reach this resort, you have to drive through a national forest campground to the property. Situated on next to the Rio Grande National Forest and the headwaters of the Rio Grande, Thirty Mile Resort has nine housekeeping cabins set in the woods and two lodge rooms. All the cabins have woodstoves for heat and cooking. This authentic 1930s style fishing and hunting camp has a central shower and generates its own electricity. The accommodations have neither telephones or televisions — the perfect place to get away from it all and experience a little peace and quiet.

Thirty Mile Resort sits at the edge of the wilderness where you can hike, mountain bike, boat and horseback ride to your heart's content. Travel along the trails through the stunning Weminuche Wilderness. A short drive away are river rafting trips and a museum explaining the area's fascinating history. The owners pride themselves on being committed to preserving the natural environment. Thus, small pets are not allowed as they attack the bears. Fish right on the property and then cook your fresh trout in a cast iron skillet on a woodburning cookstove. Gather around the evening campfires and spin your tales with other guests.

All units are non-smoking.

Location: 30 miles west of Creede on Rio Grande Reservoir Road. Entrance through U.S. Forest Service, then 30 miles past campground.

9 Cabins with Kitchens
2 Lodging Rooms
9 Woodstoves
Central Campfire Area

Lobby Phone
All Non-Smoking in Units
Elevation: 9400
No credit cards
2 people a night: $58 - $80
Open: 5/28 to 9/30

Leona Trego, Owner
SW of Creede
HCR 70
Creede CO 81130
719/658-2294

At the resort:

At resort or within 15 minutes:

Durango & Vallecito Lake Areas

Including Bayfield — Map: P-5, O-6

A city created by the railroad, **Durango** retains a "Frontier West" feeling. Surrounded by the San Juan Mountains, this town bustles with activity. Take a walk through living history down Main Street, Durango's National Register Historic District. The famous Durango-Silverton Narrow Gauge Railroad is the country's only coal-and-steam-powered train operating daily. Chug along sheer cliffs, criss-crossing the Animas River on the 45 mile trip to Silverton. The Animas River, or river of lost souls, has wild whitewater rafting during spring run-off and settles down in the summer for family jaunts. Rent a bike for a day and discover why this area is so popular with mountain bikers. Only 6 miles north is the Trimble Hot Springs where heated water from the La Plata Mountains arrives at the resort at a toasty 119• F. Set amidst reddish, sandstone bluffs, Durango is 25 miles north of Purgatory Ski Resort which offers the unpretentious skiing of the southwest. **Vallecito Lake**, located 23 miles northwest of Durango, lies under the snow-capped peaks of the San Juan National Forest. This lake is an angler's delight — fish for rainbow trout, kokanee salmon and northern pike. Several boat ramps and docks surround the 22-mile lake shoreline. The Vallecito Trail and the Pine River Trail access the Weminuche Wilderness where mountain bikes are strictly forbidden, but hikers and horseback riders are welcomed.

Fun Things to Do

- Animas School Museum (970) 259-2402
- Bar D Chuckwagon Suppers (970) 247-5753
- Durango-Silverton Narrow Gauge Railroad (970) 247-2733
- Five Branches Horse Rides, Vallecito Lake (800) 582-9580
- Hillcrest Golf Course (970) 247-1499
- Mountain Waters Rafting (800) 748-2507, (970) 259-4191
- Old Hundred Gold Mine Tour (800) 872-3009
- San Juan Rio Grande National Forest (970) 247-4874
- Tamarron Golf Course (970) 259-2000
- Trimble Hot Springs (970) 247-0111

Circle S Lodge

Journey to a high-country retreat in the picturesque San Juan Mountains. Circle S Lodge is adjacent to the Weminuche Wilderness area on the north end of Vallecito Lake and features nicely decorated private mountain cabins that can accommodate up to nine people. Each completely carpeted cabin includes all linens, a fully equipped kitchen, a microwave, a fireplace, an outdoor grill and a picnic table. For your convenience, they have a laundromat on the premises.

The kids will have fun on the playground and fishing in the small trout pond. Adults can pitch horseshoes or play volleyball, badminton and basketball. Surrounded by so much wilderness, you'll want to rent horses and boats, fish in the lakes and rivers, hike and take pictures. A grocery store and restaurant are within walking distance.

A 50% deposit of rental fee is required for reservations.

Location: Just northwest of Vallecito Lake.

7 Cabins with Kitchens
1 Vacation Home
8 Fireplaces

Pay Phone(s)
Elevation: 7850
Credit Cards: VMAD
2 people a night: $75
Open: 5/12 to 10/1

Steve & Cheryl Popely, Owners
18022 CR 501
Bayfield CO 81122
970/884-2473
970/884-0519 Fax call 1st

At the resort:

At resort or within 15 minutes:

Cool Water Ranch Cabins

Nestled beneath ancient pines beside the beautiful Pine River, also known as Los Piños Rio, are five cottage-style cabins. Two of the cabins have two bedrooms with 2 twin-beds and a double bed. Choose from two studios one with 2 double beds the other with a single double bed. The largest cabin has three bedrooms with 2 twin-beds and 2 double beds. All the cabins, equipped with kitchenettes, pots, pans, dishes and linens, offer modern comforts without modern hassles — no telephones or television, just a peaceful country environment.

Cool Water Ranch is quiet and off the highway, yet close to Vallecito Lake for restaurants and shopping. Enjoy trout fishing from your back door and in nearby mountain streams, lakes and rivers.

In July and August, rentals are by the week only. Advanced reservations recommended. RV sites are also available. Pets are welcome.

Location: 2 miles south of Vallecito Lake.

5 Cabins with Kitchens

Lobby Phone
Elevation: 7500
No credit cards
2 people a night: Call for Rates
Open: 5/1 to 10/5

Thomas W. Beuten, Operator
10643 CR 501
Bayfield CO 81122-9701
970/884-2269
970/884-9242
970/884-9242

At the resort:

At resort or within 15 minutes:

Cottonwood Camper Cabins & Camper Park

Close to downtown Durango, Cottonwood Cabins is within walking distance of the Durango/Silverton Narrow Gauge Railroad, the town's shopping district and restaurants. The two new camping cabins have access to hot showers and flush toilets. This is a "plain jane" cabin and RV resort for those who want to save money and walk to town.

You'll be able to fish nearby on the Animas River for a dinner of fresh rainbow trout. Mountain biking, horseback riding, golfing, and river rafting are among the area's outdoor attractions. In the fall, come for the big game hunting. Popular places to explore in the area include Mesa Verde National Park, Four Corners Monument and Vallecito Lake.

RV sites are also available. Pets are welcome.

Location: Just south of Durango on Highway 160, near milepost 83.

2 Camper Cabins

Pay Phone(s)
All Non-Smoking in Units
Elevation: 7000
No credit cards
2 people a night: $30
Open: 5/1 to 10/31

Norma & Jim Johnson, Owners
PO Box 1456
21636 US 160
Durango CO 81302-1456
970/247-1977

At the resort:

At resort or within 15 minutes:

Elk Point Lodge

Relax on the tranquil east shore of Vallecito Lake at Pine River. Elk Point features modern cabins with fully equipped kitchens, tucked away among tall pines. choose between a cabin on the lakefront or with a view of beautiful Vallecito Lake. Some cabins have fireplaces and all bedding and towels are provided (there are even extra blankets in each room). All cabins boast knotty pine interiors, carpet and bathrooms with showers. The cabins are decorated with rustic wood furniture. Firewood is provided. All cabins are off the main road and the only noise to boast of are the pitter-pattering feet of the friendly squirrels.

The lodge has a general store. There is also a recreation room with a pool table, foosball table, games, books and a huge rock fireplace. There is always a puzzle to be completed. Outside is a playground for the kids. Rent horses and fishing boats on the property or fish the lake and Pine River. Culminate the perfect day with a sunset dinner ride. Elk Point Lodge is adjacent to the San Juan National Forest, ideal for horseback riding, mountain biking and hiking. Weminuche Wilderness is 3 miles away, your hosts can help plan pack trips and expeditions for autumn elk, deer and small game hunting. Open all year, the resort offers a selection of winter sports as well. Snowmobile tours are available or bring your own. Cross-country ski right outside your front door. Or just come to relax, watch a beautiful sunset from your porch while barbecuing dinner and listen to the water gently lapping the shore.

The Elk Point is wonderful for a fall or winter vacation and less crowded.

Location: Follow paved road around west and north side of Vallecito lake. When pavement ends, keep going south two miles on gravel road.

10 Cabins with Kitchens
4 Woodstoves
Central Fireplace

Pay Phone(s)
Recreation Room
Elevation: 7800
Credit Cards: VMD
2 people a night: $58 - $140
Open: All Year

JR (Larry) & Lark Kokesh, Owners
21730 CR 501
Bayfield CO 81122-9703
970/884-2482 & Fax

At the resort:

At resort or within 15 minutes:

Five Branches Camper Park & Camper Cabins

Snug among 26 acres of tall pine trees, Five Branches Camper Park has 3,000 feet of frontage on the picturesque Vallecito Lake and the roaring Pine River. Across the covered, wooden bridge, you'll find camper cabins and platform tent cabins in grass surroundings, with a view of clear blue water backed by snow-capped peaks. Bring your own bedding and cooking supplies. New clean restrooms, coin hot showers, grocery, gift shop, and a coin laundry are on-site.

Take a breakfast horseback ride into the San Juan Mountains or an evening lake cruise as the setting sun casts colorful images onto the rippling water. Guest horses are welcomed here. Mountain bike trails start at Five Branches. There's plenty of river and lake fishing for avid anglers and you can rent a pontoon, canoe, paddle boat or fishing boat from the park. Side trips to Silverton and Ouray are great for those who like to explore. Photographers will love the stunning wildflower beds. A video game room and playground will keep the kids busy. The camp store has groceries, snacks, camping supplies, fishing and hunting licenses, gift shop and delicious hand dipped ice cream cones. Planned activities include bingo, horseshoes, volleyball, and potluck suppers.

An outdoor, group meeting area, full hookup RV sites, and tent sites available.

Location: On Vallecito Lake's east shore. Follow paved road around west and north side of the lake. When the pavement ends, keep going south another 3 miles on dirt road, or take the shorter but unpaved route across the dam and along the east shore.

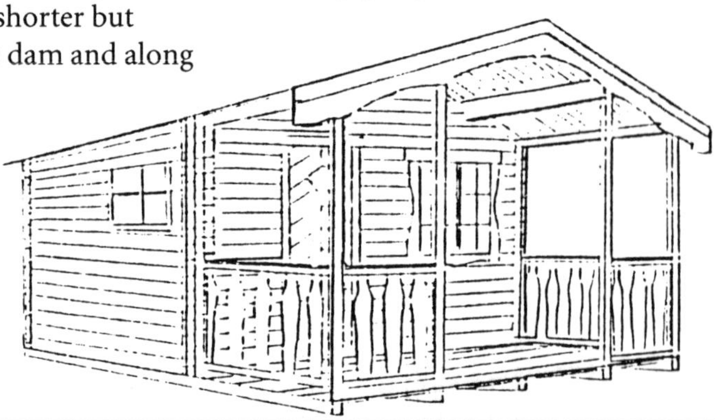

1 Cabin with Kitchen
7 Camper Cabins
Central Campfire Area

Pay Phone(s)
All Non-Smoking in Units
Recreation Room
Elevation: 7650
Credit Cards: VM
2 people a night: $25 - $45
Open: 5/1 to 9/30

Bob & Jan Davis, Owners
4677 CR 501-A
Bayfield CO 81122-9701
970/884-2582
800/582-9580
970/884-9765 Fax

At the resort:

At resort or within 15 minutes:

Forest Lakes Chalets

The chalets at Forest Lakes are tucked away among pine and spruce trees, offering comfort, peace and quiet during your vacation. The chalets have kitchens and sleeping lofts. Up to six people can stay in each chalet. Be sure to make use of the outdoor grills and barbecues for cooking up that special, freshly caught rainbow trout! Offering the best of all worlds, the resort is in the picturesque San Juan Mountains just minutes from Durango. It's close to Vallecito Lake, Lemon Lake and Durango; yet, its not right in the middle of the crowds.

An attraction at Forest Lakes are the rainbow trout and there are plenty in the private fishing lake (no license required). Other popular activities here are beautiful river hikes above Lemon Lake, long walks in Transfer Park and playing tennis. Whether you explore the river canyons, dine in Durango, spend your days fly casting, playing tennis or exploring the mountains this is the spot to do it from.

They have a hot tub and weight room available for a small daily fee. Children under six years old stay free. Ask about their weekly rates. A deposit is required when making reservations. Pets are allowed with an additional deposit.

Location: 18 miles east of Durango. Take Highway 160 to Bayfield, then north on country Highway 501 for 7 miles; or 25 minutes northeast of Durango on County Road 240 and 501.

13 Cabins with Kitchens	Pay Phone(s) Elevation: 7300 Credit Cards: VM 2 people a night: $50 - $70 Open: All Year	Greg & Beth Caldwell, Managers 260 Alpine Forest Dr Bayfield CO 81122 970/884-2411 800/525-5424 Colorado Only 970/577-4686 Fax

At the resort:

At resort or within 15 minutes:

Lake Haven Resort

Whether planning an "on-the-go" or a "get-away-from-it-all" vacation, you'll love these cabins overlooking colorful Vallecito Lake. Built of local materials and situated among shady pines, the cabins have gas heat, dishes, linens and bedding, picnic tables and tubs or showers. Some have fireplaces; most have a view of the lake.

An on-site store sells groceries, gifts, bait and tackle. Lake Haven Resort is ideal for small or large groups. The area offers many activities, from fishing and hunting, to wilderness hiking and mountain biking. Photography buffs will find plenty of subjects among the beautiful lakes, streams, forested mountains and abundant wildlife.

Make advance reservations to assure suitable accommodations.

Location: On the southwest shore of Vallecito Lake, 20 miles northeast of Durango.

15 Cabins with Kitchens
4 Vacation Homes
5 Fireplaces
5 Woodstoves

Pay Phone(s)
Elevation: 7800
Credit Cards: VM
2 people a night: $45 - $70
Open: 4/15 to 10/1

J.D. & Fern Hudgpeth, Owners
14452 CR 501
Bayfield CO 81122-9701
970/884-2517

At the resort:

At resort or within 15 minutes:

Logwood Lodge B&B, The Verheyden Inn

This luxurious 3-story, red cedar log home bed and breakfast along the banks of the Animas River is surrounded by 15 acres of quiet and seclusion. The guest rooms are attractively furnished with a southwestern flair and the queen-size beds have colorful home-stitched quilts. Rooms features private bath and large picture windows for viewing the beauty of the Animas River valley. A large river rock fireplace warms the elegant living and dining areas. The entire lodge is non-smoking.

Wake up to a full breakfast which could be country fare or a gourmet delight. In the evenings, enjoy the cozy fire and savor their award-winning desserts! Lounge on the wrap-around deck and watch the wildlife and in the evening watch the shadows climb the mountainside. Wet a hook and catch a trout lurking in the waters of the Animas while enjoying the beautiful views and sounds. Only 15 minutes from downtown Durango shopping and dining. The ancient Indian ruins of the Anasazi, Mesa Verde National Park, are an hours drive. Enjoy mountain biking and hiking on nearby trails through the San Juan Mountains. The area also offers excellent golf courses. In winter enjoy downhill skiing at Purgatory Ski Area a 15 minute drive (Logwood is the closest B&B). The area also offers cross-country skiing, snowshoeing, sleigh rides through La Plata Canyon and snowmobiling. Your hosts are happy to supply activity information to make your stay enjoyable.

Children over 8 years old are welcome. No pets allowed. Rent the entire lodge with use of kitchen for weddings, family reunions and other events, sleeps 20. Advance reservations are recommended, a deposit is required. Ask about their special winter rates and discount ski packages. Visit their Web site at http://www.fsnw.com/logwood.

Location: Twelve miles north of Durango, off Highway 550, near milepost 35.

8 Lodging Rooms
2 Fireplace
Central Fireplace
Central Campfire Area

Lobby Phone
Bed & Breakfast Available
All Non-Smoking Units
Recreation Room
Elevation: 6700
Credit Cards: VM
2 people a night: $65 - $125
Open: All Year

Debby & Greg Verheyden, Owners
35060 US 550 N
Durango CO 81301
970/259-4396
800/369-4082
970/259-7812 Fax
e-mail: logwood@hawk.scan.org

At the resort:

At resort or within 15 minutes:

Lone Wolf Lodge

North of Bayfield near lovely Vallecito Lake (5 minutes away), Lone Wolf Lodge offers one, two and three bedroom cabin homes under tall cool ponderosa and spruce trees. Each cabin at this small intimate spot has fully equipped kitchens, microwaves and color television. The fully furnished cabins can sleep up to eight and have outdoor barbecues.

You'll appreciate the free firewood while the kids will like the playground on-site. The lodge is convenient to both markets and restaurants. Nearby are horse-back rides, hiking and mountain biking trails, boat rentals, prime fishing spots and opportunities to hunt in season. Rent a four-wheel drive vehicle close by to explore scenic back roads in the mountains. In the winter, cross-country skiing, and snowmobiling are popular sports. Downhill skiing is an hour and a half drive away while you can rent snowmobiles nearby.

Location: 28 miles northeast of Durango. Take Highway 160 east to Bayfield, then north on Country Road 501 or drive 25 miles northeast of Durango on County Road 240 and 501.

LONE WOLF LODGE
VALLECITO LAKE, COLORADO

4 Cabins with Kitchens
1 Fireplace
3 Woodstoves
Central Campfire Area

Pay Phone(s)
Elevation: 8000
Credit Cards: VMD
2 people a night: $70 - $80
Open: All Year

John & Stephanie McClain, Owners
18001 CR 501
Bayfield Co 81122
970/884-0414 & Fax

At the resort:

At resort or within 15 minutes:

O-Bar-O Cabins

Disappear for a while in a secluded setting among numerous pine trees and lush grounds. These nicely decorated, river-front housekeeping cabins have stone fireplaces, covered porches or decks, fully equipped kitchens, linens and towels. Barbecue your favorite meal at the outdoor grills and picnic tables. Each cabin has been remodeled and decorated to offer comfort, while retaining a rustic touch of the past. At 1,300' higher than Durango, expect cooler air and refreshing summer evenings.

Vacation under clear Colorado skies, watch deer and elk roam through the alpine meadows bordered by tall pine trees stretching to the horizon. Be sure to cast your fishing rod on the Florida (pronounced *Flor-EED-ah*) River, right outside your door. The resort is only 12 miles from Durango, with its melodrama dinner theater and Durango-Silverton Narrow Gauge Railroad. Just a stone's throw from the national forest, two large lakes and horseback trails, O-Bar-O boasts many nearby activities, including lake and stream fishing, boating, hiking, horseback riding and fine dining.

Reservations are required.

Location: 12 miles northeast of Durango, about halfway to Vallecito Lake on the Florida River.

7 Cabins with Kitchens
7 Fireplaces
Central Campfire Area

Lobby Phone
Elevation: 7800
Credit Cards: VMD
2 people a night: $70 - $125
Open: 5/15 to 10/15

Herb & Gayle Rose, Owners
11998 CR 240
Durango CO 81301-8489
970/259-3649

At the resort:

At resort or within 15 minutes:

Pine River Lodge

Family owned and operated since 1960, Pine River Lodge features cabins overlooking beautiful Vallecito Lake. The cabins have complete kitchens — dishes, cooking utensils, linens and bedding are furnished and boast aspen-, pine- or spruce-paneled walls. Cabins have either double or queen sized beds. Many are carpeted with a porch or deck for outdoor meals and relaxing. Cabins range from small one-room cabins sleeping two people to 4-bedroom 2-story cabins sleeping 11 people. Some cabins have fireplaces. Remember to bring your own dish and bath soap. Portable barbecue grills are furnished.

Pine River Lodge has an indoor swimming pool, a game room and a large playground. The playground includes swings, slides, sandbox, jungle gym, basketball hoop, volleyball area and horseshoes. Be sure to try the excellent fishing in Vallecito Lake — anglers have set state records for northern pike and brown trout here. Hiking and horseback riding trailheads are all nearby. While visiting, step back in time with a trip on the Durango-Silverton Narrow Gauge Railroad. Visit incredible Mesa Verde National Park. Also enjoy river rafting, seeing a melodrama, playing high stakes bingo and chowing down a Bar D Chuckwagon dinner. In the winter, you can snowmobile and ski close by.

No campers, trailers, or motorhomes are allowed on the premises for sleeping. Children under 2 are free. There is an additional crib and pet fee per night. Special needs should be requested when making your reservation. When making reservations there is a two night deposit required.

Location: 16 miles north of Bayfield or 23 miles northeast of Durango. Overlooking Vallecito Lake's southwest shore.

26 Cabins with Kitchens
12 Fireplaces
Central Campfire Area

Pay Phone(s)
Recreation Room
Elevation: 7800
No credit cards
2 people a night: $61 - $84
Open: All Year

Donna & Debbie & Ermalee Atkinson, Owners
14443 CR 501
Bayfield CO 81122-9701
970/884-2563

At the resort:

At resort or within 15 minutes:

Silver Streams Lodge

At the north end of beautiful Vallecito Lake are a host of log cabins completely decorated from head to toe with wonderful country furniture (completely remodeled the summer of 1995). Each cabin has a full kitchen, open-hearth fireplace, porches and decks. Watch for deer and horses most every morning and evening during your vacation.

Sit with a cup of coffee and a snack on the main lodge's log deck overlooking mountains, ponds and meadows. The lodge is available during regular hours for reading and relaxing. A family-oriented restaurant nearby serves breakfast, lunch, dinner and cocktails. Fish — no license or tackle required — in the private pond, stocked with rainbow trout. Silver Streams has wildflowers and fishing in the spring; boating, fishing, horseback riding, hiking and mountain biking in the summer; golden aspen and hunting in the fall; cross-country skiing, snowmobiling and ice skating in the winter. A true, year-round lodge; just one minute from Vallecito Lake.

Your host can arrange hunting and pack trips for a complete wilderness vacation. The lodge serves as an additional facility to Wit's End Ranch and Resort. A European Plan is available except for July and the first 2 weeks of August, in which case Wit's End Ranch's American Plan is provided.

Location: At the north end of Vallecito Lake on county road 501 just south of Wit's End Ranch.

16 Cabins with Kitchens
2 Vacation Homes
18 Fireplaces
Central Fireplace
Central Campfire Area

Pay Phone(s)
Elevation: 7750
Credit Cards: VMAD
2 people a night: $100 - $155
Open: All Year

Jim & Lynn Custer, Owners
18645 CR 501
Bayfield CO 81122
970/884-2770
602/263-0000

At the resort:

At resort or within 15 minutes:

Steward Ranch Cabins

In the beautiful La Plata Mountains 8 miles west of Durango, Steward Ranch Cabins is on 40 scenic, private acres in Lightner Creek Canyon. The two clean and modern log cabins each have stone fireplaces, firewood, bathrooms and full kitchens with barbecues and picnic tables outside. Each features wood interiors, carpeting, linens and open-beam ceilings. Stay in the one- or two-bedroom cabin among the trees. A vacation here offers the seclusion and beauty of camping in the woods with all the comforts and convenience of home.

Steward Ranch has been a working cattle ranch owned by the same family since 1900! Hollywood has used this scenic location for scenes in two movies: "City Slickers" in 1990 and "The Abduction of Kari Swenson" in 1986.

Location: 8 miles west of downtown Durango, from Highway 160, milepost 80, on County Road 207.

2 Cabins with Kitchens
2 Fireplaces

Lobby Phone
Elevation: 7200
No credit cards
2 people a night: $52 - $58
Open: 5/1 to 10/15

Bonnie Brennan, Owner
4385 CR 207 (Lightner Creek Rd)
Durango CO 81301
970/247-8396

At the resort:

At resort or within 15 minutes:

Vallecito Resort

There's something for everyone in the cool pines of Vallecito Resort. The cabins, ranging from one to three bedrooms, are nestled in tall ponderosa pine trees where it's quiet and restful. The 10 housekeeping cabins are equipped with linens, cable tv, dishes and utensils. There's a small, private cabin for honeymooners and a large cabin suitable for family reunions. Vallecito Resort also has 6 park model trailers for you to rent. Every other day you may exchange dirty towels at the office.

You'll find everything you need here, from a grocery store and playground to a recreation hall, card room, library and craft room. Bring your square dance attire for the exciting evening dances: square (plus-C3), round (all phases), line and country swing. Vallecito Resort boasts national square dance and round dance callers. Weekly activities at the resort include Sunday church services, arts and crafts sessions, potlucks, poker, aerobics, bonfires and ice cream socials. Nearby you can play a game of tennis, golf or go bowling. Fish for state-record trout in the Pine River or take a short drive to Vallecito and Lemon lakes.

RV sites and an indoor and an outdoor group meeting area are also available. Every site has a cable tv hookup and telephone. Ask about off-season special rates.

Location: Just south of Vallecito Lake.

10 Cabins with Kitchens
Central Campfire Area

Pay Phone(s)
Recreation Room
Elevation: 7600
Credit Cards: VMD
2 people a night: $50 - $70
Open: 5/1 to 10/5

Rex & Jeannie Hornbaker, Owners
13030 CR 501
Bayfield CO 81122
970/884-9458
800/258-9458

At the resort:

At resort or within 15 minutes:

Wit's End Guest Ranch

Established in the 1860s, this ranch adjoins the 575,000-acre Weminuche Wilderness. Amid a dramatic setting of 14,000-foot peaks on all sides, the cabins, some over 100 years old, have, knotty pine interiors, living rooms, native stone fireplaces, kitchens, porch swings and queen-sized brass beds. The furnishings and decorations are exquisite and unique. The cabins are all near streams, rivers and ponds.

Wit's End provides unlimited activities: carriage rides, fly fishing, moonlight cruises on the lake, mountain biking, tennis and swimming. They also arrange horseback rides, hayrides, rafting, wilderness trips, and much more! Kids will enjoy the complete children's program. The main lodge — the original barn built in the 1870's — now contains a candle-lit restaurant, library, entertainment center and a dance floor. Listen to live music in the old-world bar, featuring mirrors from the 1836 Crystal Palace in London. Later in the evening, soak in one of the four outdoor hot tubs or the large swimming pool. The Silver Streams Lodge, adjacent to Wit's End, has additional facilities for your convenience.

If you're planning a large group vacation, inquire about the 7,000-square-foot cabin along Vallecito Lake. Ask about the full American plan (summer or winter package) when making reservations, which includes a scrumptious breakfast, lunch and dinner; and all ranch amenities and activities. The summer package activities include dinner hay rides and pontoon boat rides; while the winter package offers sleigh rides, snowshoeing, snowmobiling and cross-country skiing.

Location: North of Vallecito Lake.

30 Cabins with Kitchens	Room Phones	Jim & Lynn Custer, Owners
5 Vacation Homes	Recreation Room	254 CR 500
35 Fireplaces	Elevation: 7800	Bayfield CO 81122-9702
Central Fireplace	Credit Cards: VMAD	970/884-4113
Central Campfire Area	2 people a night: $542 - $593	970/884-3261 Fax
	Open: 5/1 to 10/15	602/263-0000

At the resort:

At resort or within 15 minutes:

Eagle County

Including Edwards, Gypsum, Red Cliff & Vail — Map: F-10, F-9, G-11 & F-11

Edwards, on I-70 past Vail, is in an open valley where the sun shines down warmly and the pace slows down. The nearby White River National Forest abounds with trails for hiking, mountain biking and horseback riding. Drive through tiny Minturn and even smaller Redcliff, mining towns steeped in history, on your way to the popular wilderness area of the Mount of the Holy Cross at 14,005'. All the ski resorts, including Vail and Copper Mountain, are accessible from here without the cost of staying in expensive, crowded condos during the ski season. Visit the numerous shops in Vail Village that aim to please the most discriminating tastes. Golfers will want to bring their clubs for some high country games in Edwards, Avon and Vail. Down the road, in the direction of Glenwood Springs is **Gypsum**, another gateway to the unspoiled White River National Forest. The forest is home to the largest elk herd in North America. Sylvan Lake State Recreation Area is not only quite scenic, but a great place to fish for brook and rainbow trout. A short drive from either Edwards or Gypsum, 40-acre Sylvan Lake is the perfect place to bring your boat and catch the big ones! Clear streams, flowing from sky-touching, snow-capped mountains, meander through wildflower meadows and into blue mountain lakes in Eagle County. Enjoy many scenic and exciting moments whitewater rafting, fishing and skiing among the wildlife and rare birds.

Fun Things To Do

- Beaver Creek Golf Club, Avon (970) 949-7123
- Eagle Vail Golf Club, Vail (970) 949-5267
- Nova Guides, Guided outdoor activities (888) 949-NOVA (6682)
- Pa & Ma's Guest Ranch (719)486-3900
- Sonnenalp Golf Club, Edwards (970) 926-3533

Cross Creek Ranch

This working cattle ranch nestled in the majestic Rocky Mountains, deep in the White River National Forest is a gem. The warmth and charm of this restored 1892 log cabin is an intimate mountain hideaway with a full country kitchen, dining area, family room, stone fireplace, bathroom with Jacuzzi tub and two bedrooms which sleeps up to six people. A large wrap around deck overlooks a cascading creek where you can fish, grill and relish in some of the high country's most spectacular scenery. In keeping with the tranquil setting and crisp clean air, Cross Creek Ranch is entirely non-smoking. There is a television and VCR, however there is no local reception. There are many pre-recorded videos to chooses from.

The picturesque ranch has private access to hiking, mountain biking, hunting, cross-country skiing and snowshoeing in the National Forest. The wooded area is alive with elk, deer and other wildlife for your viewing enjoyment. There are three ponds and two streams at Cross Creek Ranch. Make a day out of driving the scenic Glenwood Canyon and relax at the Glenwood Hot Springs Pool, there are also many nice restaurants to help finish off a perfect day. Or for winter enthusiast Alpine skiing is at its best in Vail or browse through their unique shops.

Wedding and reception areas are available. There is a two night minimum stay. Ask about their seasonal rates. Your horse can accompany you with advance arrangements. Friendly service is why people return year after year.

Location: Off I-70 between Vail and Glenwood Springs, 13 miles south of Gypsum on Valley Rd. which turns into Gypsum Creek Rd.

1 Cabin with Kitchen
4 Beds in Bunk House or Dorm
1 Fireplace

Room Phones
All Non-Smoking in Units
Recreation Room
Elevation: 8700
No credit cards
2 people a night: $125
Open: All Year

Susan & David Scott, Owners
13117 Gypsum Creek Road
Gypsum CO 81637
970/524-7557

At the resort:

At resort or within 15 minutes:

Golden Eagle Ranch

The homestead log cabins at Golden Eagle Ranch border mountain meadows of colorful aspen and blue spruce. This very private, 160-acre high-country ranch is located in the White River National Forest. The cabins, which sleep two to four people, are next to one of three clear mountain streams.

Bill Walden, a professional sculptor, offers roomy, sunlit studio space and instruction for all ages. Bring your own art supplies or purchase them at the studio. Take some time to fish for the abundant brook, rainbow and cutthroat trout in the ranch's lake and beaver ponds. Fishing and boating enthusiasts will like Lede Reservoir just 2 miles away. Hikers will want to strike out for many of the high lakes in the surrounding mountains. Bring your camera: this is the place to spot golden eagles, red-tailed hawks, elk and deer. Venture to Glenwood Springs Hot Springs pool or go whitewater rafting on the Colorado River 45 minutes away.

Advance reservations and a two day minimum stay is required. Stay a week and get the seventh day free!

Location: From I-70 take exit 140 between Vail and Glenwood Springs, 16 miles south of Gypsum on Valley Road which turns into Gypsum Creek Road, a county-maintained road.

1 Cabin with Kitchen
2 cabins without Kitchens
5 Beds in Bunk House or Dorm
4 Woodstoves

Lobby Phone
Elevation: 8500
No credit cards
2 people a night: $75
Open: 6/1 to 11/1

Linda & Bill Walden, Owners
PO Box 833
15877 Gypsum Creek Rd
Gypsum CO 81637-0833
970/524-9311

At the resort:

At resort or within 15 minutes:

Lazy Ranch Bed & Breakfast

Just down the road from the world-famous Vail Ski Resort sits a sleepy old house on the Lazy Ranch. The owner's great-grandparents homesteaded this beautiful valley site in the late 1800s and it has been owned and operated by the same family ever since. Take a step back in time when you stay in any of the four bedrooms that are uniquely decorated. Pick between the Cowboy Room, the Angel Room and the Victorian Room which share two baths or the Bert & Goldies Master Suite featuring a separate living room with a fireplace and private bath. Spend some time gazing at the horses grazing on 60 acres with a backdrop of the spectacular Sawatch Mountain Range.

The Lazy Ranch won the Colorado Centennial Farm Award and is on the Colorado Historic Registry. During your stay, wake to a full country-style breakfast made with fresh farm eggs. Animals abound on the ranch including chickens, peacocks, horses, "Pork Chop" the pig, dogs and cats. Owner Buddy Calhoun raises horses on the ranch and has an art studio where he makes custom hunting knives, walking canes, Indian shields and cowboy chaps. Fish on private trout pond and stream. Other activities include country swing dance lessons, barbecues, bonfires and barn dances. Indulge in an afternoon snack, take a moonlight stroll or relax on the gazebo swing. In addition, skiing in Vail and Beaver Creek is minutes away as are shops, restaurants and national forest trailheads for hiking and mountain biking.

Location: I-70 to exit 163 (Edward), left 1 mile to Old Highway 6, first stop light, drive west 0.75 miles to Lake Creek Road, turn left, then immediately right onto driveway.

4 Lodging Rooms
1 Fireplace
Central Campfire Area

Room Phones
Bed & Breakfast Available
All Non-Smoking in Units
Recreation Room
Elevation: 7600
Credit Cards: VMD
2 people a night: $60 - $125
Open: All Year

Buddy & Linda Calhoun, Owners
PO Box 404
0057 Lake Creek Rd
Edwards CO 81632
970/926-3876 & Fax
800/655-9343

At the resort:

At resort or within 15 minutes:

Pando Cabins & Nova Guided Year Around Outdoor Recreation

The Pando Cabins are at historic Camp Hale, during World War II the 10th Mountain Army Division's winter maneuver training, now listed on the National Historic Register. The cabins nestles amongst the pines were completed in fall of 1995. These log cabins have 2 bedrooms, a bath, full kitchens and fireplaces. The master bedroom has a queen-size bed, while the second bedroom has a full size bed, the living room has a full size sleeper sofa. Each cabin sleeps up to six people. Watch the sun rise and set on your cabins deck.

Many activities are available just steps away from your front porch. Cast your line into Eagle River or fish in their privately stocked lake. Start your mountain bike ride, cross country ski trip or snowmobile adventure from the trails right on the property. If your planning a ski vacation there are two resorts within 30 minutes drive Vail and Beaver Creek plus Ski Cooper which is only a 10 minute drive.

Pets including your horse are allowed for an additional fee. Cabin guests receive a 15% discount for tours from Nova Guides who feature rafting, fishing, jeeping, ATV, mountain bike, snowmobile and wildcat tours depending on the season.

Location: Sixteen miles south of I-70, exit 191, on US Highway 24. Six miles south of Red Cliff and 14 miles north of Leadville.

3 Cabins with Kitchens
3 Fireplaces

Room phones
Non-Smoking Units Available
Elevation: 9100
Credit Cards: VMAD
2 people a night: $85 - $95
Open: All Year

Steve Pittel & Greg Caretto, Owners
1088 Hwy 24
Red Cliff CO 81649
970/949-4232

At the resort:

At resort or within 15 minutes:

Estes Park Area

Including Drake, Glen Haven, Loveland & Lyons — Map: C-14, C-15, C-16 & D-15

Longs Peak, at a dizzying 14,255', towers over the quaint mountain town of **Estes Park.** The eastern gate to Rocky Mountain National Park, Estes Park, at 7,522', started when Joel Estes and his family moved to the valley in 1859. The public soon learned about the high mountain valley surrounded by snowcapped peaks when a journalist wrote about scaling Longs Peak. Crowds came to visit the park and stay at the famous Stanley Hotel, built in 1909. In town, stroll along the streets, sampling the numerous candy stores and craft shops, play golf, horseback ride or sail. Rocky Mountain National Park has 415 glacially-carved square miles covered with lakes, wildlife and wild flowers. Trail Ridge Road, the highest continuous paved road in the United States, traverses the park and crosses the Continental Divide. From Estes Park, you can tour the Peak-to-Peak Scenic Highway or drive through the scenic Big Thompson Canyon east to Loveland. **Loveland** has become famous for its numerous, nationally renown sculptors whose work can be seen at Benson Park. The town was named for William Austin Hamilton Loveland, the man responsible for bringing the Colorado Central Railroad's line from Cheyenne, Wyoming, through here on its way to Denver. In the early 1900s, Colorado was the leading sugar beet producing state in the country and Loveland became the sight of the first sugar mill in eastern Colorado. Nearby Carter Lake offers 100 acres of fishing and water sports. The new 38-store factory outlet mall is just west of the junction of U.S. 34 and I-25. Enjoy the easy pace in Loveland, where life moves a little slower in this "Sweetheart City."

Fun Things to Do

- Boyd Lake State Park (970) 669-1739
- Carter Lake (970) 679-4570
- Catch Wild Trout at Peter's Pond (970) 586-5171
- Enos Mills Cabin, Estes Park (970) 586-4706
- Estes Park Area Historical Museum (970) 586-6256
- Estes Park Golf Course (970) 586-8146
- Loveland Municipal Golf Course (970) 667-5256
- Loveland Museum & Gallery (970) 962-2410
- Loveland Sculpture Works (970) 667-0991
- MacGregor Ranch, Estes Park (970) 586-3749
- Rocky Mountain National Park (970) 686-1206

Anderson's Wonder View Cottages

Relax on top of the world at Anderson's Wonder View Cottages. These modern cottages and motel, with an outstanding view of the 14,256-foot Long's Peak, are scattered across seven acres of peaceful land next to Rocky Mountain National Park. All units have fireplaces, a private deck and cable television. Each cottage, spaced 50 feet apart for privacy, has a grill and a fully equipped kitchen.

Resort facilities include a heated pool, putting green, basketball court, horseshoes, shuffleboard, a picnic area and a playground. Year-round color surrounds the cottages: spring brings lush green meadows and wildflowers, while summers offer beautiful scenery and cool, refreshing mountain air. Fall abounds with golden aspen and wildlife, and mild winters showcase pristine snow and scenic splendor.

Cabins have a seven-day minimum rental during summer. Visit their Web site at http://www.estes-park.com/andersons.

Location: 2.5 miles west of downtown Estes Park, 0.25 miles north of Highway 36 (also known as Moraine Ave.).

10 Cabins with Kitchens
3 Motel Rooms
16 Fireplaces

Pay Phone(s)
Non-Smoking Units Available
Recreation Room
Elevation: 8000
Credit Cards: VMD
2 people a night: $44 - $180
Open: All Year

Tom Peter, Owner
PO Box 427
540 Laurel Ln
Estes Park CO 80517-0427
970/586-4158
800/327-0113

At the resort:

At resort or within 15 minutes:

Antler's Pointe Log Cabins "On the River"

This elite mountain retreat caters exclusively to husband-and-wife couples. The romantic, luxury log cabin suites at Antlers Pointe are approached from assigned parking, across a romantic bridge to rest on the banks of the beautiful Fall River. Each suite features a king bedroom, a private Jacuzzi for two, and step-in showers for two. Cuddle up with your honey in the cozy parlor with a fireplace and love sofa. The cabins have a southwestern decor and are complete with surround sound stereo, color cable television, VCR, and a telephone. The kitchenette is complete for a perfect candle light dinner. Walk out onto your private deck with a gas grill just 20 feet from the water's edge. Nestled beneath a grove of spruce and ponderosa pine, you can enjoy the view of snowcapped peaks, wildlife and wildflowers in your secluded river front yard.

All the activities of Rocky Mountain National Park are less than a mile away. Come to the mountains to jog, hike, mountain bike, and horseback ride. Golfers will appreciate the two picturesque courses in Estes Park. This quaint town also offers plenty of shops to explore and fine restaurants to dine in. In the winter, try snowshoeing and cross-country skiing on the pristine snow.

Ask about the 3-, 4- or 5-day romance packages, perfect for sparkling-up your special time alone. This is an ideal getaway for honeymooners, anniversaries, outdoor weddings or mountain-top marriage renewals. You will find Antler's Pointe to be the "Most Unabashedly Romantic" for your special occasion. Smoking and pets are not permitted. Advance reservations only.

Location: One block south of Fall River Road (Hwy. 34W) on Fish Hatchery Road.

8 Cabins with Kitchens

Room Phones
Bed & Breakfast Available
All Non-Smoking in Units
Elevation: 8000
Credit Cards: VM
2 people a night: $129 - $189
Open: All Year

Owner-Managed
PO Box 245
1515 Fish Hatchery Road
Estes Park CO 80517-0245
970/586-8881
800/638-8881

At the resort:

At resort or within 15 minutes:

Big Thompson Timberlane Lodge

Located on six grassy acres between Estes Park and Rocky Mountain National Park, Big Thompson Timberlane Lodge has an inspiring view of the Rocky Mountains. All of the motel, cottage units and 1,200-square-foot log homes have their own heat, carpeting, cable television with HBO and combination baths or showers. Accommodations are available with or without kitchenettes. Four of the log homes have private hot tubs or jetted tubs. The all-season log homes have gas fireplaces, a washer and dryer, fully equipped kitchens with a dishwasher and microwave — ideal for a family vacation.

The lodge is off the road along the banks of the Big Thompson River, yet within walking distance of restaurants, miniature golf and shopping areas. Cast your line into the lodges portion of the Big Thompson River — privately stocked for guests only. BBQ grills with picnic tables are spread throughout the lawn for outdoor cooking. Local activities include scenic drives to Bear Lake, Fall River Road and Trail Ridge Road. After a day's adventures, refresh yourself in the swimming pool and relax in the large hot tub.

Kids under 2 stay free, and you can have a crib added to the room for an additional charge. No pets are allowed. There is a 2 day deposit required and a 30 day cancellation policy. They cater to couples and families and therefore prefer not to host family reunions or group gatherings. They prefer not to except personal checks.

Location: Highway 36 (also known as Moraine Ave), west of Estes Park.

23 Cabins with Kitchens
7 cabins without Kitchens
11 Vacation Homes
12 Fireplaces

Room Phones
Non-Smoking Units Available
Elevation: 7500
Credit Cards: VMAD
2 people a night: $59 - $298
Open: All Year

Curt & Pat Thompson, President
PO Box 387
740 Morraine Ave
Estes Park CO 80517-0387
970/586-3137
970/586-4373
970/586-3719 Fax

At the resort:

At resort or within 15 minutes:

Colorado Cottages

Stay where you are treated like a guest of the family in true country comfort at Colorado Cottages. This is a small, intimate spot for getaways, holidays and family vacations at the edge of Rocky Mountain National Park. The charming country-style housekeeping cottages each have full kitchens, fireplaces, color cable television with HBO and in-room libraries, making it feel just like home. "At home" hospitality is extended to your family with the owners as your personal hosts.

Use the individual barbecue grills for a picnic on the grassy lawns. Expect to see plenty of wildlife, from birds in the summer to elk in the fall. Among the many local activities are fishing, hiking, golfing, miniature golfing and horseback riding. Grocery stores, souvenir shops and restaurants are located within walking distance in nearby quaint Estes Park.

A deposit for your first and last night's stay will confirm your reservation. Ask about multi-night discounts, as well as discounts for senior guests. Open and closing dates vary from year to year. Call ahead for more information. Visit their Web site at http://www.estes-park.com/colocottage.

Location: On Highway 36 (also known as Moraine Ave.), just west of Estes Park on the north side of the road.

11 Cabins with Kitchens
11 Fireplaces

Pay Phone(s)
Non-Smoking Units Available
Elevation: 8300
Credit Cards: VMD
2 people a night: $56 - $110
Open: 5/1 to 9/30

Jodi & Mark Adler, Owners
1241 High Dr - Moraine Rte
Estes Park CO 80517
970/586-4637
800/468-1236

At the resort:

At resort or within 15 minutes:

Dripping Springs Bed & Breakfast Inn and Cabins

Stay at the top of the canyon at this country-style bed and breakfast inn, built in 1936, located on five acres of aspen and pine trees on the Big Thompson River. Dripping Springs offers yesteryear's look with comfy rooms featuring a queen or full bed. Five uniquely decorated rooms have private entrances and baths, while four other charming rooms share baths. Full homemade breakfast are included. None of the rooms have a phone or television. There is also a one bedroom cabin available with a private outdoor hot tub and wood burning stove. The views of the canyon and Longs Peak from the deck and grounds are breathtaking.

In a very private location "behind the rock," Dripping Springs is three minutes from Estes Park on the way to Rocky Mountain National Park. Fish on the abundant Big Thompson River frontage at the inn and then soak away your worries in one of four large, outdoor hot tub as the sun sets behind the mountains. The national park abounds with outdoor possibilities from hiking and horseback riding to sightseeing and alpine picnicking. The lively little town of Estes Park has something to please everyone, including candy and ice cream shops to fine restaurants to theater and boutiques.

All accommodations at Dripping Springs are non-smoking. It is also an adult only resort. There is a two day minimum stay and a 50% deposit is required when making the reservation.

Location: 3 miles east of Estes Park on Highway 34 between milepost 66-67 or 16 and a half miles west of the Dam Store on Highway 34 coming from Loveland.

1 Cabin with Kitchen
9 Lodging Rooms
1 Woodstove
Central Fireplace
Central Campfire Area

Lobby Phone
Bed & Breakfast Available
All Non-Smoking in Units
Recreation Room
Elevation: 7400
Credit Cards: VMAD
2 people a night: $74 - $100
Open: All Year

Oliver & Janie Robertson, Owners
2551 Hwy 34
Drake CO 80515
970/586-3406
800/432-7145
979/586-3035 Fax

At the resort:

At resort or within 15 minutes:

Eagle Cliff House Bed & Breakfast

Nestled in ponderosa pines at the base of Eagle Cliff Mountain in Estes Park, this bed and breakfast is a warm, friendly place to stay. The rooms combine soft southwestern decor and colors with the beautiful woods used in American antiques in a warm and hospitable atmosphere. The Heritage Room is decorated with early 1900s antiques and has a queen-size iron bed. The Southwest Room features Indian artifacts and books on the culture of the American southwest as well as a queen-size bed. Both rooms have a private bath and their own entrance with a shared hot tub on the patio. For a romantic, special getaway, try the Victorian Cottage furnished in period antiques complete with a queen bed, jetted tub, fully stocked kitchenette and a sunny deck facing the mountains.

A hearty country breakfast is served in the house's sunny breakfast nook. You are welcome to dig into the "never empty" cookie jar at anytime throughout your stay. At Eagle Cliff House, you are within walking distance of Rocky Mountain National Park. Your hosts can help plan everything from a day hike into the mountains to a overnight backpacking experience into the wilderness. The popular resort town of Estes Park is nearby and offers an abundance of western history as well as unique shops and restaurants.

Ask about the individualized service for birthdays, weddings, honeymoons, anniversaries or other special occasions.

Location: On Highway 66 close to the YMCA.

1 Cabin with Kitchen
2 Lodging Rooms

No Phones Available
Bed & Breakfast Available
All Non-Smoking in Units
Elevation: 7800
No credit cards
2 people a night: $80 - $115
Open: All Year

Mike & Nancy Conrin, Owners
Box 4312
2383 Hwy 66
Estes Park CO 80517-4312
970/586-5425

At the resort:

At resort or within 15 minutes:

Elkhorn Lodge & Guest Ranch

Just two blocks from downtown Estes Park, the Elkhorn Lodge is an historical treasure — a Registered National Historical Property at the base of Man Mountain, a sacred vision-quest site. You'll experience old-West living in TV-free rooms and outlying cabins. Accommodations are a rustic reminder of yesteryear, with 1890's luxury of indoor baths. The lodge has 39 guest rooms , three housekeeping cabins, 23 non-housekeeping cabins and two vacations homes. Enjoy the views from the Lodge porch, spacious lobbies and meeting rooms. Families will appreciate the reasonably-priced breakfasts and dinners in the 1920s restaurant and the TV room with movies for the kids.

The Plains Indian Village at this 65-acre resort brings to life the rich Native American heritage. Sponsored by the non-profit Elkhorn-Man Mountain Native American Institute, the village features tipis and a look into the Plains Indian experience. Cabin guests may bring their dogs and all guests can board their horses here. Or take a trail ride with horses from the ranch's stable. One- or two-hour rides, breakfast rides and evening steak rides are available. Other amenities include a swimming pool, fee fishing and mountain bike rentals on site.

Originally a stage-coach stop for Estes Park, Elkhorn's Coach House is ideal for 200-person reunions, weddings and other special events. The Coach house also offers chuckwagon dinners, followed by adult socializing and dancing. Wilderness tent sits are also available.

Location: On West Elkhorn Avenue after US 36 turns south at the stop light.

3 Cabins with Kitchens
23 cabins without Kitchens
2 Vacation Homes
39 Lodging Rooms
4 Fireplaces
Central Fireplace
Central Campfire Area

Pay Phone(s)
Recreation Room
Elevation: 7500
Credit Cards: VM
2 people a night: $35 - $90
Open: All Year

Jerry Zahourek, Own & Kathy Durward
PO Box 1560
600 W Elkhorn
Estes Park CO 80517-1560
970/586-4416 lodge
970/586-8887 office

At the resort:

At resort or within 15 minutes:

Estes Park Center®/YMCA of the Rockies

Discover why four generations of families return to this magnificent setting every year to rejuvenate spirit, mind and body. Pick between 565 lodge rooms or the 200 modern housekeeping cabins scattered over 860 acres adjoining Rocky Mountain National Park. Each cabin has its own fully equipped kitchen and private phone; many have fireplaces. Most lodge rooms have telephones and televisions. Linens, bedding, and towels are provided in both the cabins and lodge rooms.

Depending on the season, vacation activities include hayrides, horseback rides, hikes, square dances, miniature golf, tennis and arts and crafts. "SummerFest" offers the chance to view nearly two dozen fine arts events. Kids will love the summer youth day-camp. For relaxation, try reading in the library or playing in the indoor swimming pool. During the winter, try ice skating, sledding, cross-country skiing and more. Estes Park Center is minutes away from the quaint mountain town of Estes Park. Take scenic drives through Big Thompson Canyon, over Trail Ridge Road in Rocky Mountain National Park or along the scenic Peak-to-Peak Highway.

Reservations are required for large groups — the conference and family reunion facilities can accommodate up to 2,500 people. Pets are allowed in cabins only.

Location: West of town on Colorado Highway 36 (also known as Moraine Ave.). Turn south on Highway 66.

186 Cabins with Kitchens
14 Vacation Homes
534 Lodging Rooms
136 Fireplaces
Central Fireplace
Central Campfire Area

Room Phones
All Non-Smoking in Units
Elevation: 8010
No credit cards
2 people a night: $30 - $207
Open: All Year

Dave Thomas, Dir Commun
2515 Tunnel Rd
Estes Park CO 80511-2550
970/586-3341 ext 6012
303/629-5784 Denver local
970/586-6088 Fax

At the resort:

At resort or within 15 minutes:

Fireside Cabins & RV Park

At the foot of the Rockies, just west of Loveland, are the Fireside Cabins. The cabins, sheltered among many shade trees, over look the "Devil's Backbone" of the mountains. All cabins are air conditioned and have color cable television. Some have queen beds, fireplaces and kitchenettes with cooking utensils. A fully furnished apartment with two bedrooms is also available as a motel suite for larger families.

Outside, the resort has a playground, volleyball, basketball and badminton for everyone to enjoy. A convenience store and laundry room are also available. RV sites with picnic tables and concrete patios are available year-round as well. Fireside is close to great fishing and many kinds of recreation, including hiking, mountain biking, golfing, boating, and horseback riding. After your day of fun, come back for a soak in the new, relaxing hot tub. While vacationing here, be sure to visit the town of Loveland, known for it numerous sculptors whose work grace Benson Park. If you want break from outdoor recreation, try some indoors fun at the close by 38-store factory outlet mall.

RV and tent sites are also available.

Location: 3-1/2 miles west of Loveland and 26 miles east of Estes Park. On Highway 34 near milepost 86.

4 Cabins with Kitchens
4 cabins without Kitchens
4 Motel Rooms
8 Fireplaces
Central Campfire Area

Pay Phone(s)
Non-Smoking Units Available
Elevation: 4800
No credit cards
2 people a night: $44 - $70
Open: All Year

Alan & Betty Huschka, Owners
6850 W Hwy 34
Loveland CO 80537
970/667-2903

At the resort:

At resort or within 15 minutes:

Idlewilde Cottages by the River

In a forest of 100-foot pine trees, on the beautiful Big Thompson River are the completely equipped Idlewilde cottages. The one-, two- and three-bedroom "classic Colorado" cottages have spit-log exterior and a highly lacquered, tongue-in-grove knotty pine interior. The individual cottages have been beautifully updated with quality furnishings which include fully-equipped kitchens, carpet, cable television, tile showers and screened in porches. Most of the cottages boast a river view with porch swings for your enjoyment. Each cottage has a picnic tables and barbecue grills ready for your mountain cook-outs after fishing in the Big Thompson River.

This quiet, peaceful setting is only one mile from Rocky Mountain National Park. On-site the kids can play on the swings while you play horseshoes. Anglers can fish for rainbow trout in the stocked river, if you left your equipment at home you can rent poles and tackle on-site. Nearby, you'll find entertainment and shopping in Estes Park. An outdoor hot tub welcomes you home after your mountain adventures.

Location: Three miles from downtown Estes Park and one mile from the entrance of Rocky Mountain National Park on Highway 66.

12 Cabins with Kitchens
1 Vacation Home
1 Fireplace

Pay Phone(s)
Elevation: 7828
No credit cards
2 people a night: $75 - $119
Open: 5/16 to 10/4

Al & Connie Settles, Owners
2282 Hwy 66
Estes Park CO 80517-8318
970/586-3864
303/651-7846 Nov-Apr

At the resort:

At resort or within 15 minutes:

Inn of Glen Haven

Step back in time at this historic bed and breakfast inn built in 1919. Faithfully restored to reflect its original charm, this old-world retreat maintains the romantic atmosphere of an intimate English country inn. The rooms are tastefully decorated with antiques, each with its own motif. The Queen Victoria suite has a sitting room with a fainting couch. Five of the rooms have a canopy beds. The Lillie Lantry room is decorated in a peach and green Victorian style with sunny French doors leading to the patio. Some of the rooms are spacious two-room suites with a sitting room and a bedroom. All rooms have private baths.

Continental English breakfast is included with your stay. Overnight guests may also choose to enjoy gourmet candlelight dinners and fine wines in the restaurant or pub. After dinner, relax by the huge moss-rock fireplace in the parlor. Only 7 miles from Rocky Mountain National Park, the Inn of Glen Haven is off the beaten path, yet is on an all-season highway. In the winter, the Twelve Days of Christmas are celebrated each year with "Old English" feasts. The feast is a tradition from the old English Church Kalander starting on December 26th. Explore antique shops in Estes Park and the magnificence of the national park nearby.

Well-behaved children are welcome. Open seven days a week from Memorial day through mid October; and the weeks of December 20th through January 5th for the twelve days of Christmas Feast. Open weekends the rest of the year; closed March 15th through April 15th. No pets allowed.

Location: 7 miles northeast of Estes Park on Devil's Gulch Road.

6 Lodging Rooms
Central Fireplace

Lobby Phone
Bed & Breakfast Available
Elevation: 7500
Credit Cards: VM
2 people a night: $77 - $115
Open: 4/15 to 3/15

Tom & Sheila Sellers, Owners
PO Box 219
7468 County Rd 43
Glen Haven CO 80532-0219
970/586-3897 & Fax call 1st

At the resort:

At resort or within 15 minutes:

Lazy R Cottages

From your cottage at Lazy R, you'll be able to gaze upon no less than 16 stunning mountain peaks. The sparkling clean cabins of knotty pine interiors with one, two or three bedrooms, have fully equipped kitchens, color cable television, picnic tables and barbecue grills. Many also have fireplaces stocked with free wood. Two spacious log cabins sleep up to 12 people and boast a private hot tub. The other cabins share a resort hot tub.

After a lovely morning of hiking and exploring, spend a lazy afternoon with your children at the on-site playground. Close to Rocky Mountain National Park, Lazy R is near numerous recreational opportunities, from driving along picturesque Trail Ridge Road to hiking or cross-country skiing in the untouched backcountry.

Location: Highway 36 (also known as Moraine Ave.), 1 and a half miles from Estes Park.

11 Cabins with Kitchens
2 Motel Rooms
9 Fireplaces

Pay Phone(s)
Elevation: 7800
Credit Cards: VMD
2 people a night: $45 - $255
Open: All Year

Mark Whittlesey; Owner & David Kiser
PO Box 1996
891 Moraine Park Rd
Estes Park CO 80517-1996
970/586-3708

At the resort:

At resort or within 15 minutes:

Machin's Cottages in the Pines

In a secluded location inside Rocky Mountain National Park, these deluxe, immaculately clean cottages are beautifully decorated. Scattered among tall pines and unusual rock formations, the cottages have fully equipped kitchens, fireplaces stocked with free firewood, large picture windows, carpeting, cable color television with HBO, porches and patio areas with outdoor furniture and barbecue grills. All linens are provided and exchanged when necessary.

Kids will like the children's playground on-site. Machin's Cottages is near a small brook and a hiking trail begins on the property. A short 1.25-mile hike from your cottage is Beaver Meadows and the spectacular mountain valley of Moraine Park, where other trails spread out into Rocky Mountain National Park. Fish in the nearby lake and river, or take a 10-minute drive to Estes Park for dining, shopping and golfing.

A minimum of two nights is required. One small pet is allowed, but it must remain on a leash. If bringing a small child, ask for high-chairs, cribs and bed-rails. Visit their Web site at http://www.estes-park.com/machins.

Location: Southwest two and a half miles from Estes Park on Highway 36 (also known as Moraine Avenue), then go west a half mile on Eagle Cliff Road.

17 Cabins with Kitchens
17 Fireplaces

Pay Phone(s)
Elevation: 8000
Credit Cards: VMA
2 people a night: $73 - $100
Open: 5/16 to 10/1

Lee Machin, Owner
PO Box 2687
2450 Eagle Cliff Rd
Estes Park CO 80517-2687
970/586-4276

At the resort:

At resort or within 15 minutes:

Mountain Haven Inn & Cottages

Mountain Haven offers a haven in the Rocky Mountains where you can enjoy majestic Colorado at its best. On two landscaped acres on the Big Thompson River with a view of snowcapped peaks, the new, fully furnished, two-bedroom cottages have fireplaces, cable television, kitchens and decks. Sit outside at the picnic table and grill dinner in the high country air on the barbecue provided. The Inn offers three bedrooms, two baths (one with a Jacuzzi tub), and a living room with a fireplace and cable television. In addition, those staying in the inn rooms may use the sunroom and the country kitchen/dining area with its dishwasher and microwave.

Fish the Big Thompson River that runs through Mountain Haven. One mile away is Estes Park, the gateway to Rocky Mountain National Park. Estes Park is a resort community that provides many recreational opportunities for visitors, including winter sports, hiking and golfing. Be sure to visit the many shops and restaurants in town during your stay.

The inn and cottages are open year-round for nightly and weekly rentals. Consider holding your family reunion or group retreats here.

Location: Between Estes Park and Rocky Mountain National Park on Highway 36 west (also known as Moraine Ave.).

6 Cabins with Kitchens
7 Fireplaces
Central Campfire Area

Pay Phone(s)
Non-Smoking Units Available
Elevation: 7500
Credit Cards: VM
2 people a night: Call for Rates
Open: All Year

Deanna Bleyle & Glenda Brown, Owners
690 Morraine Rt
Estes Park CO 80517
970/586-2864

At the resort:

At resort or within 15 minutes:

National Park Resort Cabins & Campground

Located next to the Fall River entrance to Rocky Mountain National Park, this resort is on a sheltered, tree-filled mountainside. The housekeeping cabins have fully equipped kitchens, bathrooms with tiled showers, sunken living rooms with fireplaces, picture windows with great views and color cable television. Linens and towels are provided and towels can be exchanged daily at the office. A delightful climate provides warm, sunny days and cool evenings. The pine-scented air, blue skies and grand views all make this a uniquely Colorado vacation.

Across the highway is a grocery store, gift shop, and riding stable. Bordering the national park, the resort has hiking trials, fishing and climbing nearby. Check out the nature walks, films and evening campfires in Rocky Mountain National Park. Estes Park boasts golf courses, sail boats, chuckwagon suppers and other entertainment. After a day spent at play, relax on the deck area in the private and semi-private hot tubs. Sit back, soak your muscles and contemplate the mountain splendor.

RV and tent sites are also available. Pets are welcome for a fee and special pet deposit. Advance reservations are suggested. You must pay first and last night's deposit; there is a 30-day cancellation policy.

Location: 5 miles west of Estes Park at the Fall River entrance to Rocky Mountain National Park on Highway 34.

4 Cabins with Kitchens
3 Motel Rooms
4 Fireplaces

Pay Phone(s)
Elevation: 8300
Credit Cards: VMD
2 people a night: $50 - $130
Open: All Year

Dan & Becky Ludlam, Owners
3501 Fall River Rd
Estes Park CO 80517-9801
970/586-4563

At the resort:

At resort or within 15 minutes:

River Forks Stage Stop Bed & Breakfast

Located in the historic site of the Forks Hotel of 1906 in Drake, River Forks offers two bed and breakfast suites on a private, wooded mountainside. The upstairs room has a king-sized bed with a separate sitting room and a pull out love seat. In addition to a full bath (shower, no tub), it has a bar with coffee for your in-room comfort. The honeymoon suite around the back features a solid redwood deck overlooking the river. The room has a queen-sized bed, full bath a sitting area. Breakfast is included in the nightly price.

River Forks offers the rustic tradition of the old west with many opportunities to escape the routines of daily life. Ye Old Mercantile and ice cream parlor will see to your simple vacation needs and sweet tooth. The restaurant where breakfast is served, also offers lunch and dinner. The lodge is at the fork of the Big Thompson River, secluded from the bustle of Estes Park. From here, Rocky Mountain National Park is a short 25 minute drive away. Right in River Forks backyard, however, is the natural beauty of Roosevelt National Forest with its own mountainous terrain and wildlife, including deer, elk and big horn sheep. Hike along the North Fork of the river looking for the perfect, deep, trout pool to cast your line into.

RV sites are also available.

Location: From I-25, exit 257 onto Highway 34, west 24.8 miles on the right near milepost 75.

2 Lodging Rooms
Central Fireplace
Central Campfire Area

Pay Phone(s)
Bed & Breakfast Available
Elevation: 6300
Credit Cards: VMAD
2 people a night: $75
Open: All Year

Jim & Annette Crill, Owners
PO Box 158
1601 Big Thompson Highway
Drake CO 80515-0158
970/635-9455 & Fax

At the resort:

At resort or within 15 minutes:

Romantic RiverSong® Bed & Breakfast Inn

Located on 27 wooded acres, RiverSong® is a small country inn at the foot of Giant Track Mountain in Estes Park. Once a luxurious summer home of the wealthy and the scene of "Great Gatsby-like" parties, the Inn now offers quaint bed and breakfast rooms. Each room, named after regional wildflowers, has a private bath, a river-rock fireplace, and large tubs. Each also comes with comfortable bathrobes in case you forget your own. The cozy bedrooms are decorated with a blend of antique and modern furniture. Jacuzzi tubs for two are also available. After a quiet evening in front of a crackling fire, curl up in bed under a warm comforter, lulled to sleep by the magical melody of the mountain stream outside your window. Awaken in the morning to the rich aroma of freshly brewed coffee and freshly made breads and unwind in the evening on candlelight dinners.

Fish the rushing trout stream, relax in the rustic gazebo by a pond, or enjoy the panoramic views from gentle hiking trails with rock benches. Catch site of elk, deer, raccoons, eagles, owls and chipmunks as you wander the grounds. Activities in this area are year-round: snowshoe and cross-country ski in the winter, hike and mountain bike in the summer. Attend a Rocky Mountain Nature Association seminar, or play golf and tennis. Estes Park is well known for all its shops and antiques, as well as its many festivals, including the Scottish Festival, the Rooftop Rodeo, Aspenfest, the Holiday Season Festival and the Spring Snow Festival.

Three rooms are wheelchair accessible. If planning an outdoor wedding ask about the snowshoe winter weddings the owner preforms. The Inn offers picnic basket dinner to enjoy in your room or out on their patio. The Inn is not suitable for small children or pets.

Location: 2 blocks south of US 36, at west end of Lower Broadview Road, on the Little Thomp son River.

5 cabins without Kitchens
4 Lodging Rooms
9 Fireplaces
Central Campfire Area

Lobby Phone
Bed & Breakfast Available
All Non-Smoking in Units
Recreation Room
Elevation: 7900
Credit Cards: VM
2 people a night: $135 - $250
Open: All Year

Gary & Sue Mansfield, Innkeepers
PO Box 1910
1765 Lower Broadview Rd
Estes Park CO 80517-1910
970/586-4666
970/577-1961 Fax
E-mail: riversng@frii.com

At the resort:

At resort or within 15 minutes:

Shelly's Cottages

Along the river and away from the road on five acres of quiet mountain splendor, these modern, comfortable cottages have private baths, excellent beds with linens, and full kitchens with dishes. Some cottages have fireplaces, while two "special occasion" units have king-sized beds and private hot tubs in their own gazebos. Another cottage sleeps up to six and also has its own hot tub and fireplace. Cook your freshly caught stream trout on the barbecue grills and eat at shaded picnic tables.

Go for a hike or drive on scenic roads through the high mountain country and dramatic front range canyons. You are only minutes from fine dining, dinner theaters and the sights of Lyons, Estes Park, Rocky Mountain National Park and Boulder.

Special occasion packages come with champagne, breakfast baskets, chocolates and dining certificates. Visit their Web site at http://www.csn.net/shellys/index.htm.

Location: Four miles northwest of Lyons, 20 minutes from Estes Park, off of Highway 36 near milepost 16.

9 Cabins with Kitchens
4 Fireplaces

Lobby Phone
Elevation: 5900
Credit Cards: VMD
2 people a night: $40 - $150
Open: All Year

Henri "Ro" & Marilyn Kinson, Mgrs
PO Box 740
16188 North St Vrain Dr
Lyons CO 80540-0740
303/823-6326
800/356-6061
303/823-9321 Fax
E-mail: shellys@csn.net

At the resort:

At resort or within 15 minutes:

Skyline Cottages

Skyline Cottages rests right on the Big Thompson River with spectacular views of Longs Peak. To ensure your comfort, the hostess provides current magazines and fresh mountain flowers in the five cottages, the one vacation home and the two small apartments which are available. Color, cable televisions and radios are furnished in each unit with irons and ironing boards available on request. Each has fully equipped kitchens and linens as well. Four of the cottages have wood-burning fireplaces set in rustic pine with tile trim. Surrounded by blue spruce trees, the cottages can accommodate from one to six people depending on the unit you chose. The vacation home will hold 12 or more comfortably and has an unusually large kitchen, living room and bedrooms. Some units have carpeted, outdoor decks — perfect for admiring the wonderful views.

Fish for rainbow, German, brown, cutthroat and brook trout right outside your cabin. Or relax in the mountain sunshine on your front porch or river front deck. Be sure to grill your fresh catch of the day or steaks on the covered, charcoal grills next to the river. Tucked between Roosevelt National Forest and Rocky Mountain National Park, Skyline is also a short drive from downtown Estes Park and the Hidden Valley Ski Area. Here the activities to choose among seem endless: hiking, picnicking, horseback riding, playing tennis and golf, riding the aerial tramway, boating, swimming, and, of course, sightseeing. Estes Park entertainment events include theater productions, chuckwagon dinners, rodeos and horse shows. Whenever you come to vacation here, be sure bring along your camera. The views as you drive over Trail Ridge Road to the Continental Divide are truly unforgettable.

Location: Two miles southwest of Estes Park on Highway 66.

5 Cabins with Kitchens
1 Vacation Home
2 Lodging Rooms
4 Fireplaces

Lobby Phone
Elevation: 8000
Credit Cards: VM
2 people a night: $50 - $85
Open: 5/15 to 10/31

Sue Lamb, Owner
1752 Hwy 66
Estes Park CO 80517
970/586-2886
602/274-6407 Winter

At the resort:

At resort or within 15 minutes:

Streamside Cabins

The luxurious cabins at Streamside are right on the Fall River and are surrounded by 17 acres of wooded meadow with the mountainside and wildlife enhancing them. AAA rated these elegant cabin suites with four diamonds and Mobil with three stars. The 19 housekeeping cabins and cabin suites are one and two bedroom with king and queen beds, living rooms with sleeping sofas, full kitchens with microwaves and a dining area. Some feature in-room steam baths, jetted tubs, private, riverfront decks and patios with gas grills. All cabins have fireplaces, free wood, color cable television, VCRs, cathedral ceilings and skylights.

Streamside is hiking distance from the beauty of Rocky Mountain National Park. Traverse the famous park on foot, mountain bike, horseback, snowshoes, cross-country skis or in your car. The herds of mule deer, elk and big horn sheep are too spectacular to miss! Fish for rainbow trout in the Fall River's rushing waters, a few steps away from your cabin. Hike Old Man Mountain trail right on the property for 45 minutes to the ancient Arapahoe Indian Nation's former ceremonial site. Near to Estes Park, you'll be able to sample the town's many restaurants and explores the numerous, quaint gift shops. No matter how you spend your day, come back to Streamside and relax in the new, enclosed, heated swimspa and hot tub.

Ask about the 3-5-7 day "Affairs of the Heart" packages for honeymoons, birthdays, anniversaries and other special occasions.

Location: Between Estes Park and Rocky Mountain National Park on Fall River Road.

19 Cabins with Kitchens
19 Fireplaces

Pay Phone(s)
All Non-Smoking in Units
Elevation: 7600
Credit Cards: VMAD
2 people a night: $70 - $270
Open: All Year

Susan & Lynn Coffman, Owners
PO Box 2930
1260 Fall River Rd
Estes Park CO 80517-2930
970/586-6464
800/321-3303
970/586-6272 Fax
E-mail: streamsd@frii.com

At the resort:

At resort or within 15 minutes:

Telemark Resort Cottages

Relax and enjoy the splendor of the outdoors while staying at the cozy cottages at Telemark Resort on the Big Thompson River. Choose from the 10 housekeeping cabins, each having a fireplace, telephone, and cable television.

Within minutes are restaurants, shops and evening entertainment in the charming town of Estes Park. Kids can frolic at the resort's playground while anglers can try fishing right on the property. Other nearby activities include horseback riding, river rafting, golfing and boating on the lake. When you need a break from the outdoors, learn a little history of the area at the local museum. In the winter, with the beauty of Rocky Mountain National Park just moments away, you can cross-country ski, snowmobile or go on a romantic sleigh ride.

Pets are welcomed to accompany you for a fee.

Location: Near Estes Park on Highway 36.

10 Cabins with Kitchens
10 Fireplaces
Central Campfire Area

Room Phones
Elevation: 7522
Credit Cards: VMA
2 people a night: $60 - $80
Open: All Year

Vigdis Lohne, Owner
PO Box 100
650 Moraine Park Rd US 36 W
Estes Park CO 80517-0100
970/586-4343
800/669-0650

At the resort:

At resort or within 15 minutes:

Tiny Town Cottages

Located on 15 acres, with breathtaking views of the snow-capped peaks of the Continental Divide, these cozy cottages are furnished with everything you need. The one-couple cottages are equipped with fireplaces and free firewood, kitchens, king or queen size beds, bath with tub/shower and color cable television with HBO. The Honeymoon Cottage has a two-person whirlpool tub. This property caters to non-smokers only in a totally non-smoking environment.

Enjoy a picnic, BBQ or just relax on the spacious grounds. Try casting your line into the privately stocked quarter mile of the Big Thompson River adjacent to the Cottages, available to guests only. Tiny Town is close to several fine restaurants, a supermarket, laundromat and a miniature golf course. Rocky Mountain National Park, one mile away, offers many scenic roads and trails, wildlife, wildflowers and waterfalls in a spectacular mountain setting.

Tiny Town Cottages caters to adults, singles and couples, who are looking for peace, quiet and privacy. To ensure their privacy, large groups or family reunions are not allowed. A minimum of three to four nights stay is required. Pets are not allowed.

Location: On Highway 36 (also known as Moraine Ave.), one mile west of Estes Park, near milepost 5.

20 Cabins with Kitchens
18 Fireplaces

Pay Phone(s)
All Non-Smoking in Units
Recreation Room
Elevation: 7644
Credit Cards: VMAD
2 people a night: $49 - $110
Open: 5/1 to 10/15

Bob & Helen Mitchell, Owners
830 Moraine Ave
Estes Park CO 80517-8005
970/586-4249

At the resort:

At resort or within 15 minutes:

Valhalla Resort

Tucked away on eleven tree-studded acres next to Rocky Mountain National Park are a wide variety of exceptionally clean, comfortable and well-furnished vacation homes, ranging from rustic to luxurious. The cottages have fully equipped kitchens with dishes, glassware, pots and pans, coffee-makers and toasters. The living rooms have fireplaces, cable television and the homes feature separate bedrooms and baths, some with whirlpool jets. Each vacation home has its own private deck or patio with a barbecue and exterior furniture.

In the summer, enjoy the swimming pool, while year-round you can soak in the private hot tub or play in the activity center. There is an on-site laundromat and gift shop. Bring your sweetie for one of the exclusive LoveScapes® vacations, with a private Love Retreat, abundant deli tray, flowers, champagne and other surprises. Besides the many activities available in Rocky Mountain National Park and the town of Estes Park, Valhalla provides shuffleboard, miniature golf, horseshoes and ping-pong. Bring hiking boots for the trails, a swimming suit for the pool, and warm sweaters for the cool, crisp mountain evenings.

Valhalla offers senior discounts and special rates during the off-peak season.

Location: One third of a mile off Highway 66, near milepost 1, off Highway 36 west (also known as Moraine Ave.).

18 Cabins with Kitchens
4 Vacation Homes
22 Fireplaces

Pay Phone(s)
Recreation Room
Elevation: 7700
Credit Cards: VMAD
2 people a night: $51 - $154
Open: All Year

Lynette & Mike Lott & Jeannine & Matt Swatzki, Owners
2185 Eagle Cliff Rd - PO Box 1439
Estes Park CO 80517-1439
970/586-3284
800/522-3284
970/586-6361 Fax

At the resort:

At resort or within 15 minutes:

Woodlands on Fall River

The Woodlands offers 16 one- and two-bedroom suites overlooking the sparkling waters of Fall River. The tastefully decorated suites feature panoramic views, spacious living rooms, separate bedrooms with queen beds and ceiling fans, wood-burning fireplaces with native flagstone hearths, and fully equipped kitchens including microwaves and coffee makers. Coffee and tea are provided. Each unit also has color cable television with HBO, VCRs and free video libraries. Some suites have Jacuzzi tubs. Enjoy the dramatic mountain setting from the large decks and patios off the suites which overlook Fall River and Castle Mountain. Grill your dinner outdoors on the gas grills provided.

In nearby Rocky Mountain National Park, spend hours enjoying nature and the abundant wildlife. Hike, fish or picnic in the park. In the winter, explore it on cross-country skis or snowshoes. The drives are scenic year-round. Estes Park, with its many shops and restaurants, is a short drive down the road. After a day's adventures, be sure to visit the outdoor spa with its large sun deck, hidden in a secluded grove of fir, spruce and pine trees. Soak in the warm waters, enjoy a crisp mountain breeze rustling the leaves and listen to the soothing rush of the river. The Woodlands is perfect for relaxing far from busy city life.

Visit their Web site at http://www.estes-park.com/woodlands.

Location: Two and a half miles west of Estes Park on Fall River Road (US 34 bypass).

16 Vacation Homes
16 Fireplaces

Room Phones
Non-Smoking Units Available
Elevation: 7600
Credit Cards: VMAD
2 people a night: $65 - $107
Open: All Year

Sandy & John Gilfillan, Owners
1888 Fall River Road
Estes Park CO 80517
970/586-0404
970/586-3297 Fax
800/721-2279

At the resort:

At resort or within 15 minutes:

Yogi Bear's Jellystone Park at Estes

Welcome to the serenity of the Rocky Mountains. Here you'll find 35 wooded acres of hillside adjacent to Roosevelt National Forest. The comfortably furnished, rustic housekeeping cabins are shaded by tall ponderosa pines whose scent fills the crisp mountain air. Wild roses, friendly chipmunks, singing birds and loitering wildlife enhance the friendly atmosphere and add to the beauty of the Meadowdale Valley. Picnic with the whole family at the group picnic areas.

Amenities include modern restrooms, hot showers, a convenience store and a coin laundry. Peaceful and convenient, Park Place is near both Rocky Mountain National Park and Estes Park for wilderness and civilized vacation activities. Explore the adjacent Roosevelt National Forest by hiking, biking or horseback riding its trails. Play a game of basketball, have fun in the video arcade or challenge your family to horseshoes, volleyball and badminton. To relax, swim in the heated pool and sunbathe on the large deck.

Formally known as Park Place Cabins & Camping Resort. An outdoor, group meeting area and RV sites are also available.

Location: 5.5 miles southeast of junction Highway 34 and 36, near milepost 5.

4 Cabins with Kitchens
2 Camper Cabins
Central Campfire Area

Pay Phone(s)
All Non-Smoking in Units
Recreation Room
Elevation: 7800
Credit Cards: VMD
2 people a night: $40 - $75
Open: 5/10 to 9/15

Tony & Kathy Palmeri, Owners
5495 US Hwy 36
Estes Park CO 80517
970/586-4230
800/722-2928
970/577-0474 Fax

At the resort:

At resort or within 15 minutes:

Evergreen

Map: F-15

In a picturesque, mountain setting, **Evergreen** offers all the outdoor adventures the Rocky Mountains has to offer near the amenities of the Queen City of the Plains, Denver. Spend your vacation visiting the museums, restaurants, art galleries and shops in downtown Denver or exploring the many wonders the mountains have to offer. Evergreen boasts a lake that has been a popular ice skating spot for decades. It usually opens by Christmas. Experience what ice skating was meant to be — outdoors in view of snowcapped peaks. Other area activities include hiking, mountain biking, fishing and cross-country skiing. From here, go down the road to Golden and tour Coors Brewery, or go north to the limited stakes gambling towns of Central City and Black Hawk. On your way west to the ski resorts of Winter Park and Loveland, be sure to stop for a relaxing soak in Idaho Springs' natural hot mineral springs. Nearby, explore any of the many historical sites, like Buffalo Bill's Grave, perched on top of Lookout Mountain.

Fun Things To Do

- Buffalo Bill's Grave and Memorial Museum (303) 526-0747
- Coors Brewery Tour (303) 277-BEER
- Evergreen Lake (303) 674-2677

Bauer's Spruce Island Chalets

On 19 roomy acres, Bauer's Spruce Island Chalets provide comfort and convenience throughout the year. All chalets have kitchens, living rooms, bathrooms, shower-tubs and have from one to four bedrooms. The larger chalets feature fireplaces and cable television.

Most of the chalets surround a large verdant lawn where the whole family can barbecue, picnic and play lawn games, including croquet and badminton. Walk along Cub Creek or fish in the property's small pond and stream. Public park lands to the east are easily accessible for hiking and fishing. In addition, a variety of stores, craft shops, churches, restaurants, art galleries, golf, horseback riding stables and tennis courts are nearby in town. If you desire solitude, take a short drive to scenic areas where you can watch wildlife and birds frolic on the mountainside.

Location: From Highway 74, go through Burgan Park to Evergreen. Turn west on Highway 73, then turn south on Brook Forest Road.

5 Cabins with Kitchens

Pay Phone(s)
Elevation: 7200
Credit Cards: VMAD
2 people a night: Call for Rates
Open: All Year

Ron & Sue Retterer, Owners
5937 S Brook Forest Rd
Evergreen CO 80439-1678
303/674-4757

At the resort:

At resort or within 15 minutes:

Evergreen Lodge

These beautifully furnished cabins are secluded below towering blue spruce trees along side Cub Creek. The spacious cabins have fully equipped kitchens, microwave ovens, cable televisions (VCRs are available), fresh linens, large fluffy towels, comfortable beds and complimentary coffee and tea. Some cabins feature fireplaces with free wood. A lovely creek-side picnic area with brick barbecue grill is available to all guests, while the playground is designed for kids.

Hike, fish and mountain bike in the resort's backyard wilderness — the lush forests around Evergreen. Visit town, where you can play golf, dance, ice skate on the lake in winter, shop and dine in fine restaurants. For limited-stakes gambling and a touch of history, take a bus from town or drive to the casinos in close by Central City and Black Hawk. Downhill ski at nearby Summit County ski resorts. Denver, a short drive down the mountains, offers many big city attractions, from its zoo and museums to numerous downtown cultural events. Evergreen Lodge is at the heart of a real mountain experience.

Location: At Highway 73 and Brookforest Road, 1 mile south of the dam on Highway 73, on the southwest side of the road.

8 Cabins with Kitchens
3 Fireplaces
1 Lodging Room or Apartment

Room Phones
All Non-Smoking in Units
Elevation: 7200
Credit Cards: VMAD
2 people a night: $70 - $115
Open: All Year

Coral Carley, Owner
PO Box 2861
5331 Hwy 73
Evergreen CO 80439-2861
303/674-6927

At the resort:

At resort or within 15 minutes:

Highland Haven Creekside Inn

Set amid spectacular rock outcroppings, towering blue spruce and 400-feet of the scenic Bear Creek, Highland Haven is in one of Colorado's most exquisite settings, yet only one block east of downtown Evergreen. This upscale bed and breakfast inn offers guest rooms, suites and deluxe cottages with fireplaces. The inn's atmosphere is enhanced by exceptional decor, tasteful landscaping, a flowered arbor and a charming fountain. The Gardener's Cottage is a special cabin with a canopy bed made from willow branches, a moss-rock fireplace, antique furnishings, a private deck overlooking Bear Creek and a Jacuzzi. All accommodations are non-smoking and have fully equipped kitchens, telephones, linens and towels. Special features in some of the rooms include CD systems, VCRs and garden patios, decks or balconies with breath-taking views.

Continental breakfast is complimentary and served on the historic "Pioneer Porch" every morning. Look for afternoon refreshments served there, too! Fish right at the inn or try some of Colorado's best skiing at Winter Park, Keystone, Loveland or Copper Mountain. If you prefer, cross-country ski in the surrounding backcountry, or ice skate and ice fish on Evergreen Lake. Visit charming Evergreen, venture to Denver, or drive west into the mountains and old mining towns.

Business needs are met with the fax and modem-ready phone system. The Inn has added the Dailey Cabin, built in 1884, as a new conference and celebration facility. Ask about the elaborate champagne packages to celebrate your special occasions. We specialize in romance. Pets are not allowed at the inn.

Location: Highway 74, near milepost 7.

10 Cabins with Kitchens
2 cabins without Kitchens
4 Motel Rooms

Room Phones
Bed & Breakfast Available
All Non-Smoking in Units
Elevation: 7000
Credit Cards: VMAD
2 people a night: Call for Rates
Open: All Year

Tom Statzell & Gail Riley, Owner
4395 Independence Trl S
Evergreen CO 80439-8516
303/674-3577
800/459-2406
303/674-9088 Fax

At the resort:

At resort or within 15 minutes:

Glenwood Springs

Including New Castle — Map: G-7 & F-7

Soaking in the large, brick-lined hot springs pool (it's 615' by 75'), gazing up at pine-covered mountain peaks, you'll understand why first the Ute Indians and then wealthy miners and European aristocrats treasured **Glenwood Springs**. When the Utes were relocated in 1882, the town sprang up, catering to the rich from around the world. With money came trouble: by 1887 there were 22 bars in a two-block area! Doc Holliday, who was wanted in Arizona for killings at the OK Corral shoot-out, is buried here. The Hotel Colorado opened in the early 1890s and was the summer White House for Teddy Roosevelt. A total of seven U.S. presidents vacationed here. Today, people come for the history and hot springs as much as the rugged and beautiful surroundings. Glenwood Canyon has a 9-mile bike path and rafters enjoy the white waters of the Colorado River flowing through the canyon. This area is also popular with spelunkers (cave explorers) because of the number of caves and one of the largest underground rivers in the country. The White River and Gunnison National Forests as well as four wilderness areas can be easily reached for day hikes or cross-country skiing.

Fun Things to Do

- Frontier Historical Society & Museum (970) 945-4448
- Glenwood Springs Golf Course (970) 945-7086
- Glenwood Springs Hot Springs Pool (970) 945-7131
- Johnson Park Miniature Golf (970) 945-9608
- Rifle Creek Golf Course, Rifle (970) 625-1093
- Rock Gardens Rafting (970) 945-6737
- Silt Historical Park (970) 876-2668 or (970) 876-2702
- Sunlight Mountain Resort (800) 445-7931
- Westbank Ranch Golf Course (970) 945-7032
- White River National Forest Headquarters (970) 945-2521
- Yampa Hot Springs Spa & Vapor Cave (970) 945-0667

Knotty Pine Lodge

Across from the Roaring Fork River, Knotty Pine Lodge is on the edge of town. Come relax and enjoy the Rocky Mountains in the modern cabins on a nice lawn or the comfortable lodge rooms. Accommodations include fully equipped kitchenettes, cable television and complete laundromat facilities. The cabins surround a park-like setting for barbecuing on gas grill, lawn games and lounging.

Be sure to relax in the Glenwood Springs Hot Springs pool between shopping, fishing, hunting, hiking and skiing. For those who like to hoof it, you can horseback ride in the surrounding area. Aspen, Sunlight, and Snowmass ski resorts are just a few miles away. Snowmobilers will love the nearly 1,400 miles of trails with pristine snow during the winter. Several snowmobile rental dealers are close by.

Ask about special ski packages during the winter. They have group rates for groups with 25 people or more.

Location: Exit 116 off of I-70, 1.5 miles south on Highway 82, bear right at fork in road. Before Sunlight bridge.

17 Cabins with Kitchens
4 Lodging Rooms
3 Fireplaces

Room Phones
Elevation: 5872
Credit Cards: VMAD
2 people a night: $55 - $70
Open: All Year

Bill & Lee Hill, Owners
2706 Grand Ave
Glenwood Springs CO 81601-4426
970/945-6446
800/726-5940

At the resort:

At resort or within 15 minutes:

New Castle/Glenwood Springs KOA & Kamping Kabins™

This A+ KOA award winning campground, located on a trout-stocked mountain creek, encompassed by woods and high mountain peaks, has Kamping Kabins™. Bring your own bedding supplies and cooking utensils. Clean restrooms with hot showers and push button locks and a coin laundry are available. Grill your dinner outdoors at the picnic tables and barbecues provided. Relax in the cool shade provided by tall firs, spruce trees and the occasional aspen trees bordering East Elk Creek.

Fish right at the resort! Kids young and old will like the horseshoes pits by the creek, the large playground and the video game room. Trails from the KOA leading into the wilderness are great for hikers. Glenwood Canyon has a path for bikers and rollerbladers. Exercise your pet in the designated dog run. Eat breakfast at the Creekside Cafe weekends Memorial through Labor Day. Everynight chow down on the cowboy steak dinners. This makes an excellent base camp for wind surfing, rafting, and horseback riding. Golfers, from the miniature to 18-hole variety, will find courses to challenge them in Glenwood Springs. Flat Top Wilderness Area is a 15 minute drive; and photographer's will enjoy the wildlife, birds, flowers and snow-capped mountains.

Ask about the RV and tent sites.

Location: Two and one half miles north of New Castle, 9 miles west of Glenwood Springs. Off of I-70, at exit 105.

9 Camper Cabins

Room Phones
All Non-Smoking in Units
Recreation Room
Elevation: 6000
Credit Cards: VMD
2 people a night: $35 - $40
Open: 5/9 to 9/28

New Castle KOA
0581 CR 241
New Castle CO 81647
970/984-2240
800/KOA-3240
970/984-0349 Fax
E-mail: rosrich@rof.net

At the resort:

At resort or within 15 minutes:

Ponderosa Lodge

The rustic log cabins and contemporary A-frames, all modern and newly renovated, are nestled among the oldest trees in Glenwood Springs. These quiet, cozy cabins have queen beds, kitchens with pots and pans, fireplaces and remote control cable television. The cabins also have air conditioning and thermostatically controlled heat. Picnic in the two-acre park, with BBQ grills and picnic tables behind the cabins.

Play volleyball, badminton and horseshoes in the family playground. Or let the kids roam the large playground on the property. During the summer, a fun mini-golf course is within walking distance. The Ponderosa Lodge is near the famous Glenwood Springs Hot Springs pool and various activities, such as fishing, hiking, jeeping, rafting, fine dining, spelunking in the vapor caves, sightseeing, golfing, horseback riding and hunting. Ponderosa Lodge is 12 miles from Sunlight Ski Area.

Location: On Frontage Road off I-70, near exit 114.

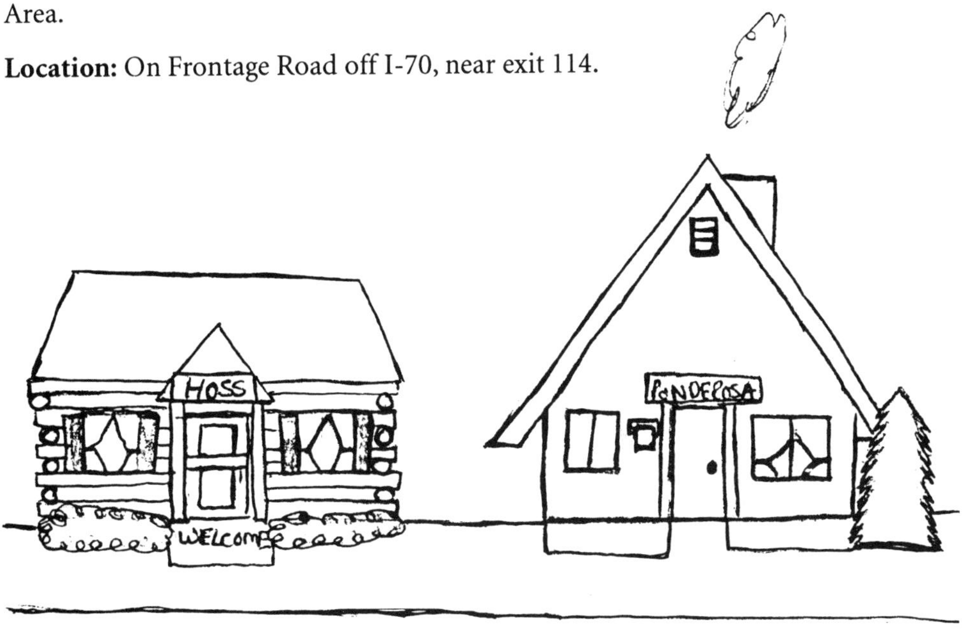

14 Cabins with Kitchens
3 cabins without Kitchens
7 Fireplaces

Room Phones
Elevation: 5700
Credit Cards: VMAD
2 people a night: $36 - $118
Open: All Year

Delbert & Lori Russ, Managers
51793 Hwy 6 & 24
Glenwood Springs CO 81601
970/945-5058
800/843-5449
970/945-1172 Fax

At the resort:

At resort or within 15 minutes:

Riverside Cottages

Located in a heavily wooded 7.7-acre site, Riverside Cottages boasts a spectacular 1,200-foot frontage on the Roaring Fork River — Glenwood Springs' only river front resort. The cottages accommodate up to 10 people, and have furnished modern kitchens, cable television with HBO, private bedrooms and linens with maid service daily! Cabins range from one bedroom to three bedrooms with queen size beds in most. Some cottages have fireplaces with furnished wood. For those who like barbecuing, there are plenty of grills, picnic tables and lawn chairs.

The Gold Medal waters of the Roaring Fork River are fishable year-round and is heavily populated with trophy-sized trout. Your hosts can arrange rafting, hunting trips and sightseeing trips for the whole family. Year-round activities include visiting the world famous Glenwood Springs hot mineral and swimming pools and Vapor Caves. In season, go hiking, biking, river tubing and rafting, kayaking, miniature and regulation golfing, and horseback riding. During the winter, enjoy skiing, sledding, snowmobiling and ice skating. For something a little different, enjoy four-wheel driving, the nearby waterslide or take a hot air balloon ride.

Groups and reunions are welcomed at Riverside. Although reservations are encouraged, drive-in visitors are welcomed when space is available. Deposits for reservation are required, be sure to check about their cancellation policy.

Location: At the southern city limits of Glenwood Springs off of Highway 82, turn right at Buffalo Valley Restaurant. Double back on County Road 154 about three-quarters of a mile.

15 Cabins with Kitchens
6 Fireplaces
Central Campfire Area

Room Phones
Elevation: 5800
Credit Cards: VMAD
2 people a night: $75 - $158
Open: All Year

Kevin Eggloff & Tristina Jackson, Managers
1287 CR 154
Glenwood Springs CO 81601
970/945-5509
800/945-5509 Reservations only
970/945-0247 Fax

At the resort:

At resort or within 15 minutes:

Spruce Tree Ranch

Along the beautiful, wooded banks of the East Elk Creek in New Castle, you'll discover modern log cabins in a magnificent, quiet setting, with views of high mountain peaks. A beautiful creek flows past the roomy cabins which have private baths, linens, two double beds and a hide-a-bed in the main room. Although you can't cook in the cabins, you can barbecue that freshly caught trout on the outside grills by one of the three ponds. Store your supplies in the social/game room's community refrigerator/freezer.

Kids will love the ranch's playground. Ranch activities include horseshoes, volleyball, croquet while nearby activities are playing golf, rock climbing and bird watching. This photographer's paradise features wildlife, birds, flowers and snow-capped mountains. Visit the Rifle Gap Reservoir and the unusual Rifle Falls. Hike in the Flat Tops Wilderness area and fish in streams and reservoirs. Hunt, horseback ride, mountain bike, whitewater raft the Colorado River, or just relax by the stream. And don't forget to visit the famous Glenwood Springs Hot Springs pool to ease the sore muscles after a day of adventure.

Children under 3 are free and a minimum deposit is required.

Location: 2 miles northwest of New Castle, I-70 Exit 105. 8 miles west of Glenwood Springs.

5 cabins without Kitchens
Central Campfire Area

Lobby Phone
Recreation Room
Elevation: 5900
No credit cards
2 people a night: $45 - $55
Open: 5/1 to 11/15

Tom & Lynn Jorgensen, Managers
2026 Road 245
New Castle CO 81647
970/984-2144 Ranch

At the resort:

At resort or within 15 minutes:

Grand Lake & Granby Area

Map: D-13

These mountain towns, at the western entrance to Rocky Mountain National Park, sit on great fishing lakes with beautiful, unspoiled views. Anglers will find rainbow, brook, mackinaw and cutthroat trout in abundance and large kokanee salmon as well. From **Granby**, Lake Granby, Shadow Mountain Reservoir and Willow Creek Reservoir are all close at hand. Resting on the shores of the largest natural lake in Colorado, **Grand Lake** is an alpine village with board sidewalks, log-front stores and the modern amenities of dining and shopping. At 8,369', this rustic town is enveloped by peaks, especially the impressive, bald Mt. Craig. Grand Lake has access to two reservoirs, two national forests, the national park and the Never Summer Wilderness Area which is accessible only by hiking trails. You can horseback ride, boat, hike, golf and river raft in this beautiful area. When the snow starts, Grand Lake and Granby become a winter playground, with groomed trails for snowmobiling, cross-country skiing, snowshoeing and close by slopes for downhill skiing. Ute, Arapaho and Cheyenne tribes used to hunt and fish in this Middle Park area and when you visit you'll see why this was land worth fighting over.

Fun Things to Do

- Arapaho National Forest (970) 887-4100
- Cozens Ranch House Museum, Winter Park (970) 726-5488
- Granby County Museum (970) 725-3939
- Grand Lake Golf Course (970) 627-8008
- Hot Sulphur Springs Mineral Baths and Pool (970) 725-3306
- Kaufman House (970) 627-3351
- Raven Rafting & Adventures (800)332-3381
- Rocky Mountain National Park (970) 627-3471

Circle H Lodge Bed & Breakfast

On the shores of majestic Lake Granby and overlooking the Continental Divide, Circle H Lodge Bed & Breakfast boasts a million dollar view from your lodge room as well as the great room, restaurant and lounge. The six individually decorated, non-smoking guest rooms have their own baths, televisions and have either one or two double beds. Two of the lodge rooms can be made into a suite with an equipped kitchen, living room and private deck, perfect for families. Breakfast — homemade muffins, cereals, warm beverages, juice and fruit, included with your room, is served in the restaurant.

Fish year-round right in front of the 8,000-square foot lodge. The lodge's restaurant specializes in deli sandwiches, soups, salad plates and mouth-watering desserts. Bring your own boat and use their courtesy dock for boating on Lake Granby or rent a boat at one of the nearby marinas. Hiking, horseback riding and golfing are within easy reach. Fall and winter activities include hunting, skiing, ice fishing and snowmobiling. Your hosts live here all year and strive to offer close and personal attention to every guest.

Circle H Lodge has a private meeting room available. Inquire about their elk hunting camp during the fall. Roll-away beds are available. Children under 5 stay free.

Location: Six miles north of Granby and nine miles south of Rocky Mountain National Park. On Highway 34 between milepost 6-7.

6 Lodging Rooms

Lobby Phone
Bed & Breakfast Available
All Non-Smoking in Units
Recreation Room
Elevation: 8300
Credit Cards: VMAD
2 people a night: Call for Rates
Open: All Year

Paul & Tricia Navarre, Owners
6732 US Hwy 34
Granby CO 80446
970/887-3955

At the resort:

At resort or within 15 minutes:

Columbine Creek Ranch B&B, Cabins & Snowmobile Rentals

Experience history in this unique bed and breakfast built in the early 1900s. Lucille Ball and Desi Arnez stayed at this charming ranch. The four rooms are filled with pine wood and each is uniquely decorated. All rooms have a private bath and television. Choose between a queen-size or full-size bed. Four cabins are available alongside the stocked trout ponds equipped with outdoor gas grills, televisions, coffee pots, dishes, silverware, dish pans and bath towels with either a kitchenette or refrigerator and cook-top.

Relax in the lodge in front of the fireplace and watch the big screen television. End your evening with a dip in the hot tub outside in the cool mountain air. Bed and breakfast guests wake up every morning to a family style breakfast, all you can eat. Cabin guests can join in for an additional charge. Enjoy complimentary coffee and tea throughout the day. Spend the days hiking, biking, shopping, dining out, boating, horseback riding and fishing. Catch all the fish you want without a license in the ranch ponds; there is a fee for the fish (per inch) and all fishing supplies are provided. This is a wonderful place to bring your children for their first fishing experience — awards are given for their first catch ever or an especially large one. Your hosts will clean them for you so you can grill them up at your cabin. In the winter, activities include skiing and snowmobiling (you can rent here).

Pets are allowed only in the cabins. The bed and breakfast and one cabin are open year round. Children under 5 stay free. Cancellation deposits will be refunded with 2 weeks notice. Columbine Creek specializes in small family reunions up to 40 people.

Location: On Highway 34 at milepost 15, near west entrance to Rocky Mountain National Park.

4 Cabins with Kitchens
4 Lodging Rooms
Central Fireplace
Central Campfire Area

Pay Phone(s)
Bed & Breakfast Available
All Non-Smoking in Units
Recreation Room
Elevation: 8500
Credit Cards: VMD
2 people a night: $60 - $85
Open: All Year

Jim & Tami Wold, Owners
PO Box 1675
14814 HWY 34
Grand Lake CO 80447-1199
970/627-2429 & Fax call 1st

At the resort:

At resort or within 15 minutes:

Daven Haven Lodge

Near the west entrance to Rocky Mountain National Park, and only two blocks from downtown, Daven Haven Lodge features two camper cabins and 16 cabins. Six of the units have fireplaces and all have cable television. Daven Haven is in a scenic setting just a half block from Grand Lake. At night, have the entire family gather around the campfire ring and outdoor barbecue area.

The main lodge has a lounge, dining room and banquet facilities. The dining room specializes in casual, affordable family meals. The resort also offers a heated swimming pool, open from June to Labor Day, horseshoes and volleyball. Grand Lake is famous for all the outdoor activities it offers, including four wheel drive tours, horseback riding, river rafting, golfing, miniature golfing, mountain biking and, of course, boating on lovely Grand Lake. Winter time features many things to do as well, including downhill and cross-country skiing, sleigh riding, snowmobiling, ice fishing and hunting. Come to Grand Lake in time for the Winter Carnival and dog sled races.

Daven Haven is ideal for family reunions, wedding receptions and business retreats.

Location: At entrance of Grand Lake go down the hill and take the first right onto Center Road to the first stop sign, then turn left onto Marina Drive, go two blocks.

12 Cabins with Kitchens
4 cabins without Kitchens
2 Camper Cabins
6 Fireplaces
Central Campfire Area

Pay Phone(s)
Recreation Room
Elevation: 8369
Credit Cards: VMD
2 people a night: $63 - $115
Open: All Year

Greg & Carey Barnes, Owners
PO Box 1528
604 Marina Dr
Grand Lake CO 80447-1528
970/627-8144
970/627-5098 Fax

At the resort:

At resort or within 15 minutes:

Elk Creek Camper Cabins & Campground

Along a snow-fed creek at the western entrance to Rocky Mountain National Park are Elk Creek's new camper cabins. Bring your own bedding and cooking supplies.

Wood, supplies, ice and snacks can be purchased at the camp store. On-site activities includes badminton, volleyball and horseshoes. Hike or mountain bike along the many trails leading out of the campground. During the snowy months, the trails are groomed for cross-country skiing and snowmobiling. Guest horses are permitted or rent one at nearby stables. The recreation room with a fireplace, playground and movies will keep the kids busy. And, of course, the ice cream socials will be popular too. The Grand Lake marina and boat launch are just down the road. Anglers will find the lake fishing fantastic and the stocked trout pond filled with fish just aching to be caught. Elk Creek welcomes snowmobilers in the winter and golfers who play the nearby 18-hole course in the summer. The campground features wheelchair accessible facilities.

RV and tent sites are also available. Ask about the off-season rates and winter storage.

Location: 0.25 miles north of Grand Lake on Highway 34, near milepost 16.

9 Camper Cabins
Central Campfire Area

Pay Phone(s)
All Non-Smoking in Units
Recreation Room
Elevation: 8500
Credit Cards: VM
2 people a night: $32 - $32
Open: All Year

Tom Stanley, Owner
PO Box 549
143 CR 48
Grand Lake CO 80447-0549
970/627-8502
800/ELK-CREEK (355-27335)
970/627-3076 Fax

At the resort:

At resort or within 15 minutes:

Kickapoo Lodge

Spend your vacation surrounded by trees, uniquely situated by both Shadow Mountain Lake and Grand Lake. The three to five room, well-spaced cottages are quiet, yet within walking distance of town. The cottages are completely equipped and furnished with every comfort and convenience for housekeeping, including refrigerators and cable television. Each also has central heating and cable television.

For guests who bring their boats, the lodge offers a private boat landing. Enjoy many activities in the Grand Lake area, such as fishing, swimming, golfing and square dancing. Summer brings local rodeos, yacht and boat races as well as buffalo barbecues. As the western gateway to stunning Rocky Mountain National Park, this part of Colorado features 50 peaks over 10,000' high to photograph, climb or simply admire.

The lodge requires a one-week minimum stay and recommends advance reservations.

Location: From Highway 34, near milepost 15, take the first right off Grand Ave. past the post office and school, across the Channel Bridge.

6 Cabins with Kitchens
2 Fireplaces

Lobby Phone
Elevation: 8369
No credit cards
2 people a night: $42 - $64
Open: 6/1 to 10/1

Dorothy Young, Owner
PO Box 486
1100 Jerico Rd
Grand Lake CO 80447-0486
970/627-3369

At the resort:

At resort or within 15 minutes:

Lonesome Dove Cottages

Come vacation where the stars are a little brighter, the skies a little bluer, the trees a little greener and the water a little deeper. Come to Grand Lake country and Lonesome Dove Cottages! The newly remodeled, spacious cottages have a bedroom, living room and dining room area. Set apart to insure comfortable vacation living and privacy, the modern units have television, fully equipped kitchens with cooking utensils, linens, bedding and towels.

Lonesome Dove caters to families with its children's playground, outdoor barbecue, and lawns edged with towering spruce trees. Located at the west end of Grand Lake Village, the cottages are walking distance from the main part of the town with its varied activities and shopping in quaint shops. Here you'll be a stone's throw from Grand Lake and near to Shadow Mountain Lakes as well as Granby Reservoir. Water sports abound, from boating and water skiing to fishing for rainbow, German brown and mackinaw trout and kokanee salmon. If you prefer stream fishing, there's plenty of mountain creeks in the area too. Warm weather activities include golfing, hiking, sightseeing, horseback riding and mountain biking. In the winter go snowmobiling or take a romantic sleigh ride.

Location: In downtown Grand Lake on Grand Avenue.

8 Cabins with Kitchens
1 Fireplace
4 Woodstoves

Pay Phone(s)
Elevation: 8500
Credit Cards: VMD
2 people a night: $68 - $120
Open: All Year

Susi & Dennis Everhart, Owners
PO Box 501
416 Grand Avenue
Grand Lake CO 80447-0501
970/627-8019 & Fax

At the resort:

At resort or within 15 minutes:

Mountain Lakes Lodge

Mountain Lakes Lodge is a nature enthusiast's dream where the only thing you'll overlook is the spectacular Continental Divide. Located on the waterway that joins Lake Granby with Shadow Mountain Lake and Grand Lake, the resort offers cozy housekeeping cabins with color cable television for your accommodations. Lofted ceilings and wood beams gives these cabins a true rustic flare. All have fully equipped kitchens with dishes, cookware, and microwave ovens. Larger cabins have woodstoves, french doors with decks, and cooking stoves.

The western entrance to Rocky Mountain National Park and the quaint village of Grand Lake with shopping and restaurants are only minutes away. In warm weather you can enjoy hiking, fishing in lakes or the canal, boating, horseback riding and golf. When the weather cools off the area becomes a winter wonderland with ice fishing, cross-country and downhill skiing and snowmobiling at nearby Winter Park and Silver Creek. Bring along a camera to capture the abundant small wildlife, from chipmunks and squirrels to hummingbirds.

Reservations are recommended. The Lodge welcomes various sized groups, receptions, reunions and weddings.

Location: Highway 34, near milepost 10.

10 Cabins with Kitchens
2 Vacation Homes
1 Fireplace
9 Woodstoves
Central Campfire Area

Pay Phone(s)
Elevation: 8300
Credit Cards: VM
2 people a night: $40 - $140
Open: All Year

Dave & Karen Mawhorter, Hosts
PO Box 160
10480 Hwy 34
Grand Lake CO 80447-0160
970/627-8448

At the resort:

At resort or within 15 minutes:

Nonehshe Cabins

Named after the Ute Indian word for dream, and pronounced "no-neh-she", Nonehshe Cabins offer peace, quiet and sweet nonehshe. The newly remodeled cabins are cozy and comfortable and each has one bedroom, a living room, a kitchenette, a shower bathroom, and a private picnic area with a barbecue grill. The cabins, which sleep up to four, are fully furnished with linens, dishes, cooking utensils and cable television.

Located in the quaint village of Grand Lake, Nonehshe is a short walk from many unique shops and restaurants. Summer activities in town include bingo, bowling, live theater and miniature golf. In the area, enjoy swimming, boating, golfing, hiking and mountain biking. Grand Lake, Colorado's deepest natural lake, is a one block stroll away. Winter activities include downhill skiing, cross-country skiing and snowmobiling. Relaxing is a year-round activity at Nonehshe. Fishing is great any season, from the spring run-off through glorious fall and on into snowy winter with ice fishing on the lake.

Location: 450 Broadway, 0.5 blocks south of Grand Avenue, behind Grand Co. Lumber.

4 Cabins with Kitchens
2 Woodstoves

Lobby Phone
Elevation: 8500
Credit Cards: VMD
2 people a night: $55 - $90
Open: All Year

Richard & Pat Farmer, Owners
PO Box 1696
450 Broadway
Grand Lake CO 80447-1696
970/627-8012
E-mail: nonehshe@rkymtnhi.com

At the resort:

At resort or within 15 minutes:

River Pines Cottages & RV Park

A beautiful setting with towering, lodgepole pines along the boulder-strewn, north fork of the Colorado River is yours for the taking at River Pines. Bordered by national forest with lovely Shadow Mountain Lake a short walk downsteam, the cabins sleep up to 8 people. All cabins have fireplaces and shower bathrooms, kitchens and cable television.

Hiking, biking and snowmobile trails begin at your cabin. Catch a rainbow traout in the river behind your cabin or take a soothing soak in the hot tub. Near the river bank are picnic tables and barbecue grills for your convenience. A volleyball net and horseshoes are provided in the large play area. Let your hosts arrange horseback rides, hayrides, snowmobile rentals or ice fishing for you. Just to the north of River Pines is Rocky Mountain National Park where scheduled programs include nature hikes, lectures and tours conducted by the Park Service Rangers. Sight-seeing boat cruises on the two lakes are available as are charter boats for the serious anglers.

RV sites are also available. A reservation deposit of 50% is required. A two night minimum stay is required; three night minimum on holidays.

Location: On Highway 34 at milepost 12.

12 Cabins with Kitchens
12 Fireplaces

Pay Phone(s)
Elevation: 8350
Credit Cards: VM
2 people a night: $39 - $96
Open: All Year

Mark Johnson, Owner
12082 US Hwy 34
Grand Lake CO 80447
970/627-3632 & Fax
800/793-0835

At the resort:

At resort or within 15 minutes:

Rocky Mountain Cabins

Ideally situated between the north fork of the Colorado River and the western entrance to Rocky Mountain National Park, this new resort features luxury cabins with porches. The cabins come with every amenity, including rock fireplaces, washer/dryer, cable television, full kitchens and baths and much more. You'll find plenty of privacy and quiet on these six acres enveloped by stunning mountain scenery. Imagine fishing right off your porch into the river and then dining on your catch while watching a colorful sunset.

From Rocky Mountain Cabins, you can cross-country ski or snowmobile on 130 miles of groomed trails as well as across Shadow Mountain Lake. Great downhill skiing is 15 to 45 minutes away at Winter Park and Silver Creek. Take a romantic sleigh ride over crisp, pure white snow. Summer activities abound here, from mountain biking, horseback riding and hiking to golfing and wildlife watching. Boat and fish on the lake or cast into any number of crystal mountain streams. The small town of Grand Lake offers gourmet dining, melodrama, bingo and shopping.

Reservations are required and there is a two night stay minimum. Cabins sleep 2 to 8 people and no pets are allowed.

Location: Just north of River Pines on east side of Highway 34.

3 Cabins with Kitchens

Lobby Phone
Elevation: 8500
No credit cards
2 people a night: Call for Rates
Open: All Year

Chris & Kathy Lorens, Owners
PO Box 835
12206 Hwy 34
Grand Lake CO 80447
970/627-3061

At the resort:

At resort or within 15 minutes:

Shadow Mountain Guest Ranch

The best of the mountain area's ambiance will be right at your doorstep at Shadow Mountain Guest Ranch. Among aspen and pine trees, all of the private cabins have queen beds and the big cabin has a fireplace. Each cabin has kitchenettes for preparing your favorite family meals. Gather around in the comfortable kitchen where folks sip coffee and discuss local hot spots after breakfast.

The central, historic, log lodge has two large, stone fireplaces and a comfortable seating area for conversation, satellite television, card games and socializing with other guests. Enjoy their brand new hot tub for the ultimate in relaxation. Anglers will like casting for trout in Willow Creek which runs through the property. Located near Rocky Mountain National Park and Lake Granby, you can hunt, fish, boat and hike to your heart's content. Summer trail rides are a great way to explore the picturesque area. Winter snow makes an ideal playground for skiers and snowmobilers.

Dogs under 20 pounds are allowed for a small fee. The lodge is a good place for groups, workshops, entertainment or just plain chat in a homey atmosphere. Take advantage of the licensed massage therapist on-call to ease your aches and pains.

Location: 5.5 miles north of Highway 40 on Highway 125, near milepost 5.

6 Cabins with Kitchens
1 Fireplace
Central Fireplace
Central Campfire Area

Lobby Phone
Bed & Breakfast Available
Recreation Room
Elevation: 8600
Credit Cards: VMD
2 people a night: $95 - $145
Open: All Year

Jim & Dale White, Owners
PO Box 963
5043 Hwy 125
Granby CO 80446-0963
970/887-9524
800/64-Shadow (647-4236)
970/887-3059 Fax

At the resort:

At resort or within 15 minutes:

Western Riviera Cabins & Motel

Located right in the quaint village of Grand Lake, Western Riviera offers a varied choice of accommodations. Relax in the comfort of one of the motel's units featuring one or two double beds or one king bed. Each has a full bathroom and telephone. The suites sleep up to 6 with two queen beds, a queen sofa bed, televisions and telephones in each room, a refrigerator and private bath. The cabins accommodate five people and have new kitchenettes with microwave ovens, televisions in each room and a full bath. There are no telephones in the cabins. Enjoy wonderful views of the lake and beach front park from the wooden decks, picnic tables and grills.

Grand Lake, the oldest tourist town in Colorado, had maintained the image of the "Old West". Wooden boardwalks, 4th of July celebration with fireworks, Western Weekend with gun fights and buffalo barbecues — it's all found in Grand Lake. Nearby are over 100s of miles of groomed snowmobile trails, huge mountain snow bowls and meadows. In the summer, these same trails can be explored on foot or by mountain bike. Gather the family for a picnic on the beach area and uses the gas grills available. Soak away your worries in the outdoor spa with a magnificent view of the lake and snow-capped mountains.

Location: On Highway 34 at milepost 15.

6 Cabins with Kitchens
19 Motel Rooms

Room Phones
Non-Smoking Units Available
Elevation: 8400
Credit Cards: VM
2 people a night: $50 - $90
Open: 5/15 to 10/16

Kathie & Tony Loeser, Owners
PO Box 1286
419 Garfield Ave
Grand Lake CO 80447-1286
970/627-3580
970/627-3320 Fax

At the resort:

At resort or within 15 minutes:

Grand Mesa Area

Including Cedaredge, Collbran, Mesa, Paonia & Somerset — Map: I-5, H-5, H-4, I-6 & I-7

At 10,000', **Grand Mesa**, the largest flat-top mountain in the world, rises more than a mile above the valley floor. Almost the entire Grand Mesa is within the Grand Mesa National Forest. Discover aspen and spruce groves, flowered meadows and over 200 cool clear lakes offering fantastic fishing for rainbow, brook and brown trout. Some lakes have boat launches and you can reach many of them from the highway. For the more adventurous, visit the lakes only accessible by four-wheel drive, foot or horseback. Utes called this the "Home of the Departed Spirits" and they brought hostages here after the 1879 Meeker Massacre. Almost entirely within the Grand Mesa National Forest, Grand Mesa has abundant wildlife, making this a popular area for fall hunting. Elk, deer and many smaller mammals roam the alpine forest. Drive the Grand Mesa Scenic and Historic Byway and tour the changing aspen in the fall. Visit Surface Creek Valley Historical Society's Pioneer Town in **Cedaredge** where you can experience the American West at the turn of the century. Hikers will want to trek along the Crag Crest National Recreation Trail, a 10-mile circular trail rising from east and west trailheads. The 6.5 mile long path stretching across the top of Crag Crest is open to foot traffic only. Escape the summer heat and relax in Grand Mesa's cool mountain air. Few places offer such a delightful combination of climate, scenery and recreation as the **Somerset** area. The natural beauty of the countryside, the clean air and the surrounding majestic mountains are the ideal vacation ingredients. The close by West Elk Wilderness is a magnificent place for hiking and hunting. The entire area is a focal point of backroads and trails leading into the wilderness. Take a drive along the West Elk Scenic By-Way and record some of this area's uniqueness with your camera. Nearby, in **Paonia**, you'll find abundant orchards filled with sweet and sour cherries, apricots, peaches, plums, pears, nectarines and a large variety of apples. The town of Paonia was founded by Samuel Wade in 1882 when he brought the first fruit trees into the valley. In addition to Paonia's farmers, the area's economy is based on coal mines and ranching.

Fun Things to Do

- Colorado Guest Ranch Horse Rides (800)521-4055, (970) 929-6260
- Deercreek Village Golf Course, Cedaredge (970) 856-7781
- Electric Mountain Lodge Horse Rides & Snowmobiling (970) 929-5522
- Grand Mesa Lodge Store & Gift Shop (800) 551-MESA
- Meander Tours (970) 487-3402
- Pomotawh Naantam Ranch Horseback Rides (970) 929-6575
- Surface Creek Historic & Pioneer Town, Cedaredge (970) 856-7554

Buzzard Creek Ranch, Cabins & Meander Tours

Stay at a private ranch in Plateau Valley at the edge of the Grand Mesa National Forest where the air is clear and the wildlife abundant. Buzzard Creek offers one housekeeping cabin and two non-housekeeping cabins. One unit has a woodstove. Join in the campfire breakfasts every morning before you start your day.

Buzzard Creek hosts cowboy dinners and evening entertainment as well as wagon and sleigh rides for the whole family to enjoy. Other activities include horseback riding, hiking nature trails, fishing on the property or many of the nearby lakes, and hunting in season. Mountain bike trails begin near your front door. In the winter, you can snowmobile, snowshoe, cross-country ski, and take a sleigh ride all right at Buzzard Creek. Nearby you can downhill ski and ice fish. Meander Tours, located on-site, offers a variety of scenic tours of this part of Colorado. Plateau Valley is situated between Battlement Mesa and Grand Mesa. The valley is prized for its beauty, serenity, and unsurpassed hunting, fishing and recreation. Working cattle ranches dot the valley floor, giving you a taste of the true West.

Tent sites are also available. Pets and horses are welcomed to accompany you to Buzzard Creek.

Location: East on Highway 30.

MEANDER TOURS
SCENIC TOURS OF WESTERN COLORADO

1 Cabin with Kitchen
2 cabins without Kitchens
1 Woodstove
Central Campfire Area

Lobby Phone
Bed & Breakfast Available
Recreation Room
Elevation: 6000
Credit Cards: VM
2 people a night: $45 - $85
Open: All Year

Sylvia Spangler, Owner
Rt 1 Box 354
5896 Hwy 330 E
Collbran CO 81624
970/487-3402
970/487-3801 Fax

At the resort:

At resort or within 15 minutes:

Colorado Guest Ranch & Chipeta Ranch

So, you wanna be a cowboy? Colorado Guest Ranch is the place to be one! Accommodations are in a restored 1902 Victorian home, a solar lodge at 8,000' and a new lodge on the mountain with the atmosphere of western casual ranch living. Thirty-two miles of trails for all kinds of adventures are within the ranch and nearby Grand Mesa offers another 200 more miles of trails.

Explore the 4,000 acres of river bottoms up to the 9,000 foot splendor of mountains on the 16,000 acres of BLM land to which the ranch has a permit. Wildlife abounds here, like elk, mule deer, mountain lion, bear, song birds and birds of prey. Family activities include daily and weekly pack trips, instruction, hiking, fishing, horseback riding, hunting, cookouts, photo safaris, arena events, and cattle work. Saddle up and ride to the mountains or four-wheel drive to spectacular views. Fish miles of a private stream on the ranch or cast into the North Fork of the Gunnison River. In season, hunt elk, track mountain lion and black bear.

Location: East of Paonia on Highway 133, between milepost 14-15.

2 Cabins with Kitchens
8 Lodging Rooms
1 Woodstove
Central Campfire Area

Lobby Phone
All Non-Smoking in Units
Elevation: 9000
Credit Cards: AD
2 people a night: $43 - $60
Open: All Year

Larry & Elaine Mautz, Owners
1938 Hwy 133
Paonia CO 81428
970/929-6260
800/521-4055

At the resort:

At resort or within 15 minutes:

Crystal Meadows Ranch, Cabins & Campground

Tucked between two mountain ranges, in a scenic river valley, Crystal Meadows has accommodations varying from a two-bedroom log house with a full kitchen and a small bath, to a one-room log cabin with three beds and a shared bathroom. The ranch is nestled serenely in the mountains where Anthracite, Coal and Muddy creeks join to form the North Fork of the Gunnison River. At Crystal Meadows, you're surrounded by the sound of cool rushing alpine-fed water and vistas of pine covered peaks.

For your convenience, there is an on-site grocery store with RV supplies, ice, limited groceries and firewood. The outdoor pavilion and indoor meeting room will be great for your conference or family reunion. The restaurant serves tasty breakfasts on weekends, hearty lunches and delectable dinners. Fish in the privately stocked lake, or in the snow-fed Anthracite Creek. Rent horses nearby, or bring your own, to ride. Horseback ride, mountain bike, or hike in the nearby West Elk Mountains and the Raggeds, two vast and scenic wilderness areas. Hunters will find abundant deer and elk here in season. Enjoy West Elk Scenic Byway as you drive over the picturesque Kebler Pass Road to Crested Butte.

Full hookup RV sites are also available.

Location: Paonia, go 16 miles northeast on Highway 133. Carbondale go southwest 47 miles. Near milepost 24, on County Road 12 (Crested Butte-Kebler Pass Road).

3 Cabins with Kitchens
3 cabins without Kitchens
1 Vacation Home
1 Camper Cabin
2 Woodstoves

Pay Phone(s)
Bed & Breakfast Available
Recreation Room
Elevation: 6200
Credit Cards: VMD
2 people a night: $40 - $135
Open: All Year

Bill & Kay Tennison, Owners
30682 CR 12
Somerset CO 81434-9625
970/929-5656
970/929-5657 Fax

At the resort:

At resort or within 15 minutes:

Electric Mountain Lodge

In the heart of the Gunnison National Forest, the historic Electric Mountain Lodge has comfortable lodge and dormitory rooms. The lodge is at the edge of Hubbard Park at the foot of Electric Mountain.

After a day exploring the forest and meadows carpeted in wildflowers, unwind in the spacious hot tub and soothing sauna. Take in the beautiful views from the restaurant and then relax by the fireplace in the large lounge while watching satellite television. The large, completely redecorated, full service restaurant also has a well-stocked bar. Rent your choice of transportation to ride the Sunlight to Powderhorn Trail: horseback, mountain bike or snowmobile. The lodge also offers snow-cat tours. You'll enjoy the excellent fishing, hunting and hiking in this area. Another popular summertime activity from Electric Mountain Lodge is A.T.V. riding the backcountry. Whether you play volleyball and horseshoes at the property, or go exploring, you'll have a great vacation here.

Location: From Highway 133, near milepost 36, go north 18.5 miles on Stephens Gulch Road.

12 Lodging Rooms
8 Beds in Bunk House or Dorm
Central Fireplace

Pay Phone(s)
Bed & Breakfast Available
All Non-Smoking in Units
Recreation Room
Elevation: 9200
Credit Cards: VMA
2 people a night: $60 - $60
Open: 6/1 to 3/31

Brenda & Lance Meagher, Owners
PO Box 370
2880 4010 Drive
Paonia CO 81428-0370
970/929-5522
970/929-5533 Fax

At the resort:

At resort or within 15 minutes:

G R Bar Ranch Cabins

If you've dreamed about an exciting vacation, high in the picturesque Rocky Mountains, this is it! The secluded, G R Bar Ranch Cabins are at 9,300' in elevation and higher, adjoining both the Gunnison and Grand Mesa National Forests. These completely furnished ranch houses rent by the week, so you can really settle into a vacation away from it all. Arrowhead Cabin, at 9,300', sleeps five and is completely modern. Red Springs Cabin, a half mile from the national forest at 9,600', sleeps eight and features a fireplace, wood-burning cook stove as well as a gas range. Newly constructed Many Penny Cabin, at 9,500', will accommodate eight and has a spectacular view of lakes and mountains. All cabins have complete kitchens, hot and cold running water, propane barbecues, and all linens. To insure privacy, the closest building, the ranch house, is at least a quarter of a mile away.

If you really want to get away from it all, spend time in an incredible setting, love nature, peace and quiet and crave a different experience from traditional cabin resorts and dude ranches, G R Bar Ranch is what you've been looking for! Take advantage of unlimited fishing in eight private lakes — no license required. Explore thousands of nearby acres by horseback, jeep or on hiking trails viewing the local wildlife. Each cabin has its own corral and tack room to keep your horse or the ranch horses happy. Swimming, golfing, and rafting activities are a mere 30 minute drive. You're in the center of nature's wonderland, with scenic views, myriad's of wildflowers and wildlife — a photographer's delight.

Cabins are rented on a weekly basis and reservations are necessary.

Location: 12 miles north of Paonia. Call ahead and your hosts will meet you and take you to the ranch.

3 Cabins with Kitchens
1 Vacation Home
3 Woodstoves

No Phones Available
Elevation: 9400
No credit cards
2 people a night: $157 - $186
Open: 5/15 to 11/15

N.W. & Barbara Grosse-Rhode, Owners
4149 N 80 Lane
Paonia CO 81428-9639
970/527-6434

At the resort:

At resort or within 15 minutes:

Grand Mesa Lodge

In the Grand Mesa National Forest, 55 miles from Grand Junction, this resort features cozy housekeeping cabins and a motel above beautiful Island Lake. These attractively furnished log cabins have fully equipped kitchens, gas heat and bathrooms with showers. One cabin features a fireplace, sauna, and lake view. All cabins are furnished with bedding, towels and barbecue. The motel units, which are non-smoking, are available for those not requiring kitchen facilities. The comfortable lodge lobby has a scenic view for relaxation, conversation and coffee.

Shop in the on-site store for groceries, gifts, antiques, authentic Indian jewelry, fishing and hunting supplies, including licenses. Island Lake, the largest lake on Grand Mesa, is an outstanding mile long and surrounded by evergreens and aspen trees. Rent boats at the lodge for memorable fishing. Deer and elk abound for hunting in season or simply viewing. Nearby are horseback riding and golfing opportunities, as well as excellent restaurants to try. The national Craig Crest Trail, a 10-mile loop, is just 0.25 miles from the lodge. Mountain bike trails abound here.

A deposit equal to 50% of the total is due within 10 days of booking. Balance is due 21 days prior to arrival. Ask about the cancellation policy. Well mannered pets are permitted in the cabins, but must be on a leash at all times.

Location: Highway 65, near milepost 28.

14 Cabins with Kitchens
3 Motel Rooms
1 Fireplace
1 Woodstove
Central Woodstove
Central Campfire Area

Pay Phone(s)
Non-Smoking Units Available
Elevation: 10500
Credit Cards: VM
2 people a night: $35 - $80
Open: 5/15 to 10/31

Chuck & Jan Harrington, Owners
PO Box 49
Cedaredge CO 81413-0049
970/856-3250
800/551-MESA (6372)

At the resort:

At resort or within 15 minutes:

Pitkin Mesa Bed & Breakfast

Near the fruit-growing town of Paonia, you'll find Pitkin Mesa Bed & Breakfast. This modern home is in a peaceful, semi-rural neighborhood one mile from downtown. Choose from three rooms; one of which has a private bath while the other two rooms share a full bath. Home-style breakfasts are served every morning at 8 a.m.

Pitkin Mesa has an indoor swimming pool and hot tub for guests to enjoy. Outdoor courts are set up for both croquet and badminton. The views from here include the North Fork Valley and surrounding mountains such as Lamborn Mountain. The townsfolk are friendly and Paonia has restaurants and shops to enjoy. From the B & B, go for a short hike, take a bike ride or simply sit on the covered porch and take in the views. If it's chilly out, you can enjoy the views from the peaceful sunroom. Area attractions include the North Rim of the Black Canyon of the Gunnison, Grand Mesa Scenic Byway with 300 lakes for fishing and recreation, a new 18-hole golf course in Cedaredge, Crawford and Paonia reservoirs, Gunnison River Pleasure Park, and the world famous quarry in stunning Marble just a short mountain pass away. Paonia is known for its fruit orchards which bloom in the spring and offer a variety of fruit throughout the summer and fall.

No pets, tobacco or alcohol are allowed. Children under 14 by special arrangement only.

Location: Near Paonia on "P" Road.

3 Lodging Rooms
Central Woodstove

Lobby Phone
Bed & Breakfast Available
All Non-Smoking in Units
Recreation Room
Elevation: 5600
Credit Cards: VM
2 people a night: $55 - $65
Open: 6/1 to 10/31

Dale & Barbara Soucek, Owners
3954 P Rd
Paonia CO 81428
970/527-7576

At the resort:

At resort or within 15 minutes:

Pomotawh Naantam Ranch

Both a fully functioning cattle ranch and a recreational ranch all in one, Pomotawh Naantam Ranch is on 3,500 acres adjacent to BLM and national forest near Somerset. The ranch's name originates from the Indian words for mountain (pomotawh) and wolf (naantam). The Basic Cabin has a double and two twin beds and can sleep up to 6 comfortably. The Anthracite Cabin is next to a creek of the same name and has double, twin and sofa sleeper beds with a kitchenette and full bathroom. The Layton Cabin is tucked away behind a cedar fence and walk way for extra privacy. Inside are a rustic, queen-size log bed, queen sofa bed, a kitchenette and full bathroom. All three log cabins are fully furnished with rustic, homemade log beds, country comforters and fresh ground coffee. Sit on your front porch and enjoy the view of Muncy Basin and the entrance to the Dark Canyon.

The ranch offers guided and unguided creek and lake fishing, hiking in summer and fall, snowmobiling and cross-country skiing in winter and spring. Take one of the ranch's experienced, well-mannered horses over spectacular mountain trails on rides that range from one hour to pack trips of several days. Bring along a camera to capture bull elk bugling in the fall and newly born calf elk and fawn deer in the spring. Keep a look out for the occasional bear and mountain goat amid fields of wildflowers as well. Only a half mile from the Raggeds Wilderness in Gunnison National Forest and 9 miles from West Elk Wilderness, you'll have plenty of the great outdoors to explore.

Location: On County Road 12, near milepost 27, to Kebler Pass.

3 Cabins with Kitchens
1 Vacation Home
1 Woodstove

Pay Phone(s)
All Non-Smoking in Units
Elevation: 6700
Credit Cards: VM
2 people a night: $70 - $150
Open: All Year

Jon & Dori Lee, Owners
26767 CR 12
Somerset CO 81434
970/929-6571 hp
970/929-6575 ranch
970/929-6585 Fax

At the resort:

At resort or within 15 minutes:

Gunnison Area

Including Almont, Crested Butte, Ohio City, Parlin, Sapinero & Sargents — Map: K-9, J-9, I-9, J-10, K-10, K-7 & K-11

Named for a topographer who was mapping a railroad route to the Pacific in 1853, **Gunnison** is surrounded by over 1.7 million acres of public land. The Gunnison River Territory stretches from one spectacular naturescape to another with plunging canyon walls, emerald lakes, imposing peaks and wildflower meadows. Ute Indians, miners, ranchers and the railroads all contributed to the western character of this area. Today, Gunnison prides itself on having some of the best outdoor recreation in the state. Blue Mesa Reservoir in the Curecanti National Recreation Area, 9 miles west, is the largest man-made lake in Colorado with 96 miles of shoreline — an angler's paradise. Gunnison National Forest has more than 750 miles of teeming trout streams and reservoirs. Nearby, the Aberdeen Quarry was in operation from 1889 to 1892 and supplied the stone for Denver's capitol. The Alpine Tunnel, 30 miles east, now abandoned, bore through the Continental Divide at 11,523', making it the highest railroad station in the country. Drive along a scenic byway through **Almont**, 30 miles north to **Crested Butte**. Surrounded by sheer beauty, Crested Butte is the place to white water raft and enjoy nature's splendor. Home of the Fat Tire Bike Week, the oldest bike festival in the world, the town is near mountain bike trails over scenic passes and four wheel drive roads to old ghost towns. Try fly-fishing in nearby streams or golfing a championship course. Savor campfire cuisine or gourmet restaurants after catching a play or climbing a peak. As the wildflower capital of Colorado, Crested Butte basks in gentle mountain warmth, an inspiration for recreationists and nature lovers. During the winter, Crested Butte, Mt. Crested Butte and Crested Butte Ski Area are connected by a free shuttle. With an average of 229 inches of snow each year, this is a great place for winter sports, including snowmobiling, downhill and cross-country skiing.

Fun Things to Do

- 7-11 Ranch (970)641-0666
- Country Club & Golf Course, Crested Butte (970) 349-6129
- Curecanti National Recreational Area (970) 641-2337
- Dos Rios Golf Course, Gunnison (970) 641-1482
- Gunnison National Forest (970) 641-0471
- Morrow Point Boat Tour, Gunnison, Summer (970) 641-0402
- Mountain Bike Hall of Fame Museum, Crested Butte (970) 349-7382
- Taylor Reservoir (970) 641-0471
- Three Rivers Rafting & Fly Fishing Shop, Almont (970) 641-1303

7-11 Ranch

The Rudibaugh family has hosted outdoor adventures at their ranch, situated on Quartz Creek and surrounded by majestic mountains, since 1958. The semi-rustic cabins have fully equipped kitchenettes with a stove and a central bathhouse.

Fish for dinner in one of the many native trout streams right outside your cabin door or in the ranch's stocked private lake. Home-cooked, ranch-style, meals are available with advanced notice, remember this is a working ranch. Join in their cattle drive, where you can be a cowhand, guiding 800 head of cattle over a 12,000-foot pass to their summer pasture. Camp under the stars and eat meals served by the camp cook with the other cowhands. Back at the ranch, choose from a myriad of horseback trips, such as day-long outings or five- to seven-day pack trips in some of the most beautiful scenery in Colorado. Your hosts also can help outfit your hunting trip for big horn sheep, elk and mule deer in season.

For weddings, ask about the carriage with the fringe on top for a memorable addition to your special day.

Location: Take Highway 50 to Parlin, then 5 miles north on County Road 76.

5 Cabins with Kitchens
1 cabins without Kitchens
6 Beds in Bunk House or Dorm
4 Woodstoves
Central Campfire Area

Lobby Phone
Recreation Room
Elevation: 8500
No credit cards
2 people a night: $25
Open: 5/1 to 11/30

Rudy & Deborah Rudibaugh, Owners
5291 CR 76
Parlin CO 81239
970/641-0666

At the resort:

At resort or within 15 minutes:

Almont Resort

The Taylor and East Rivers meet at Almont Resort to form the champion of trout rivers, the Gunnison. The resort features a newly remodeled "Riverhouse" vacation home directly on the river with a private hot tub. The vacation home has seven bedrooms, three and a half baths, and two kitchens, perfect for a small family reunion. The resort also has 16 rustic cabins, some of which are on the river. All the cabins have bathrooms and many have kitchenettes or full kitchens. Most of the smaller cabins have coffee makers and refrigerators. The largest cabin, with six double beds, one single and a hide-a-way, features two bedrooms, a loft, a full bathroom and kitchen and a wood burning stove.

A restaurant, open for breakfast, lunch and dinner, and lounge reside on Almont's 100 acres. Once an important stop on the railroad and a famous summer resort since the turn of the century, the resort established in 1893 has historical significance. Horseback ride right from the resort's stables. Take the family on a whitewater raft or float trip. Many old ghost towns await your four-wheel drive vehicle. Excellent hunting and fishing are what have brought people to this resort for nearly 100 years. In the winter, ski at Crested Butte and Monarch, take a guided snowmobile tour and explore the endless trails nearby on your cross-country skis.

Almont specializes in family and business gatherings, from outside barbecues to gourmet, sit-down dinners.

Location: Near Gunnison & Crested Butte on Highway 135, near milepost 10.

6 Cabins with Kitchens
9 cabins without Kitchens
1 Vacation Home
Central Campfire Area

Pay Phone(s)
Recreation Room
Elevation: 8026
Credit Cards: VM
2 people a night: $50 - $75
Open: All Year

Harold & Susan Seiff, Owners
PO Box 306
10209 Hwy 135
Almont CO 81210-0306
970/641-4009 Fax call 1st

At the resort:

At resort or within 15 minutes:

Big Horn Guest Ranch

Tucked away in a historic mining valley on Quartz Creek, Big Horn Guest Ranch, family owned and operated since 1971, offers 12 log housekeeping cabins — eight are adjoining. All but one of the cabins sleep five or more. One has a fireplace and non-smoking units are available. The ranch is near Ohio City and the Pitkin & Alpine Railroad Tunnel.

The Ranch has a large grassy area, partially shaded by towering trees, with a volleyball, basketball and badminton court in addition to a horseshoe pit. A serene lake, a picnic area and playground are on the ranch grounds and will add to your vacation enjoyment. Fish, hunt, hike, mountain bike, snowmobile and golf nearby. In area: swim, raft, horseback ride and go four-wheel driving.

Big Horn Guest Ranch is great for family reunions, honeymoons and inexpensive vacations.

Location: On County Road 76, 9 miles north of Parlin at milepost 9.

11 Cabins with Kitchens
1 Vacation Home
1 Fireplace
Central Campfire Area

Lobby Phone
Non-Smoking Units Available
Elevation: 8600
No credit cards
2 people a night: $29 - $46
Open: All Year

Dave & Dee Nicholl, Owners
9102 CR 76
Ohio City CO 81237
970/641-1800
E-mail: poorfarm@rmi.net

At the resort:

At resort or within 15 minutes:

Char-B Resort

Located in the beautiful secluded Spring Creek Canyon, Char-B Resort is near the tiny town of Almont. The spacious one to five bedroom housekeeping cabins come with and without wood burning stoves. All cabins are fully modern and gas heated with well equipped kitchens and a natural knotty pine interior. Bedding, bed linen, cooking and eating utensils, bath and kitchen towels, and wood for the fireplaces are furnished. Bring only your food and personal items for a worry-free vacation.

Char-B Resort is spaciously laid out among aspen and pine trees, high in the land of deer and elk. Visit the country store on-site, stocked with novelty items, groceries, hunting and fishing licenses and fishing tackle. A coin laundry is also here for your convenience. While you prepare a barbecue cooked dinner in the large cook-out shed, send the kids off to the playground which features swings, slides, badminton, volleyball, horseshoes and stilt walking for children of all ages. Fish for trout along the banks of the resort's creek. Adjoining government property, Char-B is right next to many outdoor recreation possibilities. Be sure to bring your swim suit along so you can enjoy the hot tub and sun deck. Winter offers snowmobiling, snowshoeing, and cross country and down hill skiing. Mt. Crested Butte is an easy 30 minute drive. Cross country skis and snowmobile rentals can be arranged and delivered to you at the resort.

Ask about the large recreation hall with a fireplace for your group gathering. Pets are allowed.

Location: On County Road 744, nine miles northeast of Almont off of Highway 135, near milepost 10.

18 Cabins with Kitchens
3 Woodstoves
Central Fireplace
Central Campfire Area

Pay Phone(s)
Recreation Room
Elevation: 8600
Credit Cards: VM
2 people a night: $60 - $93
Open: All Year

Tim & Shannon Wiginton, Owners
PO Box 279
1730 County RD 744
Almont CO 81210-0279
970/641-0751

At the resort:

At resort or within 15 minutes:

Island Acres Motel & Log Lodges

Make Island Acres Motel and Log Lodges your base for exploring beautiful Gunnison County. Stay in one of the 20 motel rooms or pick one of the two log lodges for your vacation. Most units are equipped with kitchenettes and all have dial-out phones, HBO and cable television. One- and two-bedroom units are available with double or queen beds. The motel and lodges are located between two bridges on an island formed by the Gunnison River. The four acres of grounds provide ample room for children to play safely on the beautiful tree lined lawn.

Step right outside your door to fish on the Gunnison River. Blue Mesa Reservoir, a short drive away, is another popular fishing hole for anglers of all ages. This area has become a mecca for mountain bikers and with good reason as there are many spectacular trails to explore. Other activities include golfing, four-wheel driving, river rafting, and horseback riding. If vacationing during the winter, ask about the ski packages and Crested Butte Mountain Resort which is only 40 minutes away. Come back after your day of fun for a pleasant walk along shaded country roads that begin at the motel. Or barbecue your day's catch under the shade of mature cottonwood and pine trees.

Small pets are welcomed to accompany you if arrangements are made in advance. Some non-smoking units are available.

Location: West of Gunnison on Highway 50.

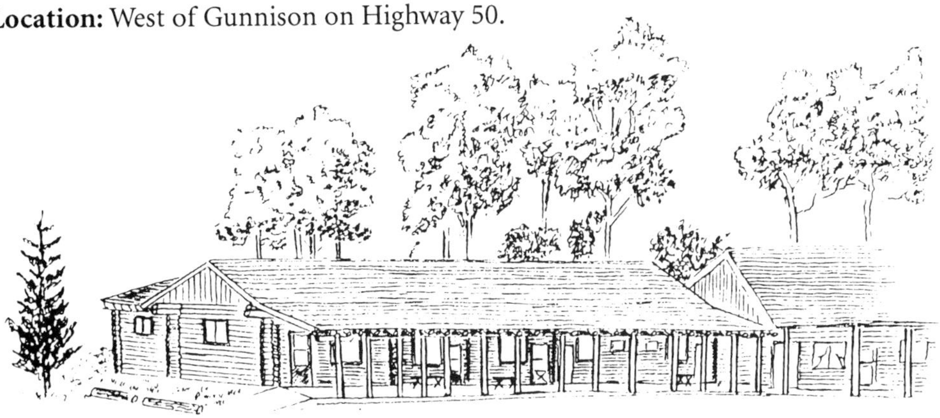

2 Cabins with Kitchens

Room Phones
Non-Smoking Units Available
Elevation: 7800
Credit Cards: VMD
2 people a night: $33 - $49
Open: All Year

Gwyn & Jaena Howells, Owner
38339 W Hwy 50
Gunnison CO 81230
970/641-1442

At the resort:

At resort or within 15 minutes:

Lake Fork Resort

Lake Fork Resort is brand new and on the Blue Mesa Reservoir between Gunnison and Montrose. The six housekeeping cabins are on 53 acres overlooking the impressive lake. The beautiful, one bedroom cabins have queen log beds, equipped kitchens with utensils and appliances, living areas and private bathrooms. Children or additional guests will be comfortable on the queen pull-down bed in the main living area. Relax on your front porch and enjoy the views of Blue Mesa Lake and Black Mesa.

A convenience store, volleyball court and a childrens playground are located on site for your enjoyment. In the summer of 1997, a full service restaurant is scheduled to open. The resort is surrounded by Gunnison National Forest and Curecanti National Recreation Center. With so much open space to enjoy, the activities are boundless — from hiking, mountain biking and fishing to water skiing, sailing, river rafting and horseback riding. Come in the fall to hunt or the winter to downhill and cross-country ski, ice fish and snowmobile.

Vacation packages are available for all seasons. Ask about the group discounts. Choose between basic cabin rentals or the American plan with all meals served in your cabin (until the opening of the restaurant).

Location: West of Gunnison on Highway 50 about 22 miles, turn left after Lake Fork bridge onto Cove Road, take first right.

6 Cabins with Kitchens
Central Fireplace
Central Campfire Area

Room Phones
Bed & Breakfast Available
All Non-Smoking in Units
Recreation Room
Elevation: 7800
Credit Cards: VMAD
2 people a night: $40 - $70
Open: All Year

Carla & David Alley, Owners
PO Box 1807
0940 Cove Rd
Gunnison CO 81230
970/641-3564
800/368-9421

At the resort:

At resort or within 15 minutes:

Ley-Z-B at Sapinero

Located 25 miles off the highway west of Gunnison, Ley-Z-B is on the Blue Mesa Reservoir. The six rental cabins offer rustic charm. A shower house is available. Linens are not supplied unless requested so bring your pillows, towels and sleeping bags for those cold nights. The cabins are heated. The two-bedroom cabin has a kitchen and sleeps up to six.

Ley-Z-B has a cafe serving all meals, bar and gas station with groceries, fishing tackle, and licenses for sale. They're famous for their "All You Can Eat" western barbecues on Saturday nights from Memorial Day to Labor Day. The Blue Mesa Reservoir has over 70 miles of shoreline, more than 30 streams, and is one of Colorado's largest lakes. Stocked with hundreds of thousands of trout and salmon, Blue Mesa is a favorite fishing hole from both bank and boat. Fish for kokanee, brook, lake, rainbow, cutthroat and brown trout. Many come to the reservoir to windsurf, water-ski and ice fish as well. Minutes away from Ley-Z-B are boat and jetski rentals, horseback riding stables, boat tours of the stunning Black Canyon and many breath-taking sights. Hunters also favor this area because nearby West Elk Wilderness, Gunnison National Forest and the Uncompahgre forest offer abundant trophy elk and deer. The same barbecue special is offered during the rifle season.

RV sites are also available. Pets are allowed. Formerly known as Sapinero Trading Post.

Location: East of the junction of Highway 92 and Highway 50. On Highway 50 near milepost 133.

5 cabins without Kitchens
1 Woodstove
Central Woodstove
Central Campfire Area

Pay Phone(s)
Elevation: 7300
Credit Cards: VM
2 people a night: $25
Open: All to Year

Leysa, Alan Brown & Natalie, Ken Zaelit
PO Box 47
16020 Hwy 50 West
Sapinero CO 81247-0047
970/641-2340

At the resort:

At resort or within 15 minutes:

Lost Canyon Resort

Lost Canyon Resort is in a peaceful and grassy setting on a beautiful 10 acres overlooking the Gunnison River. The log cabins are modern and fully equipped with private bathrooms and kitchens with ranges, refrigerators, dishes and cookware. The accommodations can sleep up to eight people. All bed linens, blankets, soap and towels are supplied. Many cabins feature fireplaces or wood stoves. Come here to really get away from the hustle and bustle of the city; the old style resort's cabins have no televisions or telephones!

Central Gunnison country is ideal for hunting, skiing and fishing. Lost Canyon Resort is on the Gunnison River and is close to three reservoirs, as well as many other smaller rivers and streams. Downhill or cross-country ski at Crested Butte ski area, only 20 miles away.

Lost Canyon Resort really lets you get away from it all. There is no RV parking or store to disturb the quiet. Pets are allowed here.

Location: 8 miles north of Gunnison, just east of Highway 135, near milepost 8.

17 Cabins with Kitchens
5 Fireplaces
4 Woodstoves
Central Campfire Area

Lobby Phone
Elevation: 8000
Credit Cards: VM
2 people a night: $55 - $64
Open: All Year

Max, Bob & Catherine Reinhardt, Owners
8264 Hwy 135
Gunnison CO 81230-9620
970/641-0181

At the resort:

At resort or within 15 minutes:

Rockey River Resort

Homesteaded in 1892, Rockey River Resort features old and new log cabins among cottonwood trees along the steady flow of the Gunnison River. The cabins have fully equipped kitchens and bathrooms. All blankets, bed linens, towels, cooking utensils, dishes and flatware are provided. You'll find modern comfort in a rustic atmosphere here.

The abundant beauty of this country is unmatched. All of nature's colors in rocks and mountain flowers are displayed throughout the many scenic circle trips designed for your enjoyment. Check out a bit of history in the numerous ghost towns, old mines and relics of a by-gone era. If you're more interested in sports, the resort is within easy access to hunting, lake fishing, skiing, whitewater rafting and horseback riding. Fish along almost a half-mile of privately owned river frontage of the churning Gunnison or try lake fishing at nearby Taylor, Spring Creek and Blue Mesa Reservoirs. The playground, with volleyball, basketball, horseshoes, and badminton will keep the children entertained while you prepare a meal of freshly caught trout. The library has books for all ages.

RV sites near the Gunnison River are also available.

Location: 6 miles north of town, 0.5 miles east of Highway 135, near milepost 6.

14 Cabins with Kitchens
5 Fireplaces
3 Woodstoves
Central Woodstove

Pay Phone(s)
Elevation: 7860
Credit Cards: VMA
2 people a night: $34 - $72
Open: All Year

Rob & Dani Wattles, Owners
4359 CR 10
Gunnison CO 81230-9606
970/641-0174

At the resort:

At resort or within 15 minutes:

Shady Island Resort, Cabins & RV Park

Stay mere feet from the banks of the Gunnison River at Shady Island Resort. The housekeeping cabins range in size from one-room cabins to a large three-bedroom vacation home, with a living room, dining room and kitchen. All cabins have a shower or tub and a kitchen or kitchenette. Some include free standing wood burning stoves. At night, the only sounds you'll hear are the steady gurgle of the river and the wind in the trees. In the morning watch the trout jump for breakfast on the river.

Send the kids off to the playground to play miniature golf, badminton, horseshoes and volleyball while you relax in the shade. Ask your hosts about organized raft trips leaving from the campground and tubing on the Gunnison River. Shady Island Resort is conveniently close to Gunnison, within 2 miles of a shopping center, service station and laundromat. Enjoy fishing the Gunnison River or on many of the other nearby lakes and streams. Guest horses are permitted or rent one at local stables. Area activities include four-wheel driving, hiking and mountain biking.

RV sites are also available.

Location: Highway 135, 2.5 miles north of Gunnison, near milepost 3.

10 Cabins with Kitchens
1 Vacation Home
3 Woodstoves

Pay Phone(s)
Recreation Room
Elevation: 7700
Credit Cards: VMD
2 people a night: $35 - $45
Open: 5/1 to 11/15

Jerry & Becky Griffith, Managers
2776 N Hwy 135
Gunnison CO 81230-9705
970/641-0416

At the resort:

At resort or within 15 minutes:

Silent Spring Resort

A newly-updated small resort, Silent Spring offers two rustic-style, fully modern log cabins with well-equipped kitchens. The cabins are located in beautiful Spring Creek Canyon and are surrounded by national forest. Discover quiet, peace and privacy in this secluded but comfortable setting. The first cabins sleeps four and has a large stone fireplace, while the second cabin sleep six and includes a wood burning stove. Firewood is provided at no extra cost. Recent improvements include newly remodeled cabin interiors, new paint, satellite television, ceiling fans, leather couches and designer window treatments — all to appeal to the discriminating vacationer. Both cabins come with bedding, towels, cooking and eating utensils, new refrigerators with ice makers, gas stoves and bathtubs and showers. A laundromat is conveniently on-site.

Try the excellent fishing on Spring Creek, the Taylor River and other reservoirs and streams close by. Take raft trips, horseback rides, hayrides and pack trips from nearby Harmel's ranch. Golf on two 18-hole courses just 30 minutes away.

Two RV sites are available. Small pets are accepted and the hosts prefer to rent by the week. Honeymooners, or any special occasion should inquire about the romantic first cabin, champagne and flowers. Ask about discounts for long-term stays.

Location: Go 18 miles north of Gunnison on Highway 135, near milepost 10. Turn east at Almont on Taylor River Road (FR 742) to Harmel's; then go 1 mile up Spring Creek Road.

2 Cabins with Kitchens
1 Fireplace
1 Woodstove

No Phones Available
All Non-Smoking in Units
Elevation: 8453
No credit cards
2 people a night: $90
Open: 4/15 to 11/15

Ron Watson, Owner
905 CR 744
Almont CO 81210
970/641-0583 Resort
E-mail: URBAN_refugee@msn.com

At the resort:

At resort or within 15 minutes:

Three Rivers Resort & Outfitting

Named for the Taylor, East and Gunnison rivers in the heart of Gunnison National Forest, Three Rivers Resort features private, rustic and modern riverfront cabins with fully equipped kitchens. All cabins have a stove, refrigerator, dishes, utensils, linens, bedding, pots and pans for light housekeeping. Some cabins have fireplaces and full baths while others retain the 'Old West' atmosphere with a central bath nearby. Sit next to the Taylor River and exchange tales about the one that *didn't* get away!

The indoor pavilion can accommodate up to 100 people and has a pool table, foosball and many other table games. It's perfect for large family reunions. Other on-site facilities include a laundromat, a general store and a professional fly, tackle and paddle shop with everything from to beginner's bait to the best fly fishing rods around. Sample the grill and deli. In the summer, participate in resort-sponsored activities such as square dances, bingo and potlucks. The resort also offers mild or wild raft trips and inflatable kayak trips. Raft down scenic Taylor Canyon to fish areas only accessible by boat. Or combine a rafting trip with fishing in those deep pools hard to reach from the shore. Hike in the national forest where you'll discover bubbling streams, clear lakes, delicate wildflowers, colorful rocks, dense forests and a variety of wildlife in abundance.

Full hookups RV sites with campfire pits, concrete patios, and picnic tables are also available. Pets must be declared and registered when making your reservation.

Location: 10 miles north of Gunnison in Almont, take Highway 135 to milepost 10, turn right up Taylor Canyon Road (County Road 742) 0.25 mile.

27 Cabins with Kitchens
6 Fireplaces
2 Woodstoves
Central Campfire Area

Pay Phone(s)
Recreation Room
Elevation: 8000
Credit Cards: VMAD
2 people a night: $30 - $85
Open: All Year

Mark & Mary Jo Schumacher, Owners
PO Box 339
130 CR 742
Almont CO 81210-0339
970/641-1303
970/641-1317 Fax
888/761-FISH (3474)

At the resort:

At resort or within 15 minutes:

Tomichi Creek Lodge

Situated high in the beautiful Tomichi Creek Valley, adjacent to the Continental Divide, is Tomichi Creek Lodge. Recently remodeled, accommodations in the rustic log lodge include three large comfortable bed and breakfast rooms, each with its own bathroom, or a cabin that sits streamside where the Buckhorn and Tomichi Creeks join together. A unique, micro hydroelectric system supplies power to the property.

Open year-round and surrounded by Sawatch Range and Gunnison National Forest, the resort has outdoor activities for everyone. Anglers of all ages can try dropping a line in the stocked trout pond (no license required) or the beaver ponds of Tomichi Creek. For that really big catch, Gold Medal fisheries are only a short distance away. Hikers, mountain bikers, and four-wheel enthusiasts will enjoy exploring the uncrowded and pristine back-country that surrounds the lodge. History buffs will enjoy investigating the numerous ghost towns and mining camps in the area for mining relics left behind. Take time to explore the Alpine Railroad Tunnel, considered one of the greatest engineering marvels of its time. Do a little rock hunting for quartz crystals or other minerals. Enjoy world record elk and deer hunting in the fall or just take in the breathtaking colors of the aspen trees. In the winter, enjoy cross-country skiing and snowmobiling. (Due to snowy conditions, the lodge is only accessible by the hosts' Snow-Cat or by your own snowmobile). After the day's adventures, soak in the hot tub and follow up with a hearty home-style dinner.

Reservations are required.

Location: 13 miles north of Highway 50 on County Road 888 (White Pine Road), near milepost 190, 1 mile northeast of Sargents, west side of Monarch Pass.

1 cabin without Kitchen
4 Lodging Rooms
Central Woodstove
Central Campfire Area

Lobby Phone
Bed & Breakfast Available
Recreation Room
Elevation: 10300
Credit Cards: VM
2 people a night: $160
Open: All Year

Frank Culbertson & Renee Cortez
Box 39
CR 888 Tomichi Creek Rd
Sargents CO 81248
970/641-5595

At the resort:

At resort or within 15 minutes:

I-70 East

Map: H-22, F-19, G-26

On I-70, there's a myriad of things to see and do. Located on Colorado's high plains, **Limon** is a convenient stopping point while traveling. Limon has a municipal swimming pool, nine-hole golf course and numerous picnic areas. Watch for the abundant wildlife on the plains surrounding Limon. The town's Schoolhouse Museum was built in 1895 and is an excellent example of early school houses in Lincoln County. Nearby, in the town of Genoa, is the Genoa Tower Museum where you can see six states from the tower on a clear day. The museum also has a large collection of fossil skulls, guns, bottles, Indian artifacts and oddities like two-headed calves and jackalopes! Northeast from Flagler is the Flagler Reservoir and State Wildlife Area where you can fish and picnic while protected wildlife wander in the reserve. The Kit Carson County Carousel in Burlington, is a fully restored and operating, hand-carved 1905 wooden merry-go-round. One of fewer than 170 such carousels left in the country, this gaily painted, charming antique was a toy of the American Victorian middle class and is a National Landmark. In **Strasburg**, visit the Comanche Crossing Museum. As you travel I-70 west, you can watch the beautiful Rocky Mountains rise majestically up out of the plains.

Fun Things to Do

- Burlington Old Town Museum (800) 288-1334, (719) 346-7382
- Comanche Crossing Museum (303) 622-4668
- Flagler Reservoir & State Wildlife Area (719) 765-4422
- Pioneer Schoolhouse Museum, Limon (719) 775-2350
- Welcome Center at Burlington (719) 346-5554

Denver East/Strasburg KOA & Kamping Kabins™

Dotted with shade trees, Denver East/Strasburg KOA has Kamping Kabins™ which offer a pleasant and inexpensive place to stay while seeing the sights of Denver. One of the seven kamping kabins™ is a new two bedroom model for families. For your convenience, hot showers and a laundromat are on-site. Two restaurants are within an easy walking distance for your dining pleasure.

Amenities include a playground, large video game room, heated swimming pool, and free nightly movies. A large meeting room is ideal for groups of up to 70. Take your pet on the dog walk for daily exercise. The camp store has groceries, pop, ice, camping supplies and souvenirs. Let your hosts help plan a visit to all of the nearby Denver attractions, including the zoo and Museum of Natural History. Check out the local Comanche Crossing Museum in Strasburg, with its restored train depot, 1904 schoolhouse, 1910 homestead and over 3,000 artifacts.

Full hookup RV sites and tent sites are also available. Groups are encouraged and welcomed.

Location: Highway 70, Exit 310, 35 miles east of Denver.

7 Camper Cabins

Pay Phone(s)
All Non-Smoking in Units
Recreation Room
Elevation: 5380
Credit Cards: VMAD
2 people a night: $29 - $35
Open: All Year

Jim & Sharon Strange, Owners
PO Box 597
1312 Monroe St
Strasburg CO 80136-0597
303/622-9274
800/562-6538 Resveravtions only

At the resort:

At resort or within 15 minutes:

Limon KOA & Kamping Kabins™

Convenient to the Interstate, Limon KOA has Kamping Kabins. Shade trees dot the campground providing cool spots to relax. Be sure to bring your own bedding and cooking equipment. The Limon KOA provides picnic tables, barbecue grills, clean restrooms, hot showers and a laundromat. Sit back and watch the colorful sunrises and sunsets flood the endless sky with color.

The heated swimming pool, playground and game room are among the on-site amenities. The sports fields have basketball, volleyball, badminton and tournament quality horseshoes. Exercise your pet on the dog walk. The camp store has snacks, gifts, souvenirs and limited groceries. The Limon KOA is a great stopover before entering Denver, Colorado Springs or the Rocky Mountains. Restaurants, shops, service stations, and stocked fishing pond are within walking distance, while golf and tennis are nearby. If you're heading east, stop and visit the Genoa Tower Museum & Antiques just a few miles away at the next I-70 exit east.

RV and tent sites are also available.

Location: Interstate 70, near Exit 361. Go to the Pizza Hut, then head two blocks north.

2 Camper Cabins

Pay Phone(s)
Recreation Room
Elevation: 5366
Credit Cards: VMD
2 people a night: $27
Open: 4/1 to 10/31

Jim & Kay McCormick, Owners
575 Colorado Ave
Limon CO 80828
719/775-2151
800/KOA-2129

At the resort:

At resort or within 15 minutes:

Strasburg Inn B&B, Sewing Basket, Gifts & Flowers

The Strasburg Inn in eastern Colorado offers late 19th-century charm in its relaxing parlor complete with a library to browse. The Inn was established in 1915 to serve the growing community which the railroads accessed in 1870. The seven bed and breakfast rooms have either king, queen or double beds, color televisions, shared baths and air conditioning for hot summer evenings. Each room is decorated with antiques and local crafts. The Comanche Suite, a large, one-bedroom suite with a sitting room and a private bath, is tucked under the eaves of the large inn which provide an at-home atmosphere. The suite also has a VCR for add convenience. The included continental breakfast for all guests features fresh, home-baked pastries, fresh orange juice and steaming hot coffee.

In days gone by, travelers staying at the inn also found a grocery store, barber shop and dining room on the first floor. Today, the Strasburg Inn has a full-service flower shop, gift shop and fabric store, each with unique items sure to please. There is also a laundry and playground on-site. The Inn is located in historic Strasburg where, on Aug. 15, 1870, the tracks were laid to connect the Atlantic Coast to the Pacific Coast. Learn all about this event and other historical moments at the nearby Comanche Crossing Museum. Other places to visit while in town are Urich's Locomotive and the Llama Ranch where you can tour and see the llamas for free. Other area attractions include fishing, golfing, boating and hunting in season. Pets are welcomed to accompany you to the Strasburg Inn.

Location: 35 miles east of Denver in Strasburg on Main St.

8 Lodging Rooms

Pay Phone(s)
Bed & Breakfast Available
Non-Smoking Units Available
Recreation Room
Elevation: 5380
No credit cards
2 people a night: $35 - $45
Open: All to Year

Linda Hobaugh, Owner & Jack Frost
PO Box 296
1406 Main St
Strasburg CO 80136-0296
303/622-4314

At the resort:

At resort or within 15 minutes:

Lake City

Map: M-7

Lake City is home to several 14,000' mountain peaks: Uncompahgre, Sunshine, Handies, Red Cloud and Wetterhorn. Tucked into the grassy canyon where Henson Creek and the Lake Fork of the Gunnison River meet, Lake City is a state secret. Hike in any of the four national forests (600,000 acres) that surround this small town. The Alpine Scenic Loop Backcountry Byway begins in town and runs through Ouray and then on to Silverton on 65 miles of dirt and gravel roads. The backcountry byway has some of the most stunning four wheel driving in the world! The Silver Thread Historic Byway (Highway 149) ribbons through the communities of South Fork, Creede and Lake City in the San Juan Mountains, once a toll road and stage route for miners, is a 75 mile paved highway. Try boating on spectacular Lake San Cristobal, Colorado's 2nd largest natural lake — approximately 350 acres. Fish for rainbow trout in the swirling Lake Fork River or explore the Victorian charm of downtown with over 75 buildings from the late 1800s — one of Colorado's largest historical districts. Lake City's history is pretty mild compared to the more notorious mining towns. But one story just won't die: Alferd Packer. In 1874, Packer convinced some prospectors to let him guide them through the snow-covered mountains. Six weeks later, he appeared 76 miles to the northeast alone with a beard and long hair. He claimed to have survived on roots and berries but the truth soon came out and Packer was accused of murder and cannibalism. He was sentenced to hang in 1883 at Lake City's courthouse but Packer got off on a legality and ended up only serving 14 years. Every September, Lake City remembers its famous cannibal with the Annual Alferd Packer Jeep Tour and Barbecue!

Fun Things to Do

- Hinsdale County Museum (970) 944-9515
- Hummer Adventure Tours (970) 944-2780
- Lakeview Resort Boat Rentals & Outfitters (800) 456-0170, (970) 944-2401
- Matterhorn Tours (800) 779-8028, (970) 944-2210
- National Historic District (970) 944-2527

G & M Cabins

Conveniently located in the historic town of Lake City, G & M Cabins offers one, two and three bedroom cabins. Here you can enjoy "family vacations the way they used to be." These fully equipped housekeeping cabins have kitchenette, private baths and color cable televisions. Some cabins have hand crafted lodgepole furniture and screened porches for relaxing.

G & M has a picnic area with a large outdoor barbecue grill and a children's playhouse. Located in downtown the cabins are within walking distance of shops, restaurants, the town park, and lovely streams fishing. Outdoor activities are boundless here, including horseback riding, jeeping, whitewater rafting, mountain biking and boating on Lake San Cristobal. If hiking is your passion there are five 14,000er's nearby; or if you enjoy a lower impact adventure drive the Alpine Loop Scenic Byway in a rental jeep for breathtaking scenery.

A minimum stay is required from the middle of May to the middle of August.

Location: Off Highway 149, milepost 72.

13 Cabins with Kitchens
Central Campfire Area

Lobby Phone
Elevation: 8671
Credit Cards: VM
2 people a night: $45 - $50
Open: 5/25 to 10/1

Annette Anthony & Jim Baker, Owners
PO Box 503
331 Gunnison Ave
Lake City CO 81235-0185
970/944-2282
602/948-5816 Winter

At the resort:

At resort or within 15 minutes:

Lakeview Resort, Cabins, Suites, Lodge Rooms & Outfitters

Lakeview resort offers what Colorado used to be — few people, deep blue lakes, bubbling streams, mountain peaks, dusty ghost towns and high mountain passes. A family resort on the shores of Colorado's second largest and one of the most beautiful natural lakes, the park has mountain cabins in the pine trees adjacent to a lodge and marina on Lake San Cristobal. The cabins have kitchenettes, living areas, woodburning stoves or fireplaces, private baths and one to three bedrooms. The cabins sleep from three to nine people depending upon the accommodation. The lodge suites have kitchenettes, living areas, private baths and an extra-large bedroom with a queen and double bed. Lodge rooms sleeping up to four people are also available. All rooms are non-smoking.

The resort boasts fishing and pontoon boats for rent, guided fishing trips, horseback riding, sunset supper rides, and all day horseback trips. The resort's outfitting service offers a variety of hunts in Colorado (CO Lic #939) and Montana (MT Lic #6299). Combine horses and fishing on high mountain rides to alpine lakes and streams where the trout are the freshest! In one of the last real wildernesses Colorado has to offer, you'll likely see elk, deer, coyotes, rabbits and numerous other wildlife. Here bald eagles soar over towering peaks and bright wildflowers dot lush meadows where babbling brooks hide rainbow trout.

RV sites are available. Ask about the complete facilities for groups, seminars and family reunions. If you're over 55 ask about their Elderhostel. Pets on a leash are allowed with a per day fee.

Location: On Highway 149, near milepost 70, Turn south on County Road 33 and drive half a mile.

10 Cabins with Kitchens
10 Lodging Rooms
3 Fireplaces
7 Woodstoves
Central Campfire Area

Pay Phone(s)
All Non-Smoking in Units
Recreation Room
Elevation: 9000
Credit Cards: VM
2 people a night: $45 - $85
Open: 5/1 to 10/1

Tom & Midge & Dan & Michelle Murphy
PO Box 1000
Lake San Cristobal
Lake City CO 81235-1000
970/944-2401
800/456-0170
970/944-2925 Fax

At the resort:

At resort or within 15 minutes:

Matterhorn Cabins, Motel & Tours

You'll enjoy the views from the Matterhorn Motel in its quiet, mountainside location, yet only two blocks from the heart of historic Lake City. Two housekeeping cabins and 12 motel rooms are available. The accommodations are clean and comfortable. Most units have fully furnished kitchenettes and cable television.

Scenic mountain tours depart right from the motel to take you on unforgettable high mountain adventures on the Alpine Loop Back Country Byway. You'll travel up to 12,800 feet over Cinnamon and Engineer passes to follow the footsteps of settlers and miners who once traversed the mountains. A knowledgeable guide will share the fascinating history of bygone days of the mining boom in this area. Be sure to bring your camera along for the panoramic views. Within minutes of the resort, anglers of all expertise levels will find plenty of cold, clear, flowing streams, beaver ponds and high alpine lakes. Hike into the San Juan Mountains to experience unspoiled, back country scenery. To catch a glimpse of Lake City's past, visit the Hindsdale Country Museum or take a walking tour among the Victorian homes dating from the 1800s.

Some non-smoking rooms are available.

Location: Two blocks from the Lake City Historic District.

2 Cabins with Kitchens
12 Motel Rooms

Pay Phone(s)
Non-Smoking Units Available
Elevation: 8684
Credit Cards: VMD
2 people a night: $40 - $45
Open: 5/1 to 10/31

Richard & Linda Walker, Owners
PO Box 603
Lake City CO 81235
970/944-2210
800/779-8028

At the resort:

At resort or within 15 minutes:

Moncrief Mountain Ranch & Lodge

In the peaks of the San Juan Mountains of southwestern Colorado, Moncrief Mountain Ranch provides visitors with a unique, enchanting group and family vacation spot. The 19,300-square-foot log cabin lodge is an impressive retreat on 320 acres of aspen-covered mountain slopes. A 28-foot-high fireplace dominates the main lounge area and is surrounded by French windows offering spectacular views of 14,000' peaks and the Lake Fork Valley. Choose from eight private rooms and two dormitory-style wings in the lodge. There are also two bunk houses with their own living area and fireplace than can accommodate up to 24 people each.

Among the activities available for package excursions, enjoy rafting, horseback riding, four-wheel drive tours, guided river fishing, and nature walks. At the ranch, pond and stream fishing, canoeing and wildlife watching are popular in the warm weather. From the lodge, it's just a short hike to Diamond Falls and the Rock Slide; a geological point of interest. For cooler weather, come for ice skating and cross-country skiing. After a full day of activities, relax with a massage or a good book from the well stocked library.

For the perfect getaway, call about the weekly packages which include 7 nights of lodging with 3 meals per day, 1 wine and cheese tasting evening, 1 day-long excursion, a 2 hour massage and all the activities at the ranch. Moncrief's is the perfect setting for corporate retreats, seminars, family reunions, weddings and workshops.

Location: On Highway 149, turn east on County Road 30 past the lake where the paved road ends. Drive 1.8 miles.

10 Lodging Rooms
48 Beds in Bunk House or Dorm

Room Phones
Bed & Breakfast Available
All Non-Smoking in Units
Recreation Room
Elevation: 9100
Credit Cards: VM
2 people a night: Call for Rates
Open: 4/15 to 12/20

Linda Barnett, Mgr
PO Box 593
CR 30
Lake City CO 81235-0593
970/944-2796
970/944-2721 Fax

At the resort:

At resort or within 15 minutes:

Ox-Yoke Riverside Resort

This resort of 12 housekeeping cabins boasts a river that runs through it. The cabins sit along the edge of the crystal waters of the Lake Fork/Gunnison River, so you can fish right outside your door. The one- and two-bedroom cabins are spacious, comfortable and clean. Each is fully equipped with cable television, picnic tables, grills and campfires.

From Ox-Yoke, walk to town and explore the intriguing history of Lake City. You can both fish and river raft right from the resort. Area activities include lake and river fishing, four wheel driving to ghost towns, hiking, climbing and mountain biking to scenic vistas. You can also go on four wheel drive tours, horseback riding tours or rent boats to take on the lake's pristine waters. Open until October first, the resort is a good place for hunters to stay as well. The opportunities for photography and observing wildlife are unlimited no matter the activity you undertake.

Location: On Highway 149, near milepost 71.

12 Cabins with Kitchens
Central Campfire Area

Lobby Phone
All Non-Smoking in Units
Elevation: 9000
Credit Cards: VM
2 people a night: $45 - $80
Open: 06/1 to 10/01

Sam & Sherry Elrod, Owners
PO Box 97
Hwy 149 S
Lake City CO 81235-0097
970/944-2252
817/279-0831 Winter

At the resort:

At resort or within 15 minutes:

Rocky Top Lodge & Hummer Adventure Tours

In a lovely, private setting, Rocky Top Lodge is conveniently close to Lake City. The four housekeeping cabins all have full kitchens. Each of the modern, log units offers cozy comfort with wood interiors and woodburning stoves or fireplaces. Towels and linens are supplied. A sofa-bed and roll-away bed in each cabin can accommodate extra family members and guests. Cabin One can sleep up to five, has a large, covered porch and is surrounded by a grassy, tree-covered lawn. Cabins Two & Three can sleep up to seven, have woodburning pellet stoves and large, covered porches. Cabin Four sleeps up to five, has a king bed in a loft bedroom overlooking the living area, brick fireplace, open front deck and lots of trees and privacy. Private barbecue grills and picnic tables at each cabin make for great outdoor dining. While away an afternoon on the gliding cedar porch chairs.

Hummer Adventure Tours is located right on the property. They offer unforgettable tours over the beautiful Alpine Loop Scenic Byway where you'll get the chance to explore old ghost towns and mines scattered across the rugged Cinnamon and Engineer passes. Or take a custom tour to places like Ouray, Silverton, Heart Lake and Poukeepsie Gulch for six or more. The Hummer comfortably seats up to 10, but will take as few as two. The Crystal Lake Trail is as close as your back door for hiking and mountain biking. The Lake City area has plenty of spots for great fishing, hiking, mountain biking, horseback riding, snowmobiling, cross-country skiing and hunting. The quaint, historic town has plays, slide shows, concerts, a movie theater, a museum, historic homes tour, restaurants and local shops.

Rocky Top Lodge is a non-smoking facility and pets are not allowed.

Location: Highway 149, near milepost 73.

4 Cabins with Kitchens
1 Fireplace
3 Woodstoves

Room Phones
All Non-Smoking in Units
Elevation: 8700
Credit Cards: VMD
2 people a night: $75 - $105
Open: All Year

Bob & Linda Inge, Owners
PO Box 232
Hwy 149 North
Lake City CO 81235
970/944-2780

At the resort:

At resort or within 15 minutes:

Texan Resort Cabins

Established in 1946 on the banks of the Lake Fork of the Gunnison River, this resort features a small beach and a 65-foot waterfall. The comfortable log cabins are set in a wooded hollow among tall spruce, fir, aspen and cottonwood trees. Surrounded by large green lawns, all of the cabins have modern plumbing with showers or tubs and completely equipped kitchens. Some have fireplaces. You might enjoy requesting their large, Scandinavian style log cabin. Your hosts supply all linens and towels. There are several barbecue areas to grill your favorite meal.

Enjoy the traditional, resort-sponsored Thursday night cookouts. They also offer guided snowmobile tours in the winter, generally from Thanksgiving through March or early April. Fishing is a year round sport here. Four-wheeling on hundreds of miles of old 1890s mining trails takes you to exciting new vistas and remote fishing locations. Lake San Cristobal is just 2.5 miles from your door, while dozens of other smaller lakes are nearby.

Texan Resort Cabins has many loyal, repeat customers so reserve early for your vacation.

Location: Highway 149, near milepost 71. South of Lake City on County Road 142.

16 Cabins with Kitchens
5 Fireplaces
Central Woodstove
Central Campfire Area

Pay Phone(s)
Non-Smoking Units Available
Elevation: 8671
No credit cards
2 people a night: $37 - $95
Open: All Year

Steve & Gayle Meredith, Owners
PO Box 156
860 CR 142
Lake City CO 81235-0156
970/944-2246

At the resort:

At resort or within 15 minutes:

Woodlake Park Cabins & Campground

Near the Alpine Loop Scenic Backcountry Byway, on the Silver Thread Scenic Byway and at the foot of beautiful Slumgullion Pass, Woodlake Park is adjacent to the river and far enough from town for quiet, but close enough for convenience. It has two camper cabins with a double bed and bunk bed. An outdoor grill and picnic table are provided, but you supply bedding, lantern and cooking utensils. The luxury vacation home facing the Lake Fork of the Gunnison River sleeps up to 10 in its two bedrooms and on sleeper sofas. It also boasts a full bath downstairs, a half bath upstairs, a kitchen with new appliances and a dining area. Woodlake Park is surrounded by river and mountain vistas and shaded by tall pine trees. You'll only hear the babble of the Lake Fork of the Gunnison River as it runs its course.

Get the whole family involved in the fun, organized pavilion activities such as line dancing (instruction given). There's no end to the exciting adventures this mountainous area has to offer: bird watching, fishing, hiking, hunting, mountain biking, horseback riding, Jeeping, ATVing and exploring areas of geological interest and old ghost towns. Check out historic Colorado lore at the Alferd Packer massacre site nearby.

RV camping with uncrowded, spacious sites is also available.

Location: Two and a half miles south of Lake City on Highway 149, between milepost 69-70.

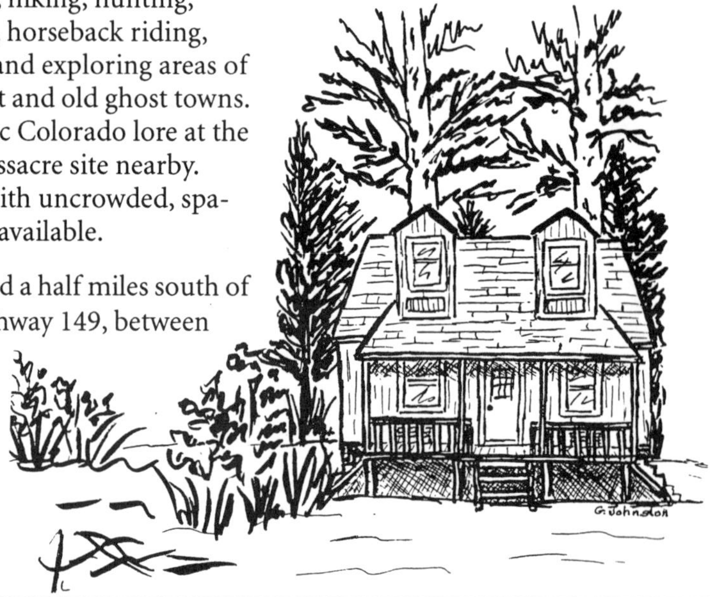

1 Vacation Home
2 Camper Cabins
Central Campfire Area

Pay Phone(s)
Elevation: 9000
No credit cards
2 people a night: $25 - $60
Open: 6/1 to 10/1

Latellya Smith, Owner
PO Box 400
Hwy 149 South
Lake City CO 81235-0400
970/944-2283
800/201-2694

At the resort:

At resort or within 15 minutes:

Meeker

Map: E-5

Meeker, gateway to the White River National Forest and the Flattops Wilderness (accessible only by foot or on horseback), attracts many visitors who come for the excellent fishing and hunting. The White River Forest, with one of the largest elk herds in Colorado, has 111 miles of fishable streams and 780 acres of lakes. Named for Nathan C. Meeker who arrived in 1878 to head White River Indian Agency, the town sits amidst hidden valleys, hot springs and quiet retreats which prompted Utes to call it the land of shining mountains. Meeker is still a ranching community with old brick buildings and relaxed, small-town atmosphere. In 1919, Arthur Carhart, a Forest Service landscape architect working east of Meeker, wanted to create wilderness preserves which would be conserved forever, untouched by man and civilization. His idea was the core of the 1964 Wilderness Act which was fought by most Colorado politicians. Today, however, it's the designated wilderness areas that bring a steady stream of tourists. Wildlife in Piceance Basin includes thousands of animals that pick their way through sagebrush, cedar, piñon-juniper, and douglas fir. The basin has some 1,200 elk, 350 species of wildlife, 22 species of raptors, ranging from owls to eagles, and even a wild horse herd.

Fun Things to Do

- Buford Sore & Museum (970) 878-4745
- Dinosaur National Monument (970) 374-3000
- Flattops Wilderness Area (970) 878-4039
- Pollard's Outfitting (970)878-4669
- White River Museum (970) 878-9982

Buford Hunting & Fishing Lodge and Store

On the Scenic Flat Tops Byway, Buford Lodge is adjacent to the beautiful White River in the center of the White River National Forest. Some of the rustic and modern housekeeping cabins have fireplaces or wood stoves and televisions. The cabins date back to 1908 and the new Buford White River Historical Museum, filled with a growing number of artifacts of every kind, is on the property in an 85-year-old log building. Wander among old agricultural equipment, cream separators and antique slot machines while proprietor Harry Tucker relates tales of friendly Utes and the last of the mountain men in the time honored traditional of oral history.

The on-site grocery store, which is on the National Registry of Historic Places, is stocked with sporting goods, gifts and gas. Excellent fishing and hunting abounds in White River National Forest. Buford Lodge will help arrange hunt/drop camps and provide guides to those interested in a real wilderness experience. The resort also offers women's clinics in fly fishing. Dine at the nearby restaurant, then rent a horse from the local stables and trek through the backcountry's magnificence.

Location: 22 miles east of Meeker on Trappers Lake Road (County Road 8) at Buford, near milepost 20.

12 Cabins with Kitchens
1 Fireplace
10 Woodstoves

Pay Phone(s)
Non-Smoking Units Available
Elevation: 7000
Credit Cards: VMD
2 people a night: $45 - $65
Open: 5/15 to 11/15

Harry Tucker, Owner & Betty Morlen, Manager
20474 CR 8
Meeker CO 81641
970/878-4745

At the resort:

At resort or within 15 minutes:

Pollard's Ute Lodge Cabins

At the quiet end of the road up the White River Valley near the Scenic Flat Tops Byway, Pollard's Ute Lodge has cabins in a secluded forest of pine and spruce trees. Prepare your favorite evening meal in a modern kitchen, then listen to the crackling fire while you relax and watch the stars. Cabins range from one to three bedroom cabins. The Spruce Cabin is a two-story, three bedroom cabin which sleeps 9 people ideal for large family or small groups. The Oak and Wild Rose Cabins are one bedroom with a bathhouse near by for the more adventuresome. Picnic during the day outside under azure skies. Some cabins and bathhouse are equipped with handicap facilities.

Pollard's has unlicensed fishing on their private, snow-fed mountain lake. Ask your hosts, licensed outfitters #502, about the experienced guides and top-quality horses that will take you to drop camps for superb fishing and hunting trips in the back country. You can mountain bike, horseback ride or hike through the Flat Tops Wilderness area and the White River National Forest. There are mountain bike trails accessible from the property. Ride your horse or take a guided horseback tour to the world's largest aspen tree grove where, in the fall, the shades of ruby red, brilliant yellow and soft amber will amaze you.

RV sites are also available. Ask about the discounts for seniors, firemen and policemen. They also offer an weekly and monthly rate. There is an additional charge for more than 2 people.

Location: 28 miles east of Meeker on County Road 8 and follow the signs.

6 Cabins with Kitchens
2 cabins without Kitchens
1 Fireplace
4 Woodstoves
Central Campfire Area

Lobby Phone
Elevation: 8000
Credit Cards: VM
2 people a night: $25 - $60
Open: 5/15 to 11/15

Buck & Gloria Pollard, Owners
393 CR 75
Meeker CO 81641
970/878-4669

At the resort:

At resort or within 15 minutes:

Stagecoach Cabins, Lodging & RV Resort

Along the 27-acre, shaded grounds of Stagecoach runs a half mile of the scenic White River. The two rustic camper cabins are in the cool shade and guests use the new central bathhouse facilities there is a picnic table and grill out front. One cabin is completely modern and has a fireplace. Motel rooms with kitchenettes are also available. At Stagecoach, sit back, relax, watch the wildflowers grow and listen to the river flow.

Stagecoach has horseshoes and volleyball. Fish near your cabin for whitefish, brook and rainbow trout on the rolling White River. The surrounding area has over 900 acres of lakes and ponds and 200 miles of fishable streams. During the season, take guided hunting trips for large elk and mule deer herds. Close by, are a challenging golf course, a riding stable and heated swimming pool for more summer fun. Rent a horse or bring your own for unforgettable trips into the high country. The Rio Blanco Ranger District offers 17 trailheads, 250 miles of hiking trails and 280 miles of snowmobile trails. Mountain bikers will discover plenty of trails into the wilderness. The new owners have made lots of improvements.

RV and group camping sites are also available. Ask about the outdoor group meeting area. Ask about their off season rates.

Location: 2 miles south of Meeker on Highway 13, near milepost 39 at junction west of Highway 64.

3 Cabins with Kitchens
1 Motel Room
1 Fireplace

Pay Phone(s)
All Non-Smoking in Units
Elevation: 6200
Credit Cards: VMAD
2 people a night: $20 - $65
Open: 4/1 to 12/1

Dell & Linda Herring, Owners
PO Box 995
39084 Hwy 13
Meeker CO 81641-0995
970/878-4334
800/878-4334

At the resort:

At resort or within 15 minutes:

Mesa Verde Area

Including Cortez, Dolores & Mancos — Map: O-2, O-3 & O-4

The ruins of the Anasazi, a Navajo word meaning "Ancient Ones," are what bring people to this quiet, sun-drenched area. At **Mesa Verde** National Park visitors walk among the incredible cliff dwellings of these prehistoric Pueblo people. The Anasazi culture flourished here from approximately A.D. 1 to 1300, leaving behind a priceless legacy of their achievements in the famous cliff houses and mesa top villages. The reasons the Ancient Ones abandoned the area remains an enigma, despite decades of research. At one point, more than 40,000 Anasazi lived here. Ten miles away is **Cortez**, once called by the Navajo "Tsaya-toh" (rock-water) for its spring. Lowry Indian Ruins, 26 miles north of Cortez, contain the largest and best preserved painted Anasazi kivas in world. Hovenweep National Monument, 40 miles west, has its unique Anasazi ruins. Nearby is Four Corners Area Monument, located on Ute Mountain Ute and Navajo Indian reservations, the only place in the United States where four states meet. **Dolores** boasts the second largest lake in Colorado, McPhee Lake whose sloping, timbered shore makes for interesting views. Fish from a boat for large and small-mouth bass, blue gills and crappies. Or try the Dolores River, named by two Spanish friars in honor of "Our Lady of Sorrows," where the nutrient-rich waters are teaming with rainbow, brown, cutthroat and brook trout. This area also has excellent hunting, with an abundance of wildlife and big game. See the area's beautiful archeology in the nearby Anasazi Heritage Center which has over 2 millions artifacts, educational and participatory exhibits. Hike, jeep, or horseback ride in the San Juan National Forest, from the Dolores River Valley to 14,000-foot peaks in the Mount Wilson Primitive Area. Or take the scenic byway that goes northeast to Telluride on Highway 145 or southeast to Durango. The drive from Dolores to Telluride is especially magnificent.

Fun Things To Do

- Anasazi Heritage Center, Dolores (970) 882-4811
- Conquistador Golf Course, Cortez (970) 565-9208
- Cortez/University of Colorado Center & Cultural Park (970) 565-1151
- Crow Canyon Archeological Center (800) 422-8975, (970) 565-8975
- Galloping Goose Museum & Dolores Visitor Center (970) 882-4018
- Hovenweep National Monument (970) 529-4465
- Lowry Indian Ruins (970) 247-4874
- Mesa Verde Cortez Information Center (800) 346-6528
- Mesa Verde National Park (970) 529-4465
- San Juan National Forest, Dolores District (970) 882-7296
- Ute Mountain Casino (800)258-8007
- Ute Mountain Tribal Park (970) 565-3751

Alice Ann's Bed & Breakfast

Moments after you enter the magnificent Wrightsman House mansion, built in 1903, you'll know you've found a home while vacationing in Mesa Verde County. Alice Ann's B&B has five rooms that are individually decorated to fit the name of the room: Mesa Verde Country — country, Mancos Cowboy — western cowboy, Navajo Room — Indian, Victorian Rose — classic victorian with a splash of roses, Southern Belle — victorian with dancing belles (ladies). Some rooms have romantic fireplaces and private baths. Guest rooms are all on the second floor except the Grand Suite on the third floor. Double doors open up to winding stairs that take you to the Grand Suite, elegantly decorated with many sitting areas. The Grand Suite has a wet bar, glass top tables, love seats and a queen size bed ideal for honeymoons and anniversaries; however, there are beds to accommodate up to 6 people.

The Wrightsman House's therapy spa and garden are the perfect place to relax after a visit to Mesa Verde National Park, Cortez, Durango and the many attractions of Colorado's southwest area. Enjoy a full breakfast in the large dining room. Join in the daily afternoon gatherings to meet the other guests and nibble on complimentary refreshments. The common rooms have televisions, VCRs, books, and magazines for your enjoyment. At night, join your hosts in the evening for a unique, personal music show.

Ask about the romance package. Reservations need to be paid in advance, cancellation fee applies. Smoking area are limited. Call for a brochure. No pets allowed.Visit their Web site at http://www.swcolo.org/Tourism/Lodging/AliceAnns.html

Location: Exit Highway 160, the San Juan Scenic Skyway, at milepost 56 (Highway 184). Turn south into Mancos past visitor center, then right on Bauer. Go one block. Corner of Mesa & Bauer.

6 Lodging Rooms
3 Fireplaces
Central Fireplace

Lobby Phone
Bed & Breakfast Available
All Non-Smoking in Units
Recreation Room
Elevation: 6800
Credit Cards: VM
2 people a night: $75 - $150
Open: All Year

Alice & Abe Saunders, Owners
PO Box 775
209 Bauer Ave
Mancos CO 81328-0775
970/533-1083
800/425-4234 reservation only

At the resort:

At resort or within 15 minutes:

Circle K Guest Ranch

Snuggled in the San Juan National Forest on the Dolores River, Circle K Ranch has a spacious lodge, bunkhouses, housekeeping cabins and motel units. The lodge with a huge sunken fireplace, meeting room and dining hall, has six rooms - each sleep four people. There are two shared baths down the hall. The three bunkhouses are ideal for large groups and will accommodate up to 130 people. The housekeeping cabins have modern gas heat, fully equipped kitchens and full baths. There are one-, two- and three-bedroom cabins sleeping 4 to 9 people. The motel units have three-quarters bath, a queen bed and a twin bed. Circle K also provides full meals throughout your stay.

Family owned and operated since 1981, Circle K offers a special bargain in winter — stay here and ski Telluride for half-price! Ranch activities include trail rides, fishing, river tug-of-war and swimming, an obstacle course and a mountain cable slide. The ranch specializes in horseback rides —take a 1 to 7 hour trail ride. Facilities also include pool and ping pong tables for indoor entertainment on cool nights. There are also many four-wheel drive roads and mining camps nearby.

Circle K is an alcohol-free family resort specializing in family reunions and church retreats; they have group rates. Children 5, 6 and 7 years old are half price, and 4 and under stay free. The full-service plan provides big savings. RV and tent sites are also available. Pets are not allowed. A deposit is required when making a reservation.

Location: Highway 145, near milepost 36, 26 miles northeast of Dolores.

3 Cabins with Kitchens
6 Lodging Rooms
8 Motel Rooms
130 Beds in Bunk House or Dorm
Central Fireplace
Central Campfire Area

Pay Phone(s)
Recreation Room
Elevation: 8000
No Credit Cards
2 people a night: $35 - $68
Open: All Year

Al & Joan Cannon, Owners & Cindy Beecher, Owners
27758 Hwy 145
Dolores CO 81323
970/562-3826 & Fax
800/477-6381
E mail: crkranch@fone.net

At the resort:

At resort or within 15 minutes:

Dolores River Cabins & RV Park

In the beautiful Dolores River Valley, this park features camper cabins, housekeeping cabins and on-site trailers. Along the Dolores River in a valley, the accommodations have barbecue grills and firewood is available. Pick among cabins and trailers in the open or shaded by trees along the tumbling river. Hot showers, clean restrooms and a coin laundry are available. Come here to simply relax.

Fish right on the river, at the pond or down the road at McPhee Reservoir. The playground is great for the kids while the adults can enjoy the game room with exercise equipment, card tables and color TV. The lounge and commercial kitchen are ideal for family reunions. Exercise your best friend at the pet walk and then exercise yourself along the picturesque river walk. Nearby, you can take a four-wheel drive tour, horseback ride, whitewater raft, golf and mountain bike. End the day with a visit to the soda fountain for a refreshing drink and snack.

Weekly and month rates are available. Groups are welcomed. Ask about the wooded and open RV and tent sites.

Location: From junction of Highway 184 & 145, 14 miles northeast of Highway 145 between milepost 13 and 14. 2 miles north of Dolores.

6 Cabins with Kitchens
6 Camper Cabins
2 Woodstoves
Central Campfire Area

Pay Phone(s)
Non-Smoking Units Available
Recreation Room
Elevation: 7200
Credit Cards: VM
2 people a night: $24 - $69
Open: 4/1 to 10/31

Tomas & Sharon Kurpius, Owners
18680 Hwy 145
Dolores CO 81323
970/882-7761
800/200-3299
970/882-4829 Fax

At the resort:

At resort or within 15 minutes:

Echo Basin Dude Ranch Resort & RV Park

Formerly a working ranch on more than 600 acres, Echo Basin is lush with meadows, streams and high timber forests. The deluxe A-frame cabins with fireplaces are nestled in the forest next to the dude ranch and resort's bunk house rooms. Gather your own firewood to toss on the campfire during the cool nights. Rent cabins by the night or the week, meals included.

The Ranch has everything you need — a laundromat, a rustic, family-style restaurant, a swimming pool and a country store. In between the ranch-sponsored activities like horseback rides, hayrides, weekend rodeos and western cookouts, you can fish on the two stocked lakes or in the swift Mancos River which runs deep and fresh through the ranch. Hunt in the fall and rent snowmobiles or strap on your cross-country skis during the winter. In spring and summer, tennis, volleyball, basketball and baseball are popular activities. Venture into the San Juan National Forest on foot or by mountain bike on some spectacular trails. Be sure to see the many southwest Colorado landmarks, including Mesa Verde National Park, the mountains around Durango and the southwestern desert.

Full hookup sites in the forest are also available. Ask about the lodge for family reunions, weddings, youth camps and company picnics.

Location: Three miles north of Highway 160, near milepost 59, on County Roads 44 and M.

20 Cabins with Kitchens
20 Beds in Bunk House or Dorm
Central Fireplace
Central Campfire Area

Pay Phone(s)
Bed & Breakfast Available
Recreation Room
Elevation: 7800
Credit Cards: VM
2 people a night: $90 - $120
Open: All Year

Lee & Lori Large, Managers
43747 Rd M
Mancos CO 81328-9214
970/533-7000
970/533-9103 Fax
800/426-1890 Reservations only

At the resort:

At resort or within 15 minutes:

Green Snow Oasis Cabins & Shop

In the heart of the San Juan Skyway, about 6 miles south of Rico on the Dolores River, you'll find log cabins that sleep four to six, with full baths, kitchens, wood-burning stoves and outdoor barbecue areas. Complete housekeeping, so bring only your own food.

Green Snow Oasis' gift shop has homemade quilts of all sizes, local crafts, Indian jewelry and antiques. Other items in stock are nostalgic prints, Mexican items, dolls, clowns, yard sale treasures, miniatures, books, cast iron bells and chimes. The Green Snow Oasis is near Telluride, Cortez, Mancos and Durango. Enjoy the excellent trout fishing nearby. Hike, mountain bike and four-wheel drive in the surrounding forests. Come visit during the hunting season! Ask your hosts about hunting trips with meals. Explore Mesa Verde National Park, the Anasazi Heritage Center, the San Juan Scenic Highway and the historic Galloping Goose Train in Dolores. Walk back in time when you visit the turn-of-the-century mining camps of Rico, Ophir, Dunton and, of course, Telluride.

Daily, weekly, monthly and seasonal rates are all available

Location: Highway 145, near milepost 40.

5 Cabins with Kitchens
5 Woodstoves
Central Campfire Area

Lobby Phone
All Non-Smoking in Units
Elevation: 8300
No credit cards
2 people a night: $60 - $75
Open: 5/15 to 11/15

Ouida North
28434 Hwy 145
Dolores CO 81323-9715
970/562-3829

At the resort:

At resort or within 15 minutes:

Groundhog Fishing Camp & Outfitter

In the heart of the San Juan Mountains, Groundhog Lake is 32 miles north of Dolores. The two rustic cabins have kitchen facilities. This resort overlooks unspoiled and beautiful Groundhog Lake — nature at its best. Slip away from the crowd and step out your door to great trout fishing beneath the shadow of Lone Cone Mountain.

Groundhog Resort features excellent fishing, camping and hunting off the beaten path. Rent pontoon boats and use the launch ramp on-site. Buy gas, bait, tackle, fishing and hunting licenses and food at the convenience store. Enjoy the weekly fish fries, where you'll hear great fish stories and can share your own. The resort also offers an outfitter guide service (lic#478) during elk and deer season and can set up drop camps. The resort guides and provides muzzle loading and archery, combination hunts and mountain lion hunts. With advance registration, you can take a one- to three-day mountain horse pack trip during the summer. Group activities at the camp include horseshoes, volleyball, campfire songs and festivities.

RV and tent sites are also available. The cabins book up quickly, so make your reservations early!

Location: In Dolores, turn on 11th Street at the General store; go 28 miles north on gravel Dolores/Norwood Road. Then turn right on Route 533, 4 miles to the lake.

2 Cabins with Kitchens
2 Woodstoves

Lobby Phone
Elevation: 9000
No credit cards
2 people a night: $24 - $30
Open: 5/25 to 11/1

Jim, Louanne & Wendy Wagoner
PO Box 27
15525 CR 32
Dolores CO 81323-0027
970/565-8974, pause20184
970/882-4379 Answering Service

At the resort:

At resort or within 15 minutes:

Kelly Place B&B and Archælogical Preserve

Kelly Place offers a unique bed and breakfast experience at Four Corners, in the heart of Anasazi (ancient Indian) country on 100 acres of red-rock canyons that includes over 25 archaeological sites! The lodge is an adobe-style building dating from the 1960s. The ten private, carpeted guest rooms have queen beds and private baths. Three cabins with kitchens are also available. All cabins are non-smoking. A satisfying hot breakfast is served daily in the guest house.

Take advantage of a chance to explore ancient history while vacationing at Kelly Place. Half and full day tours of the Anasazi ruins on the property are available. Other unique activities includes archaeological programs, Anasazi pottery reproduction, guided botany, ethno-botany and rock art hikes in addition to horseback riding. The B&B also hosts weddings, family reunions, covered wagon trips and Elder hostel programs. The whole family will enjoy the free movies in the Adobe Lodge. Come be a part of living history at Kelly Place.

Kelly Place can accommodate groups of up to 24 people. Ask about their week long educational programs.

Location: 10 miles west of Highway 160 at milepost 35, on County Road G.

1 Cabin with Kitchen
1 cabin without Kitchen
8 Lodging Rooms
1 Fireplace
Central Fireplace
Central Woodstove
Central Campfire Area

Pay Phone(s)
Bed & Breakfast Available
All Non-Smoking in Units
Elevation: 5500
Credit Cards: VM
2 people a night: $69 - $99
Open: All Year

Rodney & Christie Carriker, Owners
14663 CR G
Cortez CO 81321
970/565-3125
800/745-4885

At the resort:

At resort or within 15 minutes:

Lost Canyon Lake Lodge

In a beautiful contemporary log home sheltered by tall pines and overlooking Lost Canyon Lake Reservoir, are four comfortable bedrooms with private baths just waiting for you. Relax by the fireplace in the lounge and enjoy an evening coffee or hot cider. Room rates include full breakfasts with homemade muffins, seasonal fruits, fresh-ground coffee and various hot dishes that may be enjoyed indoors or on the wrap-around deck.

Lost Canyon is only 20 minutes from Mesa Verde National Park. Your hosts are happy to give sightseeing tips and help arrange memorable adventures, from canoeing and horseback riding to archaeological digs and hot-air ballooning. After a day's adventure, relax in the hot tub (winter only) beneath a starry sky.

Reservations are recommended. Children are welcome at this non-smoking lodge.

Location: Between Dolores and Mancos, north of Highway 184, near milepost 16.

LOST CANYON LAKE LODGE

5 Lodging Rooms
Central Fireplace
Central Campfire Area

Room Phones
Bed & Breakfast Available
All Non-Smoking in Units
Recreation Room
Elevation: 7300
Credit Cards: VM
2 people a night: $60 - $95
Open: All Year

Beth Newman, Owner
15472 CR 35.3
Mancos CO 81328-1289
970/882-4913
800/992-1098

At the resort:

At resort or within 15 minutes:

Outpost Cabins, Motel & RV Park

Breathe in cool mountain air at the Outpost resort along the sparkling Dolores River. Surrounded by tall shade trees, these rustic, cozy cabins come equipped with everything including cooking utensils — housekeepers even clean daily. Motel rooms with kitchens are available and the on-site laundromat is convenient. Relax on the grassy lawn during your barbecue picnic.

Fish right from Outpost's spacious deck overlooking the Dolores River. Or try for some of the best bass and trout in Colorado at McPhee Reservoir. If fishing isn't your game, try water skiing, boating, sailing or jet skiing on the reservoir. In the surrounding national forest you can hike, hunt and four-wheel drive. For those who like to get wet, try a river rafting trip or inner tubing down the Dolores. After a day of Colorado fun, guests can sit on the deck overlooking the Dolores River. The restaurants in town are walking distance away.

RV sites and seasonal rentals are also available.

Location: In Dolores, 10 miles north of Cortez on Highway 145.

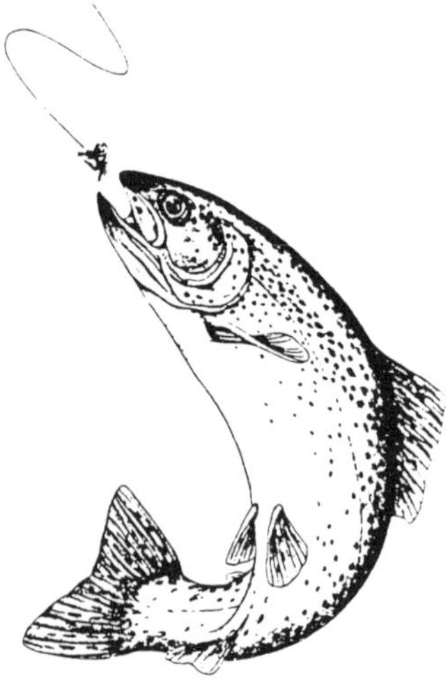

3 Cabins with Kitchens
6 Motel Rooms
Central Campfire Area

Pay Phone(s)
Elevation: 6900
Credit Cards: VMAD
2 people a night: $46 - $85
Open: All Year

Ray & Darlene LeBlanc, Owners
PO Box 295
1800 Hwy 145
Dolores CO 81323-0295
970/882-7271
800/382-4892
970/882-7194 Fax

At the resort:

At resort or within 15 minutes:

Ponderosa Cabins

A short drive from either Mancos or Dolores, Ponderosa Cabins are near Summit Lake's eastern side. The cabins are on eight acres snug under tall ponderosa pine trees and a short distance from the main road — ideal for families with children and pets. The cabins have modern electric ranges, wood burning stoves, cooking utensils and dishes, refrigerators, hot and cold running water, full size baths and gas heat. Cabin 1 sleeps up to four people, while Cabin 2 sleeps up to seven. Both cabins are non-smoking.

Near the San Juan National Forest and next to Summit Lake, Ponderosa Cabins are great for fishing and big game hunting. This resort is great for hunters, with deer passing near the property. Elk are plentiful in this part of the high country. Hunt famous "Lost Canyon" area with easy access to the vast national forest's miles of roads and trails, only 30 minutes from your cabin. If lake fishing doesn't appeal, try casting your line into the Dolores River. McPhee Reservoir, a short drive away, offers water skiing, boating, pontoon excursions and more lake fishing. Cross-country ski within ten minutes of Ponderosa Cabins or downhill ski at Purgatory and Telluride. Visit nearby Mesa Verde National Park, just 20 minutes away.

A 50 percent deposit is required when making reservations.

Location: From US Highway 160, turn north on Highway184 and drive 8 miles. Near milepost18, turn south on County Road 37 for 0.2 miles.

2 Cabins with Kitchens
2 Woodstoves

No Phones Available
All Non-Smoking in Units
Elevation: 7500
No credit cards
2 people a night: $55 - $60
Open: All Year

Jack & Ressa Muller, Owners
PO Box 457
848 Bauer
Mancos CO 81328
970/882-7396
E-mail: ponderos@fone.net

At the resort:

At resort or within 15 minutes:

Red Elk Lodge

Between Cortez and Telluride, Red Elk Ranch offers a log duplex in a secluded alpine location on the picturesque Dolores River. The two units are fully equipped with central heat, a barbecue grill, a kitchen, a living room, a master bedroom with a queen sized bed and a full bath downstairs. The loft upstairs has two twin beds and a roll-away. The larger unit also has a queen sized futon and a half bath upstairs in the loft. You bring the food and charcoal; they provide the linens, towels and soap.

Red Elk Ranch is on a12-acre location on the San Juan Skyway and boasts spectacular scenery all year. The ranch abuts the San Juan National Forest, convenient for hiking, fishing and 4-wheel touring. If you tire of casting your line into the Dolores River, drive just 22 miles to McPhee Reservoir for the best trout and bass fishing around. The ranch is 40 miles from Mesa Verde National Park with its ancient cliff dwellings and 40 miles from Telluride, with its famous downhill skiing in the winter as well as summer and fall festivals.

A $50 deposit is required when making reservations. Daily, weekly and monthly rates are available. Ask about the Telluride ski package, when you stay at Red Elk, you can ski for half price. This ranch was formerly called Rag O'Muffin Ranch. In addition to conventional means, the owners may be contacted via e-mail at redelk@sisna. com.

Location: On Highway 145 close to milepost 32.

2 Cabins with Kitchens
Central Campfire Area

Lobby Phone
Elevation: 7800
No credit cards
2 people a night: $95 - $125
Open: All Year

Martin & Melanie Halstead, Owners
27060 Hwy 145
Dolores CO 81323
970/562-3849
E-mail: redelk@sisna.com

At the resort:

At resort or within 15 minutes:

Riversbend Bed & Breakfast

Riversbend is a two-story log inn fashioned after earlier times when life seemed a bit quieter and where hospitality is still a way of life. Conveniently located on the scenic San Juan Skyway just 7 miles from Mesa Verde National Park, the inn has four loft-style guest rooms that share two full baths and are comfortably furnished with antiques and quilts, reflecting the ease and simplicity of days gone by. Set among tall cottonwood trees, the inn is on 6 acres where you're free to wander. Two common areas are available to guests at all times for reading or joining in conversation with other guests.

Guests begin each day with a scrumptious breakfast. Walk along the Mancos River, visit Mesa Verde National Park or ride the Durango & Silverton Narrow Gauge Railroad. McPhee Reservoir is 18 miles away and offers water sports and fishing. Special activity packages include winter snow sleigh rides, cross country skiing, massages, deluxe dinners, river rafting, stagecoach rides, chuckwagon dinners and shows, fly-fishing, horseback riding, etc. When you return to Riversbend, sit on a porch swing or wooden rocker before taking a relaxing dip in the hot tub.

No smoking and no pets are allowed at Riversbend. Visit their Web site at http://www.subee.com/rb/home.html

Location: North of Highway 160, near milepost 58, east of town.

4 Lodging Rooms
Central Woodstove

Lobby Phone
Bed & Breakfast Available
All Non-Smoking in Units
Recreation Room
Elevation: 6900
Credit Cards: VMD
2 people a night: $62 - $85
Open: All Year

Gaye & Jack Curran, Proprietors
PO Box 861
42505 Hwy 160
Mancos CO 81328-0861
800/699-8994
970/533-7353

At the resort:

At resort or within 15 minutes:

Willowtail Springs

Willowtail Springs features log cabins secluded amid the sunwashed landscapes of Montezuma County in the southwestern corner of Colorado just minutes off the San Juan Scenic Skyway Loop. Vacation here on 40 acres of pastures, woods and streams. Choose between two one-bedroom log cabins, a two bedroom log home, each with a fully equipped kitchen and full bath. The charming, comfortable interiors, furnished with antiques, are ideal for romantic get-a-ways, honeymooners, and family vacationers. Accommodations include decks overlooking a bass-filled lake with a canoe available to guests for fishing and swimming.

From here, you'll be mere steps from the wilderness of the La Platta Mountains in the San Juan National Forest. Peacocks, deer, waterbirds, coyotes and other wildlife live at Willowtail Springs. During the summer, spend your vacation hiking, mountain biking, canoeing, fishing and horseback riding. In the winter, go downhill and cross-country skiing, ice skating, fish on the pond or go on a sleigh ride. The resort is 10 minutes from the ancient wonders of Mesa Verde, 60 minutes from Hovenweep National Monument, Four Corners, and the natural beauty of Canyon Lands. Less than 40 minutes from the city amenities of Durango, the Anasazi Heritage Center, and Purgatory ski area. And just 75 minutes from Telluride's ski resort and summer/fall festivals.

No smoking and no pets are allowed at the resort. Senior discounts available. There is studio space which is ideal for artists, writers or group workshops. A deposit is required 30 days prior to your stay. Visit their Web site at http://subee.com/willowtail/home.html.

Location: About 5 miles west of Mancos.

3 Cabins with Kitchens
3 Fireplaces

Room Phones
All Non-Smoking in Units
Elevation: 6500
Credit Cards: VMD
2 people a night: $95
Open: All Year

Peggy Conklin, Owners
PO Box 89
10451 CR 39
Mancos CO 81328-0089
970/533-7592
800/698-0603

At the resort:

At resort or within 15 minutes:

Pagosa Springs

Map: P-9

Pagosa Springs was named by the Utes who called the hot springs "Pagosah," or "healing waters." This little town, surrounded on three sides by the San Juan National forest, is a good place to get away from it all. Explore the mystery of the only mountain home of the Anasazi at nearby Chimney Rock where these ancient farmers lived some 1,000 years ago. The twin pinnacles were once a scared shrine to the "Ancient Ones". Later, the unusual formations were a landmark for prospectors, missionaries and conquistadors who settled this rugged country. While clambering among the ruins, keep an eye out for the endangered peregrine falcon which nests here. Enjoy the town's hot springs, considered to be the hottest in the world. Windsurf, water-ski and sail on Navajo Lake, which extends southward 35 miles into New Mexico. The Weminuche and South San Juan wilderness areas' untouched beauty are only accessible on foot or horseback. The nearby Echo Lake Park and Lake Capote are stocked with rainbow and cutthroat trout, large-mouth bass and yellow perch. Other nearby places to go include hiking to Treasure Falls, prospecting on Treasure Mountain, fishing in Williams Creek and visiting the local museums. Let the land of healing waters soothe you and the breathtaking wilderness inspire you.

Fun Things to Do

- Chimney Rock Archeological Area (970) 264-2268
- Crazy Horse Outfitters (970) 731-2300
- Fairfield Pagosa Golf Course (970) 731-4755
- Fred Harman Art Museum (970) 731-5785
- Lake Capote (970) 731-5256
- Navajo State Park (970) 883-2208
- Pagosa Ranger District Office (970) 264-2268
- Piedra River Resort & Horse rides (970) 731-4630
- Rocky Mountain Wildlife Park (970) 264-5546
- San Juan National Forest (970) 247-4874, (970) 264-2268
- Upper San Juan Historical Museum (970) 264-4424

Bruce Spruce Ranch & Faris House Lodge

Surrounded by thousands of acres of national forest, Bruce Spruce Ranch is a wonderful retreat at the base of Wolf Creek Pass. If you're looking for the log cabin atmosphere that Colorado is known for, this is the place for you. Most of the cabins are full log with chinking, wood floors, and furnished with a country flair. The clean, rustic cabins are ideal for groups of up to 10 and have modern half-baths, kitchens with gas stoves, wood stoves for heat and centralized, clean hot showers. All kitchen utensils and bed linens are furnished. You may use the on-site washers and dryers as often as necessary. The Faris House Lodge is great for family reunions, church retreats and workshops. The lodge accommodates up to 31 people and has a large kitchen, dining room and living room areas, 5 bedrooms, 3 baths as well as a washer and dryer.

This scenic ranch offers many activities, including volleyball, horseshoes, horseback rides, nature hikes and pack trips for trout fishing in lakes, streams and rivers. The private fishing pond on the ranch requires no state license; there is a fee ($12/3 fish). During the season, take a hunting pack trip for deer, bear and elk. Rent a horse by the hour or day or bring your own. Close by, enjoy the four-wheel drive roads, Mesa Verde and other Indian ruins, narrow-gauge railroad trains, hot mineral baths, wilderness hot springs and more.

Ask about the group meeting areas, RV sites and group camping sites.

Location: 16 miles northeast of Pagosa Springs on Highway 160, near milepost 158. Go 0.25 miles northwest on the gravel road.

14 Cabins with Kitchens
1 Vacation Home
14 Woodstoves
Central Woodstove
Central Campfire Area

Pay Phone(s)
Non-Smoking Units Available
Recreation Room
Elevation: 8200
Credit Cards: VM
2 people a night: $34 - $49
Open: 5/20 to 10/31

Craig & Eugenia Hinger, Owners
PO Box 296
231 West Fork Rd
Pagosa Springs CO 81147-0296
970/264-5374
806/622-1346 Nov-Apr

At the resort:

At resort or within 15 minutes:

Elk Meadows Camper Cabins & Campground

The beautiful San Juan River flows through the valley portion of the campground. Camper cabins, RV pull-thrus, and secluded tent sites occupying the upper levels, Elk Meadows is a great base for hikers, mountain bikers, and fisher folks. The camper cabins offer an inexpensive way to see Colorado at its best. Bring your own bedding and cooking supplies. Clean restrooms, hot showers and a laundry are on-site for your convenience.

Only 17 miles from the Continental Divide and Wolf Creek Pass Summit, the possibilities for outdoor adventures here are endless. Pasture your horse on the 22 acres and ride from here on the endless national forest lands. Hunters will find a concentration of wild game: elk, deer, bighorn sheep, turkey and grouse. Fish for rainbow, cutthroat, brook and brown trout or swim in the San Juan River. Other Elk Meadows' sports include badminton, horseshoes, volleyball and a playground. Hiking the trails and participating in the ice cream socials are also popular activities.

Family reunions and groups are welcomed. RV, tent and group camping sites are available.

Location: Five miles northwest of Pagosa Springs on the San Juan River and Highway 160 at milepost 149.

3 Camper Cabins
Central Campfire Area

Pay Phone(s)
All Non-Smoking in Units
Recreation Room
Elevation: 7300
Credit Cards: VM
2 people a night: $25 - $30
Open: 5/1 to 10/31

Donald & Barbara Palmer, Owners
PO Box 238
5360 Hwy E 160
Pagosa Springs CO 81147-0238
970/264-5482

At the resort:

At resort or within 15 minutes:

Fireside Inn

Fireside Inn, built in 1996, has 15 modern housekeeping cabins on seven acres beside the San Juan River. A lot of love and care went into designing and decorating the cabins, with a western decor which includes branded walls, old horse tack hanging up, homemade Latilla bedposts and handmade quilts on the walls — its truly the western experience your looking for. Each cabin has a living room, one or two bedrooms, fully equipped kitchens, gas fireplaces, cable televisions and phones. The two bedroom cabins sleep up to six people, while the one bedroom cabins sleep four people. All kitchen utensils and linens are furnished.

The Inn offers horse corrals, and guests are welcome to bring their horses with them. The San Juan River offers wonderful trout fishing. In summer the area has something for the entire family with horseback rides, Indian ruins , whitewater rafting, tennis, hiking and mountain biking. In fall watch the aspen turn golden or hunt for big game. Winter offers downhill skiing at Wolf Creek Ski Area only 25 minutes away, cross country skiing, sleigh rides, snowmobile trails and tours , and ice fishing. After a day of outdoor adventure enjoy the hot tub. For your convenience there is a community washer and dryer.

The rate for a one bedroom cabin is $90.00 for up to four people. The rate for a two bedroom cabin which sleeps up to six people is $110.00. Ask about their ski packages. Pets including your horse are welcome.

Location: A quarter mile east of Highway junction 160 and 84 on Highway 160 near milepost 145.

15 Cabins with Kitchens
15 Fireplaces

Phones in Rooms
All Non-Smoking Units
Elevation: 7100
Credit Cards: VMAD
2 people a night. Call for Rates
Open: All Year

Betty & Ken Santo, Owners
PO Box 1614
1600 E Hwy 160
Pagosa Springs CO 81147
970/264-9204 & Fax

At the resort:

At resort or within 15 minutes:

Pagosa Riverside Cabins & Campground

On the scenic, majestic banks of the San Juan River, Pagosa Riverside is away from the highway and offers a peaceful and quiet vacation. Bring your own bedding to the camper cabins under tall shade trees. One cabin has a kitchenette (bring your own utensils), a bathroom and sleeps 5. Hot showers, clean restrooms and a laundry are on-site. Evenings are quiet and cool, the perfect accompaniment to days of sunshine and adventures.

Fish near your cabin for trout in the river. Amenities include paddle boats for cruising the private pond, a game room for the kids, a swimming pool for refreshing dips and a store for your convenience. There's plenty of northern New Mexico and Colorado to see from here. It's only an hour to the famous Durango-Silverton or the Cumbres & Toltec Scenic Narrow Gauge Railroads. There's great fishing on the San Juan River. Indulge in nearby horseback rides, explore the Indian ruins at Chimney Rock or whitewater raft, play tennis, hunt, hike or mountain bike. The therapeutic Pagosa Hot Springs are less than 5 minutes away.

Ask about the RV sites, and the weekly and monthly rates.

Location: 1.5 miles east of Pagosa Springs on Highway 160, near milepost 146.

1 Cabin with Kitchen
2 Camper Cabins

Pay Phone(s)
Non-Smoking Units Available
Recreation Room
Elevation: 7100
Credit Cards: VMD
2 people a night: $24 - $28
Open: 4/1 to 11/15

Ron & Julia Jones, Owners
PO Box 268
2270 E Hwy 160
Pagosa Springs CO 81147-0268
970/264-5874 & Fax

At the resort:

At resort or within 15 minutes:

Piedra River Resort

Snug among tall pines on banks above the Piedra River, and surrounded by the San Juan National Forest, these cozy, secluded log cabins come with linens, dishes and cooking utensils. Pick between housekeeping, with kitchenettes, and non-housekeeping cabins.

The cowboy cookout area is a short horse ride up the trail, where you'll be served delicious food cooked outdoors during the breakfast and supper rides. Fish, ride horses or just relax at Piedra River Resort. The resort offers daily summer horseback rides, longer pack trips, fishing trips, plus hunting and outfitting in season (licenses #102). You'll journey along the river that Anasazi Indians once roamed and cowboys still ride. Your hosts, who have lived here since 1967, can direct you to excellent hiking trails, fishing holes and other "inside" secrets of this Rocky Mountain region. Charter a fishing boat to catch kokanee salmon and northern pike — the resort owns a 20-foot cabin cruiser on Lake Navajo, 30 minutes away on the Colorado-New Mexico border.

Location: 20 miles west of Pagosa Springs and 35 miles east of Durango, on Highway 160, near milepost 121.

BACKCOUNTRY
OUTFITTERS
INC.

6 Cabins with Kitchens

Lobby Phone
Elevation: 6500
Credit Cards: VMD
2 people a night: $36 - $50
Open: 4/15 to 11/15

David & Nancy Guilliams, Owners
PO Box 4190
Hwy 160 and Piedra River
Pagosa Springs CO 81157-4190
970/731-4630
800/898-2006

At the resort:

At resort or within 15 minutes:

Sportsman's Supply Camper Cabins & Campground

In the San Juan National Forest north of Pagosa Springs, Sportsman's is far enough from town to feel secluded. The campground is 18 miles north of U.S. 160 on Piedra Road, the first 6.2 miles of which are paved and the rest are gravel. Vacation under the shade of fragrant ponderosa pines in cabins or the rental travel trailer. You'll find comfort at the edge of the wilderness here.

Join in the weekly pot luck suppers to meet your fellow vacationers. Satellite television and a recreation hall are among the camp amenities. Sportsman's boasts badminton, horseshoes, hiking trails and volleyball. Anglers will want to try their lines in the nearby Williams Creek Lake or the many nearby rivers and streams, while others may want to hunt in season. Bring your own or rent a horse here for a ride to alpine meadows and beaver ponds. Crazy Horse Outfitters on-site provide high country adventures, guided horseback rides, and fishing and hunting trips into the wilderness. Take the time to explore the nearby Weminuche Wilderness where the back country splendor has remained un-tarnished by civilization.

RV, tent sites, and one on-site trailer are also available.

Location: In the San Juan National Forest, 18 miles north of Highway 160 on Piedra Road, the first 6.25 miles are paved, the rest are gravel.

5 Camper Cabins
1 Woodstove
Central Woodstove
Central Campfire Area

Pay Phone(s)
Non-Smoking Units Available
Recreation Room
Elevation: 8100
Credit Cards: VMAD
2 people a night: $35 - $55
Open: 5/15 to 11/15

Karen Benson and Bonnie & Don Reed, Owners
2095 Taylor Lane
Pagosa Springs CO 81147
970/731-2300
970/731-9600 Fax

At the resort:

At resort or within 15 minutes:

Pawnee National Grasslands

Including Stoneham — Map: B-22

Without a doubt, your visit to Colorado wouldn't be complete without a drive on the Pawnee Pioneer Scenic and Historic Byway. The 125-mile route passes through the agricultural towns of Sterling, Stoneham, and Raymer on your way to the **Pawnee National Grasslands.** Once there, explore the subtle diversity of the prairie, in contrast to the majestic mountains. Become acquainted with the Pawnee Buttes —300' sandstone towers that have survived years of erosion in the prairie. These landmarks, a long since familiar site to the Pawnee and the occasional marauding band of Cheyenne Indians, have yielded many important fossil finds. Camels, rhinoceri & prehistoric animals fossils have all been found there. The geographical characteristics of the Buttes also indicate that the land you are standing on was once underwater. The area, previously composed of old farms ruined by the dust bowls of the 1930's, is now gradually returning to its original grass cover supporting hundreds of species of wildlife and grazing animals. Hike or mountain bike the four-mile trail to the Buttes, or for something less rugged try Jackson Lake State Park in nearby Fort Morgan for fishing, pleasure boating, water skiing and sailing. Come experience the solitude and peace of the prairie. Watch the elk and buffalo roam the plains again, where the silence is broken only by the wind and the melodious sounds of songbirds and raptures.

Fun Things To Do

- Jackson Lake State Park (970) 645-2551
- Pawnee National Grasslands Office (970) 353-5004

Elk Echo Ranch Bed & Breakfast

Elk Echo Ranch offers old west hospitality near the Colorado/Nebraska border. Relax in the newly-built, contemporary log home's beautiful, theme-oriented guest rooms, all with private baths. Pheasant Landing has a queen-size bed, a whirlpool tub and private balcony. Elk Escape features two king beds and a sofa hide-a-bed in the family room with large trapezoid windows overlooking the elk pasture. The Lodge Pole offers exposed-beam log interior, Indian decor, and two queen beds in this main floor, wheelchair accessible room. The Buffalo Bungalow is at the garden level, featuring the largest whirlpool tub, queen bed and full-sized futon with private patio viewing of the elk pasture. Complimentary VCRs and wildlife videos are available to ranch guests. The adventurous might want to try a summer night in the teepee! Start your day off with a scrumptious home cooked breakfast featuring specialties from family recipes. Dinner can be arranged with advance reservations for an additional charge.

Located in the Pawnee National Grasslands region, Elk Echo is a private ranch on nearly 2,000 acres where a herd of 400 elk and buffalo roam. This area is superb for hiking and bird watching. Your stay includes an elk plus buffalo tour as well, so be sure to bring your camera. This premier elk ranch boasts viewing big bulls in hard antler in the winter, a chance to witness the velvet stage of antler growth in the spring and new born elk calves playing throughout the summer. In the fall, listen for the spine chilling mating calls of the bull's bugles. Come for pheasant and quail hunting from October to April.

Ask about the group rates and reduced rates during the week.

Location: Five miles north of Colorado Highway 14 and 71, on County Road 155.

4 Lodging Rooms
Central Fireplace

Lobby Phone
Bed & Breakfast Available
All Non-Smoking in Units
Recreation Room
Elevation: 4700
Credit Cards: VM
2 people a night: $89 - $99
Open: All Year

Craig & Noreen McConnell, Owners
47490 WCR 155
Stoneham CO 80754
970/735-2426

At the resort:

At resort or within 15 minutes:

Peak-to-Peak Scenic Highway Area

Including Allenspark, Boulder, Eldora & Nederland
Map: D-14, D-16 & E-14

This highway, which stretches along the Front Range from Central City to Estes Park, highlights Colorado's mountain scenery, history and culture. Railroad buffs will want to drive up the grade of the Rollins Pass railroad, or seek out the route of the Switzerland Trail narrow-gauge to the small towns where Colorado's first gold strikes were made. The Central City and Black Hawk mining area boomed during the late 19th century. Its gold helped build the mansions of Denver as well as its own glamorous historic hotels and saloons. Recently, many of the old hotels and saloons have been restored as limited-stakes gambling casinos. To the north, you'll pass through **Eldora** and **Nederland**, old gold mining towns that produced tungsten through the 1940s. This small mountain town was the supply center to the silver camp of Caribou nearby which is now a ghost town. Down the canyon from Nederland is the university town of **Boulder** featuring the Boulder Reservoir where you can swim, sail and water ski during the summer months. Hiking, mountain biking and cross-country trails abound in and around town. In addition to all the culture and art events this college town offers, Boulder is becoming known for its many coffee shops, bagel bakeries and micro-breweries. Back up the canyon, passing by Boulder Falls and heading north on the highway again, you'll pass by **Ward**, an old gold camp that now harbors those who crave peace and quiet. **Allenspark** is along the scenic route into Estes Park, where majestic Longs Peak presents its most dramatic face. This highway is particularly popular during the fall when the aspen turn golden under crisp blue skies.

Fun Things to Do

- Boulder Reservoir (303) 441-3468
- Colorado Shakespeare Festival (303) 492-0554
- Eldora Ski Area (303) 440-8700
- Eldorado Artesian Springs 9303) 499-1316
- Eldorado Springs State park (303) 494-3943
- Flatirons Golf Course (303) 442-7851
- Leanin' Tree Museum of Western Art (303) 530-1442
- Nederland Visitor Center (303) 258-3575
- Twin Peaks Municipal Golf Course (303) 651-8401
- University of Colorado Museum (303) 492-6892

Allenspark Lodge & Crystal Springs Cabins

This classic, high-mountain bed and breakfast lodge is set in the flower-starred village of Allenspark. The three-story, hand-hewn log lodge, constructed of native stone and ponderosa pine, offers the time and the place to create sweet memories to last a lifetime. The lodge's spacious front porch welcomes you to step into the golden-hued, log entry, relax before a crackling fire, enjoy the candlelight. Four of the comfortable, rooms have private baths with a shower or a big tub. The other 8 rooms, all homey and each different (some with sinks, some not) have access to a large, private shower. All rooms have mountain views and are furnished with original, handmade pine furniture from the 1930s. The Hideaway Room which has decorator linens, lace-edged pillows, a big brass bed and mountain views from windows on three sides has a bear-claw footed bath and fireplace–prefect for a romantic weekend or honeymoon. Or stay in the newly decorated cabins for an especially private visit. Your hosts offer warm hospitality, creating a special magic to make your stay unforgettable.

Relax your muscles in a private hot tub or enjoy the quiet game room and eclectic library. Find something special for someone special in the small gift shop on-site. The Allenspark Lodge serves delicious continental breakfasts and lunches, featuring robust and fresh bread along with wine and imported beer. In nearby Estes Park, explore the wonders of Rocky Mountain National Park.

Ideal for small weddings of 75 people. Reservations are strongly recommended.

Location: Off of Route 7 in Allenspark, near milepost 15.

3 Cabins with Kitchens
13 Lodging Rooms
1 Fireplace
Central Fireplace

Pay Phone(s)
Bed & Breakfast Available
All Non-Smokingin Units
Recreation Room
Elevation: 8500
Credit Cards: VM
2 people a night: $50 - $90
Open: All Year

Mike & Becky Osmun, Owners
PO Box 247
184 Main
Allenspark CO 80510-0247
303/747-2552

At the resort:

At resort or within 15 minutes:

Alps Boulder Canyon Inn

The Alps is a historic, luxury country inn located 2 miles from downtown Boulder in scenic Boulder Canyon. Twelve elegant guest rooms are furnished with down comforters, period antiques and include a sitting area, a deluxe bathroom and a Victorian fireplace. Several rooms feature double whirlpool tubs, two even have old-fashioned, claw-foot tubs. All rooms have unforgettable mountain views and many have private porches. Formerly a stagecoach stop, a bordello and a gateway for miners, the inn has played an historical role in the pioneer history of this area. The entire inn is non-smoking.

Enjoy the gourmet breakfasts, afternoon teas and nightly desserts included with your stay in the dining room. Relax in the lounge's social area, furnished in the warm and homey style of the Adirondacks. Venture outside to roam the 25 acres of beautiful forest on the local hiking and bike trails. The property adjoins the Boulder County Parks and Open Space Betasso Preserve, a 715 acre park featuring miles of scenic hiking trails, picnic and camping areas as well as fantastic cross-country skiing. Located at the very edge of the Front Range of the Rocky Mountains, from the inn you can head down the canyon to Boulder or Denver for shopping, cultural events and sight-seeing year round. Take a leisurely drive up the canyon to view the snow-capped peaks of the great divide, visit old mining towns, drive the Peak-to-Peak Scenic Highway, or hike to high mountain passes, glaciers and lakes. If you want to relax, fish in Boulder Creek and bask in the scenic beauty of the high canyon walls.

All reservations require deposit equal to one night's stay.

Location: In Boulder Canyon (Highway 119), near milepost 38.

12 Lodging Rooms
2 Fireplaces
Central Fireplace

Room Phones
Bed & Breakfast Available
All Non-Smoking in Units
Recreation Room
Elevation: 5700
Credit Cards: VMAD
2 people a night: Call for Rates
Open: All Year

John & Jeannine Vanderhart, Owners
PO Box 18298
38619 Boulder Canyon Dr
Boulder CO 80308-8298
303/444-5445
800/414-2577
303/444-5522 Fax

At the resort:

At resort or within 15 minutes:

Arapaho Ranch Cabins

Pleasantly situated in a valley between Nederland and Eldora, on the Middle Boulder Creek, Arapaho Ranch is in Roosevelt National Forest. The cabins are 0.5 miles inside the gate, away from the highway. Most cabins are along the creek, while others are close by with a panoramic mountain view. Featuring roofed porches and rustic charm, each cabin has two to four bedrooms with double beds and plenty of blankets and pillows, gas heat, a bathroom, refrigerator, stove and equipment for light housekeeping. *Bring or rent sheets, pillowcases and towels.*

Kids will like the playground, while groups can participate in activities in the new recreation hall. Be on the lookout for deer, racoons or beavers that occasionally meander through the ranch. Everyone likes Monday night cookout. Fishing enthusiasts will appreciate the exclusive fishing rights to Middle Boulder Creek. Hike or drive to the many high mountain lakes for more alpine casting. While hiking up to the Continental Divide, notice the many beautiful and unfrequented pine dells, meadows and scenic points. If you're in the mood for old-time casino gambling, Arapaho Ranch is an easy drive from Central City.

Location: 17 miles west of Boulder on Highway 119, near milepost 25. Turn off on Eldora Road (County Road 130). Go 1 mile to the gate.

10 Cabins with Kitchens

Lobby Phone
Recreation Room
Elevation: 8200
No credit cards
2 people a night: $60
Open: 5/1 to 10/1

Kayla Evans & Maryanne Flynn, Managers
1250 Eldora Rd
Nederland CO 80466-9525
303/258-3405

At the resort:

At resort or within 15 minutes:

Goldminer Hotel, Rocky Ledge Cabin & The Nederhaus

The 1897 Goldminer Hotel is the centerpiece of the Eldora National Historic District. Stay in one of the fully modernized, Gold-Rush style rooms or suites, some with private bathrooms and fireplaces in this historic bed and breakfast. Rooms with a large screen television and direct-dial phones are available. All rooms include a delicious breakfast to start your day right. The "Rocky Ledge" cabin sleeps six and has a full kitchen, a fireplace, a patio and an old-fashioned bathtub on legs. The Nederhaus is a modern hotel with suites, kitchens, rooms and conference facilities. Rooms are furnished with antiques and have the modern conveniences of cable television and direct-dial phones.

Depending on the seasons, take back-country jeep, cross-country ski, snow cat and horseback tours. Eldora Mountain Resort is nearby and offers downhill skiing the whole family can afford. Ride the free shuttle to the limited-stakes gambling casinos of Central City and Black Hawk. The Goldminer and Nederhaus are adjacent to the Indian Peaks Wilderness, where you can hike to the Continental Divide. The bustling town of Boulder is only 30 minutes away. At night, soak your road-weary muscles in the communal hot tub.

Location: Off of Highway 119, near milepost 25.

1 Cabin with Kitchen
5 Lodging Rooms
12 Motel Rooms
1 Fireplace
Central Fireplace
Central Woodstove

Room Phones
Bed & Breakfast Available
Non-Smoking Units Available
Recreation Room
Elevation: 8600
Credit Cards: VMA
2 people a night: $75 - $149
Open: All Year

Carol Rinderknecht & Scott Bruntjen, Owners
601 Klondyke Ave
Eldora CO 80466-9542
303/258-7770
800/422-4629
303/258-3850 Fax
303/444-4705 Denver local

At the resort:

At resort or within 15 minutes:

Pikes Peak Area

Including Chipeta Park, Colorado Springs, Cripple Creek, Lake George, Manitou Springs & Woodland Park — Map: I-17, I-16, I-17 & I-15

Catch the excitement of Pikes Peak purple mountain majesty and see why Katharine Lee Bates was inspired to write "American the Beautiful" when she stood on the mountains overlooking **Colorado Springs**. From a ride on the Pikes Peak Cog Railway to the dramatic 14,110' summit, to the sunny charm of an afternoon hike through an alpine forest near **Manitou Springs**, the Colorado Springs area offers a myriad of activities. Visit the out-of-this-world natural red rock formations of the Garden of the Gods or tour the U.S. Air Force Academy. Explore Old Colorado City, the original site of Colorado Springs, where restored 1800s architecture made it a registered National Historic District. Fish for Rocky Mountain trout and enjoy the fresh, pine-scented air of this high-country region. One of the most famous towns in this area is **Cripple Creek**, nestled in an extinct volcano crater riddled with gold fields in a remote region on the backside of Pikes Peak. The town and its surroundings eventually produced $600 million in gold. Cripple Creek's limited stakes casino gambling offer the opportunity to strike it rich. **Lake George** was founded in 1887 a few miles from the dam at the mouth of Eleven Mile Canyon. Six miles east, Florissant Fossil Beds National Monument was once a raging volcanic field whose lava and ash preserved insects, leaves and fish. Numerous fossils were discovered in 1874 — the monument was established in 1969, encompassing ancient Lake Florissant which existed some 38 million years ago. At the nearby 7,000-acre Dome Rock State Wildlife Area, see Rocky Mountain bighorn sheep, deer, elk, bobcats, coyotes, eagles and wild turkeys. Eleven Mile State Recreation Area, 9.5 miles from Lake George, offers excellent fishing plus boating, sailing and hunting.

Fun Things to Do

- American Adventure Expeditions (800) 288-0675
- Broadmoor Golf Club, Colorado Springs (719) 577-5790
- Cheyenne Mountain Zoo & Will Rogers Shrine (719) 475-9555
- Cowhand Western Wear & High Country Cattle Drives (800) 748-3837
- Cripple Creek District Museum (719) 689-2634
- Cripple Creek Mountain Estate Golf Course Summer (719) 689-7850
- Eleven Mile State Park (719) 748-3401
- Florissant Fossil Beds National Monument (719) 748-3253
- Flying W Ranch (800) 232-FLYW or (719) 598-4000
- Garden of the Gods (719) 578-6640
- Mueller State Park (719) 687-2366
- Mule Creek Outfitters (800) 289-4868, (719) 748-3398
- Pikes Peak Highway (719) 684-9383
- Rainbow Falls Trout Fishing & Stable (719) 687-9074
- U.S. Olympic Complex (719) 578-4644/4618
- United States Air Force Academy (719) 333-8723

Camper Cabins & Campground at Woodland Park

In the mountains close to Colorado Springs and all its attractions, the Cabins at Woodland Park are in lots of shade and have great views. Bring your own bedding and supplies to one of the eight camper cabins nestled on a hillside, surrounded by aspen trees. A laundromat, restrooms, and clean, hot showers are on-site. You're welcome to enjoy a campfire with the supplied firewood. An family-oriented park, this resort also caters to seniors with special senior discounts.

Relax in heated swimming pool, play 18-hole miniature golf or on playground and in the video game room. Evening summer activities include chuckwagon suppers and free nightly movies. Chow down on a hearty, chuckwagon breakfast before setting out to fish, four-wheel drive or horseback ride nearby. Rent a mountain bike and explore the bike trail beginning at the entrance to the campground. Shuttle vans run to historic Cripple Creek's casinos. Ask about the discount casino coupons.

Teepees, RV sites, an outdoor, group meeting area and group tent sites are also available.

Location: Half a mile north from the intersection of Highways 24 and 67. Look for the sign on the left-hand side of the road through the trees. Turn left and drive three blocks west on Bowman Avenue.

6 Camper Cabins

Pay Phone(s)
Recreation Room
Elevation: 8500
Credit Cards: VMD
2 people a night: $30
Open: All Year

Craig & Karen Stewart, Owners
PO Box 725
1125 West Bowman Ave
Woodland Park CO 80866-0725
719/687-7575
800/808-CAMP (2267) Reserv. Only

At the resort:

At resort or within 15 minutes:

Cripple Creek Gold Camper Cabins & Campground

Just around the bend from the 'Old West' town of Cripple Creek and next to Pike National Forest, these camper cabins are a great way to visit the former gold-mining town which has been newly revitalized by casino gambling. Bring your own bedding and cooking supplies. Firewood is furnished for a fee. This is a family-oriented resort with nearby hot showers and a laundromat.

On-site amenities include a playground with horseshoes. Hike or horseback ride in the nearby national forest. Guest horses are welcome to join you. Elk, deer, mountain sheep and antelope can be seen from time to time just short distances your camper cabin. A visit to historic Cripple Creek is a must. Museums, mine tours, train rides and gambling casinos abound in this living legend of the old American West.

Large, rustic RV sites among aspen trees are also available.

Location: 6 miles north of Cripple Creek on Highway 67, near milepost 58,12 miles south of the Divide.

2 Camper Cabins

Lobby Phone
Elevation: 10200
No credit cards
2 people a night: $18
Open: 5/1 to 10/31

William & Linda Buckhanan, Owners
PO Box 601
12654 Hwy 67 N
Cripple Creek CO 80813-0601
719/689-2342

At the resort:

At resort or within 15 minutes:

Cripple Creek Hospitality House

This is truly a unique accommodation — the 17 guest rooms are in an award winning, restored Victorian county hospital which has been converted into a gracious guest house. The hospital building was built in 1901 to house the medical practitioners. In 1963 the Mackins purchased and restored it to its original glory. Set amidst the mountain splendor of the Pikes Peak region and next to the city limits of Cripple Creek, the charming, red-brick hospital with sunshine yellow columns takes you back to Teller County's glory days. These rooms range from small, old-fashioned singles with an antique corner washbowl to large, family units with full private baths. All rooms have color televisions. You can stay in the maternity ward or Emergency room. The Outpatient corner room is huge with several windows, 2 queen-size beds and a private bath. In Ward Two, there are two rooms. One is the Intensive Care with a queen-size bed and private bath; the other is the Lying In a corner room with a queen-size bed, private bath and enclosed private porch. There are hospital antiques scattered throughout facility.

Facilities include a laundromat, children's playground, and a family recreation room with cable television (Disney and Cinamax) and pool table. Enjoy the enclosed solarium, hot tub and on-site beauty shop. In the adjoining 3 million acres of Pike National Forest, you'll find plenty to do from fishing and horseback riding to hiking. And, of course, Cripple Creek offers every thing from slot machines to live theater. It's an easy stroll or shuttle to the downtown museums and casinos.

There are RV and tent sites adjacent to the guest house. Indoor and outdoor group meeting areas are available. Reservations are recommended. Pets are allowed on a leash.

Location: West on Bennett Ave. to "B" St., north 6 blocks.

17 Lodging Rooms

Pay Phone(s)
Recreation Room
Elevation: 9500
Credit Cards: VMD
2 people a night: Call for Rates
Open: 4/1 to 10/15

Steve & Bonnie Mackin, Operators
Box 577
600 N "B" St
Cripple Creek CO 80813-0577
719/689-2513
800/500-2513

At the resort:

At resort or within 15 minutes:

Eleven Mile Motel Cabins

Surrounded by the Pike National Forest, Eleven Mile Motel Cabins are located in the town of Lake George. Some of these modern, comfortable log cabins have kitchens. Cabins range from one to three bedroom. All feature television, carpets, modern bathrooms with showers and great views of the Tarryall Mountain Range. The rustic furnishings in combination living room and bedroom cabins are complete with a modern kitchen. Cabins sleep from 2 to 6 people. Cook up your fresh catch on the grill and dine on the picnic table right outside your door. Enjoy the convenience of private parking beside your cabin.

The Pike National Forest, only 0.25 miles away, is known for its scenic beauty. Possibilities for horseback riding, hiking, biking, stream and lake fishing and rock hunting here are endless. Only 22 miles from Cripple Creek, you make an easy day trip to its historic buildings and casinos. Fish in the South Platte River or in nearby Eleven Mile, Spinny, Tarryall and Antero reservoirs. Visit the famous Royal Gorge and the nearby Florissant Fossil Beds National Monument. Colorado Springs and its many attractions are less than an hour away.

Location: In town on Highway 24, near milepost 267.

6 Cabins with Kitchens
4 cabins without Kitchens

Room Phones
Elevation: 8100
Credit Cards: VMAD
2 people a night: $40 - $60
Open: All Year

Tom & Pat Brown, Owners
Box 146
38122 Hwy 24
Lake George CO 80827
719/748-3931

At the resort:

At resort or within 15 minutes:

Green Willow Motel Cottages

Cross the bridge on Fountain Creek and discover clean, rustic-style modern cottages at Green Willow Motel — a family business since 1953. All cottages have refrigerators, cable television and showers; some have tubs and six have equipped kitchens. All cottages have double beds. Light daily maid service provided. The Heruth's create a welcoming atmosphere with spacious grounds with trees, flowers and well landscaped lawn areas complete with views of magnificent Pikes Peak. Chairs on each porch allow a relaxing view of the scenery. A stream runs right through the resort. The creekside picnic area has chairs, picnic tables, grills and a swing set. There's even an adult swing for those young at heart. Daily morning coffee is served for your enjoyment.

Explore the hiking trail that begins at the back of the property through the park and into Garden of the Gods. Royal Gorge and Cripple Creek are only an hour's drive away, or you can take a relaxing, sightseeing bus tour. Walk from your cottage to Manitou Springs city parks or the Olympic-sized pool with kiddie-pool and hot tub. Visit the nearby quaint shops and restaurants. Green Willow offers guests old fashioned, country hospitality and friendship.

Prices vary depending on the time of year. There is a nominal charge for baby beds, cots and roll-aways. There is a campground next door. Tour pickup is available from here. Pets are allowed with permission. Call for information or email at: greenwilow@aol.com

Location: Within city limits; on a bus and trolley line. Off of Highway 24, on Manitou Avenue (business Highway 24).

6 Cabins with Kitchens
8 cabins without Kitchens

Pay Phone(s)
Elevation: 6450
Credit Cards: VMAD
2 people a night: $35 - $60
Open: 4/15 to 10/31

Ron & Bev Heruth, Owners/ Operators
328 Manitou Ave
Manitou Springs CO 80829-2506
719/685-9997
719/685-1645
E-mail: greenwilow@aol.Comm

At the resort:

At resort or within 15 minutes:

Historic El Colorado Lodge

Enjoy the tranquil mountain beauty and adventure of the Pikes Peak Region in the family-owned and operated Historic El Colorado Lodge. The lodge is the oldest continually-operated business in Manitou Springs. On four acres of rolling lawns dotted with mature Colorado blue spruce trees, the resort has a distinct southwestern flavor. The resort features adobe-style, modernized "casitas" that sleep from one to six people and have one or two bedrooms. All cabins have heat, air-conditioning, color cable television, direct-dial telephones and fireplaces. Some cabins offer kitchens and beamed ceilings.

Picnic with the whole family on the patio after a round of basketball and shuffleboard. Pleasant amenities include the largest outdoor, heated swimming pool in Manitou Springs, a pavilion, outdoor barbecue grills and a children's playground. Historic El Colorado Lodge is centrally located for all Pikes Peak Region attractions and sights such as Garden of the Gods, Pikes Peak Cog Railway, Cliff Dwellings Museum and the Buffalo Bill Museum. A short drive away are Seven Falls, Cripple Creek and the Cheyenne Mountain Zoo.

Your hosts will help you make reservations at area attractions. Family reunions are a specialty.

Location: Off of Highway 24, near milepost 299, on Manitou Avenue.

9 Cabins with Kitchens
17 cabins without Kitchens
21 Fireplaces

Room Phones
Non-Smoking Units Available
Elevation: 6035
Credit Cards: VMAD
2 people a night: $34 - $58
Open: All Year

Wally & Stephanie Hornik, Owners
23 Manitou Ave
Manitou Springs CO 80829
719/685-5485
800/782-2246

At the resort:

At resort or within 15 minutes:

Historic Ute Pass Cabins & Motel

Historic Ute Pass Cabins is your gateway to Colorado. Cabins sleep 2 to 11 people with color cable television and air conditioning. The family-sized, equipped kitchen in the cabins feel like home. The motel, originally built in 1895, has been recently expanded and restored decorated with antique furniture. Each room is different and some are connected. Fall asleep to the soothing sounds of the ever-gurgling mountain stream meandering through the resort. The outdoor picnic area borders Fountain Creek, where you can dine outdoors amid scenic splendor.

A laundromat is available for your convenience. Explore historic Manitou Springs on a walking tour. Visit many of the sights of the Pikes Peak area nearby. Drive Ute Pass to the gambling casinos at Cripple Creek. Fish in Fountain Creek right on the property or at other nearby mountain streams and lakes. Meals are available one block away.

Your hosts will be happy to help you with local Pikes Peak area attraction tour reservations. There is group meeting area for family reunions.

Location: In Manitou Springs on business route 24, one block from downtown.

4 Cabins with Kitchens
6 Motel Rooms

Room Phones
Non-Smoking Units Available
Elevation: 6400
Credit Cards: VMAD
2 people a night: $35 - $55
Open: All Year

Helena & Jerzy Gudel & Zbigniew & Irena Konaszewski, Owners
1132 Manitou Ave
Manitou Springs CO 80829
719/685-5171
800/845-9762
719/685-0529 Fax

At the resort:

At resort or within 15 minutes:

Mule Creek Outfitters & M Lazy C Ranch

The M Lazy C Ranch is an actual working cattle ranch, homesteaded in the early 1900s by the Thatcher Family. The original house and out buildings, with a few added modern conveniences, still exist to provide an 'Old West' setting for guests. Stay in individual log cabins, complete with antiques and woodburning stoves. Home cooked meals are served daily, family style in the main ranch house.

The ranch offers a variety of activities including horseback rides, chuck wagon meals, hay rides, carriage rides, fishing, overnight pack trips into the wilderness, cattle drives, cross-country skiing and sleigh rides in the winter. Hunters will want to join in for big game hunting in season. Pack trips venture into the Gore Wilderness Range or the Lost Creek Wilderness. More locally, visit historic Cripple Creek, South Park City Museum, Royal Gorge and Florissant Fossil Beds. Anglers will find plenty of fishing spots to choose from with Eleven Mile, Spinney and Tarryall Reservoirs a short distance away.

Although only ten to twelve overnight guests can be accommodated in the cabins, your hosts can provide for larger groups up to 200 in the authentic Indian teepees and outfitters' wall tents. For large groups, choose from western reenactments, rodeos, picnics and chuck wagon meals as entertainment.

Location: 5 miles west of Lake George, on Highway 24 between milepost 260-261, on right is a sign M Lazy C Ranch, make a right and go 0.75 miles. Approximately 35 miles west of Colorado Springs.

3 cabins without Kitchens
3 Woodstoves
Central Campfire Area

Lobby Phone
Bed & Breakfast Available
All Non-Smoking in Units
Recreation Room
Elevation: 8300
Credit Cards: VMA
2 people a night: Call for Rates
Open: All Year

Randy & Brenda Myers, Owners
PO Box 461
Lake George CO 80827-0461
719/748-3398
800/289-4868
719/748-3250 Fax

At the resort:

At resort or within 15 minutes:

Pinehaven Lodges & Red Stone Castle

These lodges rest literally in the shadow of majestic Pikes Peak. The beautiful Ute Pass area stretches out in both directions, furnishing a constantly changing and always restful scene of unmatched beauty. These clean and comfortable cabins, located in Chipita Park and Cascade, are unique and can accommodate five to seven people each. All have fireplaces, living rooms, bedrooms, family rooms, televisions, basic kitchens and decks or patios with wonderful views. One luxury bed and breakfast suite is also available. Red Stone Castle was built in the 1890s by William Davis, this magnificently restored Victorian luxury bed and breakfast in Manitou Springs is one of Colorado's finest historic residences. The Castle is on 20 acres overlooking the National Historic District of Manitou Springs. The elegant rooms of the Castle offer a memorable experience for individuals, couples and small families.

The lodges' close proximity to Green Mountain Falls and Manitou Springs allows for hiking, jogging, fishing, horseback riding, swimming, golfing, bicycling and tennis. Dine at nearby restaurants. Pinehaven Lodges is only 20 minutes from Colorado Springs and near to most Pikes Peak area attractions.

Nearly all reservations are weekly and made from Saturday to Saturday or Sunday to Sunday mid-May through Labor Day. A 5 night minimum stay is required in the summer. Pets are not allowed in either facility.

Location: Pinehaven Lodges are 8 miles west of Manitou Springs on Highway 24. Exit Green Mountain Falls for Chipita Park Road, go left 1.4 miles on Chipita Park Road then left for three miles on Mountain Road. For Red Stone Castle, take Manitou Avenue to Pawnee Avenue and left on Southside Road to the gate.

7 Cabins with Kitchens
7 Fireplaces

Room Phones
Elevation: 7400
No credit cards
2 people a night: Call for Rates
Open: All Year

Cavan-Daly McGrew, Owner
Red Stone Castle
Manitou Springs CO 80829
719/685-5070
719/684-9844

At the resort:

At resort or within 15 minutes:

Rainbow Falls Park

Bring your family to relax at Colorado's first trout hatchery, established in 1871. The cabins overlook 25 acres of crystal-clear lakes and streams, offering a fantastic view of Pikes Peak. Bring your own bedding, cooking utensils and water jugs.

Fry your freshly caught trout for breakfast at your cabin. Best of all, no license required in the stocked ponds! There is a charge per day and fish are weighed in at the store. No catch and release — these are catch and eat fish! The waters are brimming with rainbow, brook, cutthroat, golden and brown trout. Other activities include hatchery tours, hayrides, and a taste of the 'West' with chuckwagon suppers. Guided horseback rides will take you through majestic pine forests and mountain meadows with a view of the towering, north side of Pikes Peak. The more adventurous will want to explore on their mountain bikes or go climbing. A complete fishing store with snacks is also on-site. Discover a Ute Indian cave, explore a gold mine or hike into the Rampart Range.

Reservations are required for chuckwagon breakfasts and dinners. RV and tent sites and an outdoor, group meeting area for family reunions are also available.

Location: West from Colorado Springs on Highway 24 to Woodland Park, north 10 miles on Highway 67, near milepost 87.

2 Cabins with Kitchens
1 Fireplace
Central Campfire Area

Pay Phone(s)
Elevation: 7440
Credit Cards: VMAD
2 people a night: $34 - $59
Open: All Year

Christine & Larry Posik, Owners
PO Box 9062
Woodland Park CO 80866-9062
719/687-9074
719/687-9389 Fax

At the resort:

At resort or within 15 minutes:

Timber Lodge & Twin Bears Creekside Restaurant

Timber Lodge is nestled among the pine trees beside Fountain Creek, in the foothills below stunning Pikes Peak. Choose between separate and duplex cabins, all of which are individually decorated with rustic exteriors and modern knotty pine interiors. All cabins have heating, air conditioning, direct dial phones and cable color television. Courtesy coffee is available for all guests. Ask about the larger units for family vacations. Eleven units have fully equipped kitchenettes and two units have fully equipped, complete kitchens.

The Lodge also offers a playground and heated swimming pool from Memorial Day to Labor Day. Picnic and barbecue areas are available for everyone. Close to all the attractions of Colorado Springs and Manitou Springs, guests can enjoy the Pikes Peak Cog Railroad, river rafting, horseback riding, and the Flying "W" Ranch Dinner and Show. The Twin Bears restaurant, immediately adjacent to the lodge, specializes in steak, prime rib, pasta, seafood and chicken dishes as well as offering a children's menu.

Location: Within city limits; (on the border of Colorado Springs and Manitou Springs) on a bus and trolley line. Off of Highway 24, on Colorado Avenue.

TWIN BEARS
Creekside Inn

13 Cabins with Kitchens
12 cabins without Kitchens

Room Phones
Elevation: 5500
Credit Cards: VMAD
2 people a night: $45 - $105
Open: All Year

John & Cindy Hooton, Owners
3627 W Colorado Ave
Colorado Springs CO 80904
719/636-3941
800/448-6762

At the resort:

At resort or within 15 minutes:

Town & Country Resort — The Suites

The Suites at Town & County Resort offer a touch of class for those looking for a quiet mountain retreat in a wooded setting. The eight luxurious, two-bedroom private suites offer a special vacation in Woodland Park. The Suites are well adorned with vaulted beamed ceilings and fans in each room. Amenities include a complimentary breakfast bar, satellite television plus VCRs, kitchenettes with microwaves and coffee makers, free local calls and laundry facilities.

Relax by the wood stove in the lodge with beer or wine that is available as the day winds down and dusk settles over this mountain town. Rent mountain bikes at the resort to explore the backcountry roads. On-site amenities include a new hot tub. Partake in game nights, potlucks and poker nights. Area activities include playing golf and tennis, horseback riding, hiking local trails, cross-country skiing and lake or stream fishing just minutes away. Shuttle vans to the Cripple Creek Casinos are available. In the heart of Pikes Peak country, you'll find the nights cool and quiet, the days sunny, and your vacation perfect.

Ask about the personalized, romantic getaway and golf packages which can be tailored to suit every occasion. Pets are not allowed in the suites. RV sites are also available.

Location: 18 miles west of Colorado Springs on Highway 24, then 2 blocks north on Highway 67 at milepost 77.

8 Cabins with Kitchens
Central Campfire Area

Room Phones
Bed & Breakfast Available
All Non-Smoking in Units
Recreation Room
Elevation: 8500
Credit Cards: VMD
2 people a night: Call for Rates
Open: All Year

Gwen Collins, Manager
PO Box 368
510 N Hwy 67
Woodland Park CO 80866
719/687-9518 & Fax
800/600-0399

At the resort:

At resort or within 15 minutes:

Triple B Western Resort

Adjoining Pike's Peak National Forest with a breathtaking view of "The Peak", Triple B Western Resort has a wholesome family atmosphere. This full service resort has three housekeeping cabins, four non-housekeeping cabins and eight lodge rooms. Two cabins have fireplaces and two have wood-burning stoves to keep you cozy on cool summer nights. There are no phones in the cabins, so you can truly get away from city life.

The resort offers a wide range of outdoor activities to enjoy summer or winter. Horseback rides and chuckwagon dinners are great family activities along with tennis, volleyball, basketball and horseshoes. The playground is a nice area for the kids while mom and dad are lounging at the swimming pool or relaxing in the hot tub. In winter take a sleigh ride, go ice fishing at the nearby reservoir or snowmobile the areas trail. The Ranch House Restaurant offers guests an all-you-can-eat salad bar and a full service menu from specialty hamburgers to steaks and pasta. The area offers hiking and biking in the National forest, tours of the Air Force Academy, gold mining camps, Pikes Peak and many other National attractions.

RV and tents sites are available. Pets are allowed for an additional fee. The indoor and outdoor meeting areas make a nice place to hold a family reunion. There is a Chapel at the resort for weddings, Sunday service or daily Bible studies.

Location: Eighteen miles west of Colorado Springs on Highway 24 to Woodland Park, then three miles north on Highway 67.

6 Cabins with Kitchens
1 Vacation Home
8 Lodging Rooms
32 Beds in Bunk House or Dorm
3 Fireplaces
4 Woodstoves
Central Campfire Area

Pay Phone(s)
Bed & Breakfast Available
All Non-Smoking in Units
Recreation Room
Elevation: 8600
Credit Cards: VMD
2 people a night: $60 - $175
Open: All Year

Ron & Jackie Bullard, Owners
PO Box 5339
27640 N Hwy 67
Woodland Park CO 80866
719/687-8899
719/687-8762 Fax

At the resort:

At resort or within 15 minutes:

Ute Trail River Ranch

Escape to the peaceful and relaxing beauty of a rustic fishing camp tucked into Pike National Forest and the Lost Creek Wilderness. Ute Trail River Ranch has seven cozy, hand-hewn log cabins that sit on the Tarryall River beckoning you to settle in for a quiet retreat. The cabins take you back in time with their woodstoves, antique iron beds and western lodge decor. All are fully furnished from snugly flannel bed linens to coffee pots and mugs. The cabins sleep from two to eight people; some have private baths while others share a convenient shower house (flannel robes are provided in shared bath cabins). Ute Trail River Ranch is a non-smoking facility.

The natural surroundings invite you to slow down and enjoy the tranquil beauty of the forest and the relaxing sounds of the rushing Tarryall River. Streamside fishing is a must, especially since the Ranch was featured on the cable network ESPN's "Fly Fishing America" show. Experience the breath-taking scenery exploring the mountain hiking trails or enjoying a trail ride at a local riding stable year-round. Try a little rock hunting or bird watching.

Reservations are strongly recommended. A confirmation deposit equal to 50%of the entire stay is required. Be sure to inquire about the Ranch's off-season Bed, Breakfast and Dinner packages. Visit their Web site at http://www.owa.com/tarryall/ute.html.

Location: From Highway 24, go 1 mile west of Lake George. Take Tarryall Road north (County Road 77) for 21 miles. From Highway 285 at Jefferson, take County Road 77 south for 21 miles.

7 Cabins with Kitchens
2 Lodging Rooms
2 Woodstoves
Central Fireplace
Central Campfire Area

Lobby Phone
Bed & Breakfast Available
All Non-Smoking in Units
Recreation Room
Elevation: 9000
Credit Cards: VM
2 people a night: $50 - $90
Open: All Year

Debra Baxter & Jim Fagerstrom, Owners
21446 CR 77
Lake George CO 80827-9302
719/748-3015
E-mail: utrr@aol.com

At the resort:

At resort or within 15 minutes:

Wildhorn Inn & RV Park

A small creek runs through the property at this inn just minutes away from the historical gold mines of Cripple Creek. Wildhorn Inn offers newly remodeled log cabins with private baths, kitchenettes and color television.

Pike National Forest surrounds Wildhorn and offers the best in hunting, fishing, mountain biking, hiking and cross-country skiing. Wildlife in this area includes elk, deer, bighorn sheep, black bear, bobcat, mountain lions, wild turkey, blue grouse and other small game. The Lake George area is the trophy fishing capital of Colorado with fishing opportunities in the South and Middle Fork of the Platte River, in Tarryall, Antero, Skagway, Spinney and Eleven Mile Reservoirs. The limited stakes gambling casinos of Cripple Creek are 23 miles away. The historic town has maintained the look of the boom days of yesteryear when gold was plentiful and gambling legal.

RV and tent sites along the creek are also available. Ask about the reduced weekly and monthly rates during the winter.

Location: Off Highway 24, near milepost 265, on Park County Road 90, across from South Platte River. 40 miles west of Colorado Springs.

10 Cabins with Kitchens

Pay Phone(s)
Non-Smoking Units Available
Elevation: 8000
Credit Cards: VMA
2 people a night: $52 - $72
Open: All Year

John & Uvonne Orcutt, Owners
PO Box 220
8966 CR 90
Lake George CO 80827
719/748-3822
719/748-3630 Fax

At the resort:

At resort or within 15 minutes:

Poudre River Canyon Area

Including Bellvue, Livermore and Red Feather Lakes — Map: B-16 & B-14

Designated Colorado's first National Wild and Scenic River in 1986, the **Poudre River Canyon**, also known as Cache la Poudre, is in the midst of the Roosevelt National Forest. In 1840, French trappers camped at the mouth of the canyon west of Fort Collins. A heavy snow fell, forcing them to reduce their load, so they buried their gun powder, or "cache la poudre," along the river's banks. In 1879, settlers built a rough road along the river, soon leading to a steady stream of more cabins. With water rushing east from Rocky Mountain National Park, the crashing Poudre River runs along Highway 14 and is teaming with brown and rainbow trout. Some areas of the river are Wild Trout sections where bait fishing is not allowed. Where there are rapids, there are white water rafting trips — the river is a hot spot with both rafters and kayakers. Accessible from the canyon, the Cache La Poudre Wilderness Area ranges in altitude from 6,000' to 8,600' and its steep, rugged terrain is seldom traveled. Hiking is popular in the Comanche Peak Wilderness, the Rawah Wilderness, the Neota Flat Tops Wilderness and in Roosevelt National Forest. While fishing is the number one draw here, hiking comes in a close second. In the winter, try one of the many cross-country ski trails in the breath-taking high peaks of the Cameron Pass area at 10,276'. **Red Feather Lakes**, a group of 14 lakes, are about 50 miles northwest of Fort Collins. Six of the lakes are open to the public for trout fishing and boating. The scenic beauty of the San Isabel and Roosevelt National Forests boasts abundant wildflowers and wildlife. Look for elk, antelope, mule deer, bears, quail, grouse, mountain lions, big horn sheep and wild turkey. Wintertime brings cross-country skiers, snowmobilers, snowshoers and ice-fishing enthusiasts to the area.

Fun Things to Do

- Glen Echo General Store, Gift Shop(800) 348-2208,
- Roosevelt National Forest Visitors Center (970) 498-2770

Alpine Lodge

Located near Roosevelt National Forest, Alpine Lodge has two modern cabins with kitchens and bathrooms. One cabin sleeps five to six people and the other sleeps three. A third cabin is rustic with a kitchen, but no bathroom and only cold running water. A two-bedroom mobile home that sleeps six is also available. For all cabins, all supplies are provided except groceries. Each cabin has a small black and white television.

A gift and souvenir shop is on the premises or visit the small town of Red Feather Lakes with its few small shops, only 0.5 miles away. A rather unique, high country golf course with old-fashioned sand greens is nearby. Fishing in the six public lakes and nearby streams will keep the anglers happy. Head out on the hiking trails, rent a horse for riding in the forest, or go snowmobiling and cross-country skiing in the winter. Come and enjoy the scenic and unspoiled beauty of the Colorado Rockies!

There is no charge for children under 3 years of age. Ask about there special weekly rate. A deposit is required with advance reservations. They do not except credit cards. RV and campsites are also available.

Location: 45 miles northwest of Fort Collins, about 26 miles west of Highway 287, south 0.5 miles from Red Feather Lakes Village, between Dean Man Road and Red Feather Village.

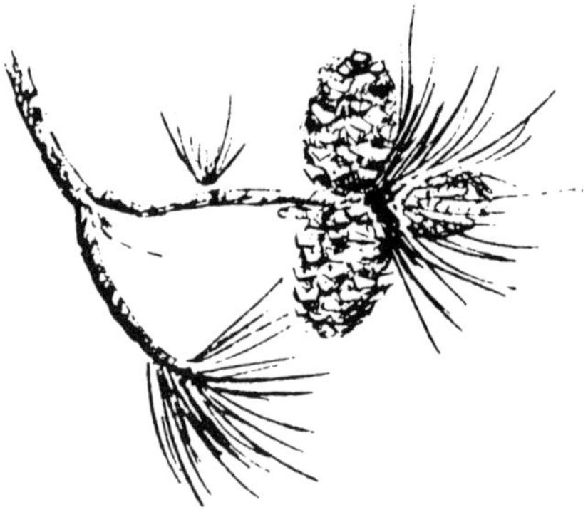

3 Cabins with Kitchens

Pay Phone(s)
Elevation: 8363
No credit cards
2 people a night: $35 - $45
Open: All Year

Emma & Lowell & Tammy Grauberger
PO Box 180
157 Prairie Divide Road
Red Feather Lakes CO 80545
970/881-2933

At the resort:

At resort or within 15 minutes:

Glen Echo Resort

In the heart of Roosevelt National Forest, quiet Glen Echo Resort is on the beautiful Poudre River, Colorado's "trout route." Choose among modern cottages with full kitchens and baths, rustic cabins with kitchens and shared bathroom-shower facilities or family mountain homes with large living rooms and everything but food. All cottages have dishes, cooking supplies, bedding and linens. Several cabins have decks overlooking the Cache La Poudre River where you and your family can relax while listening to the water's murmur. Tall pine trees and a lawn with attractive flower beds abound this landscaped resort.

Amenities include a laundromat, picnic pavilion and a general store with fly fishing and tackle, picnic supplies, sporting goods, groceries and Texaco gasoline. Enjoy the casual, non-smoking, family restaurant with tasty home cooking with made-from-scratch pies and rolls. Be sure and try the restaurant's peanut butter malts and pies. The upscale gift shop has a wide variety of T-shirts and the largest selection of authentic Native American jewelry and crafts in northern Colorado. While browsing, check out the Native American and African wildlife exhibit. Glen Echo sports a playground, recreational hall and horseshoes. Enjoy fishing on Colorado's only designated wild and scenic river near your cabin. Hike the stunning Comanche Peak Wilderness in the Mummy Mountain Range, the Rawah Wilderness or the Neota Flat Tops Wilderness.

Under the same ownership since 1957, you'll find Glen Echo's hosts friendly. Level, shaded, full hookup RV sites are also available.

Location: 41 miles west of Fort Collins on Highway 14, near milepost 90.5.

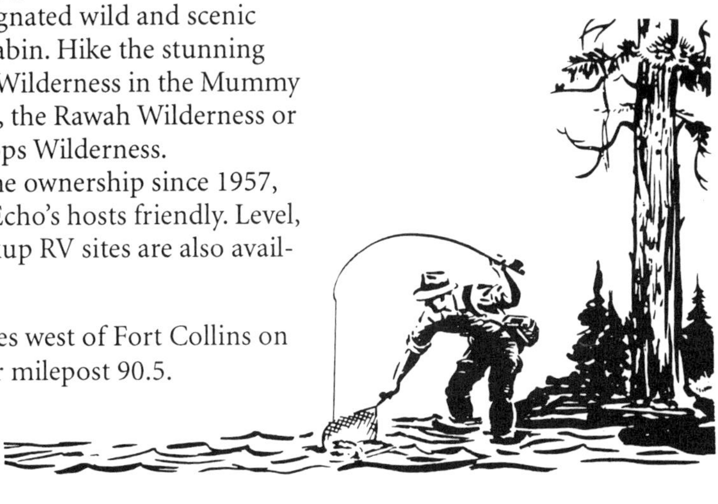

16 Cabins with Kitchens

Pay Phone(s)
Non-Smoking Units Available
Recreation Room
Elevation: 7200
Credit Cards: VM
2 people a night: Call for Rates
Open: 5/10 to 11/1

Sam Shoultz & Ken Matzner, Owners
31503 Poudre Canyon Dr
Bellvue CO 80512-9312
970/881-2208
800/348-2208 Reservations only
970/881-2066 Fax

At the resort:

At resort or within 15 minutes:

Gypsy Terrace Bed & Breakfast

On the banks of the scenic Cache La Poudre River near Bellvue, Gypsy Terrace is a rambling, ranch-style home built in an earlier era and lovingly restored and refurbished. The Loft is reached by an open wooden staircase leading to a warm, sunny room furnished in antique wood furniture and the private bath has a walk-in shower and separate vanity area. French doors open onto a secluded deck from which you can step into the hot tub. The Hideout is tucked away on the main floor and features oak floors, heirloom quilts and country charm. Its private bath has a clawfoot tub and walk-in shower. Gypsy Terrace is smoke, telephone and television free.

Located on the nationally designated wild and scenic Cache La Poudre River, the Gypsy Terrace offers a quiet, comfortable retreat. Included with your stay is a full, hearty breakfast served whenever you'd like. In addition to the private rooms, guests are welcomed to use the spacious, non-smoking great room with its wood stove, the sunlit dining room and the expansive redwood deck. The deck with its hot tub and wonderful views, is also accessible from the Loft room's deck. While this small B & B makes for a peaceful retreat away from it all, it also offers an opportunity for fantastic river fishing. Explore the many wonders of the Poudre Canyon whether you hike it, mountain bike it or cross-country ski it.

One night's deposit is required within 7 days of making the reservation. Ask about their gift certificates.

Location: 25 minutes northwest of downtown Fort Collins, Four miles west of Highway 287 (Poudre Canyon), on Highway 14, between milepost 118-117.

2 Lodging Rooms
Central Woodstove

Lobby Phone
Bed & Breakfast Available
All Non-Smoking in Units
Recreation Room
Elevation: 5300
Credit Cards: VM
2 people a night: $65 - $75
Open: All Year

Bernie Alexy & Barb Gibbens, Hosts
4167 Poudre Canyon Hwy
Bellvue CO 80512
970/224-9389
970/224-9388 Fax
E-mail: gypsy@frii.com

At the resort:

At resort or within 15 minutes:

Indian Meadows Lodge

Open year round, Indian Meadows Lodge has been recently renovated and the grounds fully landscaped. Stay in cabins along the river or have an adventure in a teepee, with a shower house providing the modern amenities. The Lone Star is a single cabin by the river with a double bed, fully equipped kitchen with a propane stove and bathroom with a shower. The Pueblo is a large guest house on the river that can sleep up to seven people. It has a living room with a fireplace, a full bath and a kitchen with a hot plate and small refrigerator. Its many windows provide spectacular views of the Poudre River. The 8-plex is a line of 8 kitchenette units consisting of three rooms: a fully equipped kitchen, a bathroom and a bedroom. The new duplexes have a queen bed, a queen hide-a-way, a small table and chairs and a bathroom with a shower. The teepee is unfurnished–bring your camping gear minus the tent.

Indian Meadows boasts excellent food prepared by renowned chefs, a comfortable, quiet lounge, friendly service and cleanliness. Enjoy the fine, candlelight dining while listening to live music when you eat dinner at the lodge. Spend your vacation relaxing and photographing the wildlife. Plenty of fishing spots and hiking trails abound in the Poudre River Canyon.

Campsites are available. Ask about seasonal discounts when making your reservations. Pets are allowed for an additional fee per night. A 50% deposit is required with reservations.

Location: On Highway 14, Poudre Canyon Road, near milepost 92.

10 Cabins with Kitchens
2 cabins without Kitchens
1 Woodstove
Central Campfire Area

Pay Phone(s)
Recreation Room
Elevation: 7400
Credit Cards: VMAD
2 people a night: $45 - $125
Open: All Year

Tim & Patty Brown, Owners
29839 Poudre Canyon Rd
Bellvue CO 80512
970/881-2281 office & Fax

At the resort:

At resort or within 15 minutes:

Inn at Boxer Ranch

Surrounded by 160 acres of grassy meadows amidst a sprinkling of moss rock, aspen and pine, the Inn at Boxer Ranch is snuggled away in the rolling foothills of the northwestern Rocky Mountains. Originally founded in 1896 as the Sloan Ranch (the first family to homestead in Rabbit Creek), the present owner, Drew Stein, renamed the still working cattle ranch after his beloved boxer, Tex. Guests can choose from the five bedrooms with two shared baths, all comfortably furnished and decorated with antiques and western memorabilia. There are no phones or televisions in the rooms to insure a true country experience.

Relaxation and fun are the primary concerns of your host, Hank. Choose to sit in the shade of a Willow tree and read or fish in the 2 acre pond and soak up the fresh air and warm sunshine. Hike or mountain bike to your heart's content; there's plenty to explore. Later, after Hank has created an incredible family-style meal and delicious dessert, take a dip in the hot tub beneath the starry skies. This is a year round vacation retreat: in summer its ideal for weddings and outdoor events, September and October offer the golden colors of fall, from November though March the ranch is a winter wonderland, and spring is lush and green with the birth of wildlife. You are assured an abundance of peace and tranquility here.

Specializing in weddings, reunions, company picnics or just a quick weekend getaway, a trip to the Inn at Boxer ranch won't soon be forgotten. Come relax and enjoy the quiet atmosphere and good ole down-home cooking. Bring your swimsuit and leave your worries behind! Your horse is invited to join you with prior arrangement.

Location: Thirty-five minutes northwest of Fort Collins

5 Lodging Rooms
Central Woodstove
Central Campfire Area

Lobby Phone
Bed & Breakfast Available
All Non-Smoking in Units
Recreation Room
Elevation: 6200
No Credit cards
2 people a night: $70 - $115
Open: All Year

Dawn Kaseoru, Mkt Dir
2221 CR 82E
Livermore CO 80536
970/498-9726
970/224-9720 Fax call 1st

At the resort:

At resort or within 15 minutes:

Mountain Greenery Resort

Mountain Greenery Resort is snuggled on the banks of The Cache La Poudre River, Colorado's first National Wild and Scenic River. The resort offers clean, modern rooms ranging from one bedroom with no cooking facilities to two bedrooms with kitchenettes, living rooms and tub-showers. There are also six mobile homes for rent.

Mountain Greenery's restaurant features home cooking, feast on a hearty breakfast, a quick lunch and a leisurely dinner, be sure to leave room for their home baked pies and mouth watering cinnamon rolls. The small country store offers fishing supplies and gifts. Children will enjoy the large lawn and playground, while all will relish casting a line into the Poudre River. After catching a trout fry it up in the picnic area by the river. There are no televisions at the resort, so family time is spent escaping into the great outdoors. The area offers four-wheel-drive trails, horseback riding, mountain biking and ample hiking trails. Or drive Highway 14 (Poudre Canyon Drive toward Walden and relax as you meander on this scenic and historic byway. The winter offers quieter time in the canyon with snowshoeing, cross country skiing and snowmobiling.

This is a perfect resort for family reunions and weddings. RV sites are available. Pets are allowed for an additional fee per night. When you stay seven nights, the seventh night is free. They offer a Senior's discount on lodging.

Location: Forty-two miles from Ft Collins, on Highway 14, Poudre Canyon Road, near milepost 90.

3 Motel Rooms
Central Fireplace

Lobby Phone
Elevation: 7205
Credit Cards: VM
2 people a night: $45 - $60
Open: All Year

Vic & Sharon McLachlan, Owners
32595 Poudre Canyon
Bellvue CO 80512-9415
970/881-2242
970/881-2723 Fax

At the resort:

At resort or within 15 minutes:

Poudre River Resort

Adjacent to the spectacular Poudre River, high in the Rocky Mountains, the resort has modern cabins with ample bedrooms, linens, bathrooms, showers, towels and fully equipped kitchens with electric or gas ranges. One cabin sleeps up to 10 people and has a fireplace. The comfortable cabins are well spaced for privacy and picnics. Fall asleep in the cool mountain air and wake to birds chirping in the trees along the river. You'll find the Poudre a quiet mountain getaway.

For relaxation, soak outdoors in the community hot tub or rent a movie from the on-site video service. For added convenience, there's a well-stocked store with craft items, groceries, fishing licenses, tackle, books and souvenirs as well as a playground, snack bar and a coin-laundromat. Meander along a path from your cabin to the river. Hike one of the excellent trails and fish in stocked lakes, both at the resort and in the nearby mountains. If you get tired of cabin cooking, dine at one of the local restaurants nearby. In the winter, pristine back country areas are accessible by cross-country skis or snowmobile. Whether you hike it or ski it, Poudre River country is refreshingly un-crowded and the mountainous terrain where pine forests and wildlife abound is Colorado at its best.

Full hookup RV sites are also available. The resort specializes in family reunions, birthday bashes, anniversary celebrations, religious and company retreats and outdoor weddings. A one night deposit is required with reservations. One pet per cabin is allowed for some cabins. There are non pet and non smoking cabins. Children four and under stay free.

Location: 45 miles northwest of Fort Collins, on Highway 14, near milepost 89.

9 Cabins with Kitchens
1 Vacation Home
1 Lodging Room or Apartment
1 Woodstove
Central Campfire Area

Pay Phone(s)
Non-Smoking Units Available
Elevation: 7200
Credit Cards: VMD
2 people a night: $50 - $135
Open: All Year

Janet & Venus, Owners
33021 Poudre Canyon Dr
Bellvue CO 80512-9426
970/881-2139

At the resort:

At resort or within 15 minutes:

Sportsman's Lodge

Since 1931, Sportsman's Lodge has been an ideal setting for families and reunions. The lodge's beautiful location and modest furnishings, many from the 1930s, will make you think time has stood still, in fact the first cabin was built in 1931. The rustic housekeeping cabins are clean and charming, featuring wood burning stoves "just like Grandma cooked on." Modern bathrooms and showers are in separate buildings. One cabin has a kitchen, sleeping room and a bathroom with a shower. Sit in the shade along the river and watch rainbow trout jump for flies.

The on-site country store sells licenses, gifts, groceries, fishing supplies and snacks. Located in the Poudre River Canyon, the lodge is within minutes of Poudre Falls, Chambers Lake and Cameron Pass. In the spring and summer, take advantage of river and lake fishing, hiking, whitewater rafting, horseback riding, mountain biking and simple, quiet, relaxing. Join your hosts in the evenings around their large campfire and join in the fun of swapping adventures and tales for your vacation. You'll have ample opportunities to photograph the abundant wildlife, including moose, bighorn sheep, and birds, especially humming birds. Fall brings a color tour of turning aspens and big game hunting. At Sportsman's Lodge, you'll escape to the past where time moved a little more slowly and the wilderness awaited exploration.

Full hookup RV sites are available. Pets are allowed for a fee. A deposit of 2 nights is required when making reservations. Ask about their weekly rates.

Location: 54 miles west of Fort Collins on Highway 14, near milepost 79.

Sportsman's Lodge, Inc.

12 Cabins with Kitchens
12 Woodstoves
Central Fireplace
Central Campfire Area

Pay Phone(s)
Recreation Room
Elevation: 7880
No credit cards
2 people a night: $38 - $60
Open: All Year

John & Lee Ann Schenk, Owners
44174 Poudre Canyon Hwy
Bellvue CO 80512-9604
970/881-2272
800/270-2272

At the resort:

At resort or within 15 minutes:

Trout Lodge

This lodge wasn't named for nothing! Be sure to bring your fishing rods along when you vacation here. The private, romantic cabins come with fireplaces, bathrooms and fully equipped kitchens. Set in a scenic, quiet atmosphere, the modern, completely furnished cabins feature comfortable rooms for your enjoyment. Chose among nine cabins, some of which have wood stoves and one is a non-smoking unit. Spend an afternoon relaxing on your front porch and an evening of candlelight dinner in the privacy of your own cabin. Or dine out in nearby restaurants.

Trout Lodge is in a wooded area, near meadows and adjoining the national forest, five state lakes and a rustic, mountain-top golf course. A central meeting room can accommodate larger groups or be a sports center for family games. Enjoy endless trout fishing on the lakes and three nearby streams. Try boat fishing on the many lakes. Hikers and photographers alike will appreciate the numerous forest and mountain trails where wildflowers and wildlife flourish. Rent mountain bikes on site or bring your horse along for some backcountry riding. In the winter, bring your skis, snowshoes and ice-fishing gear. Historic Red Feathers Lakes village has quaint country stores, restaurants and friendly town folks.

Location: 45 miles northwest of Fort Collins, about 26 miles west of Highway 287. West of Livermore 24± miles to Red Feather Lakes, turn right on Prairie Divide Road, then left on Main Street.

9 Cabins with Kitchens
4 Fireplaces
5 Woodstoves

Pay Phone(s)
Non-Smoking Units Available
Elevation: 8200
Credit Cards: VMAD
2 people a night: $49 - $99
Open: All Year

Dennis & Patti McMillan
PO Box 126
1078 Ramona Dr
Red Feather Lakes CO 80545-0126
970/881-2964

At the resort:

At resort or within 15 minutes:

Pueblo, Colorado City & Westcliffe

Including Rye — Map: K-18, M-17 & L-15

At the eastern edge of the Rocky Mountains, **Pueblo** has historically been known as a natural crossroads and melting pot for diverse ethnic groups since the dawn of time. Ute, Cheyenne, Arapaho and Kiowa tribes as well as Spanish troops, mountain men, and gold seekers would often came to do business. In 1806, Capt. Zebulon Pike built a log fort — the first structure built by Americans in Colorado. Eventually the railroads found their way to Pueblo and in the late 1880s the town built smelters. The Pueblo Reservoir sits on semi-arid plains encircled by limestone cliffs and buttes with mountain vistas. The man-made lake, with its clean, cool water and great fishing along its 60 miles of shore, is ideal for sailing. Enjoy the 73% of sunshine a year in Pueblo. When silver was king in 1881, the Denver & Rio Grande Railroad expanded from Cañon City west and built **Westcliffe.** After silver went bust, Westcliffe managed to hang on as a ranching and farming community. Just north of town is Lake DeWeese, in the bowl of the Wet Mountain Valley, which offers fishing and water sports. Grape Creek, which flows below the reservoir, has rainbow and brown trout. Lake Isabel, in the San Isabel National Forest, is ideal for picnicking, fishing and hiking. Lakes of the Clouds, at 11,200', are accessible by four-wheel drive or hiking in 5 miles. But the trip is worth it as the remote beaver ponds below the lakes have brook and cutthroat trout while the upper lake has rainbow trout. In the winter, try downhill or cross-country skiing at the Mountain Cliffe Ski Resort. No visit to **Rye** is complete without at stop at the Robbers Roost Western Museum where you can see Buffalo Bill's saddle and the guns that won the 'West'. The Wet Mountains has one of Colorado's most intriguing attractions: Bishop's Castle built solely by Jim Bishop. The artist has created a huge stone and iron castle complete with a metal dragon whose nose is a woodstove chimney. If you're nearby, a visit to the ever expanding castle promises to be memorable.

Fun Things to Do

- Bishop's Castle, Rye (719) 564-4366
- City Park Golf Course, Pueblo (719) 561-4946
- Colorado State Fair & Events Center, Pueblo (800) 876-4567
- El Pueblo Museum (719) 583-0453
- Greenway & Nature Center, Pueblo (719) 549-2414
- Hollydot Golf Course, Colorado City (719) 676-3341
- Lake Pueblo State Recreation Area (719) 561-9320
- Pueblo West Golf Course (719) 547-2280
- Robbers Roost Western Museum, Rye (719) 489-3559
- Rye Mountain Park (719)583-6011
- Walking Stick Golf Course, Pueblo (719) 584-3400

Alpine Lodge, Cabins & Dinner Restaurant

Bordering the San Isabel National Forest, Alpine Lodge is nestled among pine and aspen trees in the Sangre de Cristo Mountains. The quaint mountain cabins sleep up to four people in two bedrooms. All have kitchens equipped with stoves, refrigerators, cooking utensils and dishes. The cabins also feature private baths with all towels and linens provided. The cabins are electrically heated and insulated for year round comfort.

For your evening meal try Alpine Lodge's restaurant, specializing in charbroiled steaks, seafood, sandwiches and delicious homemade soup and pies. The only television at the lodge is in the lounge. Over 100 miles of trails in the San Isabel National Forest and Sangre de Cristo Wilderness area await you for hiking and horseback riding during the summer and snow-shoeing and cross-country skiing in the winter. Start hiking on the trails from your cabin door to dozens of mountain streams and lakes. Or drive to Lake DeWeese for fishing or boating. Climb many of the nearby 13,000' to 14,000' peaks in a day without technical equipment and don't be surprised to see eagles soaring high above you. Photograph the wildflowers splashing color through the meadows and mountainsides. In the fall, hunt elk, antelope, deer, bighorn sheep and wild turkey.

Cabins are available for daily or weekly stays. Alvarado Campground is adjacent to lodge for camping.

Location: 10 miles southwest of Westcliffe on County Road 140, off Highway 69, near milepost 55-56.

5 Cabins with Kitchens
Central Fireplace

Pay Phone(s)
Recreation Room
Elevation: 9000
Credit Cards: VM
2 people a night: $44
Open: All Year

David Leugers, Owner
6848 CR 140
Westcliffe CO 81252
719/783-2660

At the resort:

At resort or within 15 minutes:

Lodge at San Isabel

Snug in the mountains next to the trout-stocked Lake San Isabel, these cabins are ideal for groups and family reunions. The lodge is a well-established and family run. Each cabin sleeps up to eight people. Bring your own dishes and cooking utensils; the Lodge provides towels every three days and linens once a week. Some cabins feature fireplaces. Four of the cabins have kitchens for housekeeping and sleep from four to six people. Get away from it at all this scenic, quiet mountain lodge just a few steps from picturesque Lake San Isabel.

The Lodge's full service restaurant, open from 7 a.m. to 10 p.m. daily, specializes in great burgers and Mexican dishes. If you'd prefer, you can order take-out and eat your meal in your cabin. Also on-site are a grocery store, a service station and a small gift shop full of curios. Ask your hosts about summer whitewater rafting tours. Rent rowboats and paddle boats for lake excursions on Lake San Isabel. Go horseback riding, hiking and mountain biking in the surrounding national forest trails. Catch a glimpse of the past when you explore the old gold mines. Enjoy jeeping, motorcycling or ATV riding on Greenhorn Mountain. In the fall, hunt elk, antelope, deer, bear, mountain lion, big horn sheep and wild turkey. Or enjoy the yearly turning of the apsen.The lodge is on the Ophir Creek snowmobile trail system which consists of 90+ miles of groomed trails running from Ophir Creek to Greenhorn Mountain. You can access the trail from your cabin from mid-December through mid-March.

One nights rent deposit is required with reservations. RV spaces are also available.

Location: 10 miles north of Rye on Highway 165, near milepost 19. Eighteen miles from I-25.

5 Cabins with Kitchens
9 cabins without Kitchens
1 Woodstove
Central Fireplace

Pay Phone(s)
Elevation: 8600
Credit Cards: VM
2 people a night: $45 - $95
Open: 4/1 to 11/1

Dave & Shirley Harmon, Owners
HCR 75 Box 123
Rye CO 81069
719/489-2280

At the resort:

At resort or within 15 minutes:

Pueblo KOA & Kamping Kabins™

At the Pueblo KOA, the Kamping Kabins are among shade trees and there are wooden shade shelters, picnic tables and barbecue grills to enjoy outside. Bring your own bedding and cooking supplies. The KOA features a desert setting with views of the towering Pikes Peak. Hot showers, clean restrooms and a coin laundry are on-site. With sunny, dry days and cool, quiet nights, this is desert lodging at its best.

The recreation room, arcade and equipped pavilion are great for entertaining large groups. Other amenities include a heated swimming pool, basketball and volleyball courts, badminton, horseshoes, a playground and sports fields. The camp store has groceries, ice, sundries, clothing, jewelry, souvenirs and toys. The Pueblo KOA is centrally located to the beautiful Pikes Peak area, the stunning Royal Gorge and the gambling casinos of Cripple Creek. Several golf courses and a dog track are also nearby for your leisure-time relaxation. The Pueblo Reservoir, only 12 miles away, has fishing, boating, swimming and sun bathing on its beach.

RV sites are also available.

Location: Six miles north of Pueblo, on I-25 at exit 108.

2 Camper Cabins

Pay Phone(s)
Recreation Room
Elevation: 5000
Credit Cards: VMD
2 people a night: $28
Open: All Year

Rolland & Genet Anderson, Owners
4131 I-25 North
Pueblo CO 81008
719/542-2273
800/KOA 7453

At the resort:

At resort or within 15 minutes:

Pueblo South/Colorado City KOA & Kamping Kabins™

Relax in the shade and enjoy incredible views of the Rocky Mountains from Pueblo South/Colorado City KOA Kamping Kabins Resort located in the Greenhorn Mountain Valley. Bring your own bedding (or have it provided) and cooking supplies to the Kamping Kabins here. Vacations in this accommodating campground are peaceful year-round.

Entertain the kids on the playground. Families will like playing basketball, volleyball and horseshoes at the resort. In the evening, enjoy a movie, a sing-a-long around the campfire, pie and ice cream socials, and barbecues. Other amenities include a gift shop and general store with snack bar, and a hot tub with patio area for relaxing. Avid golfers will appreciate Hollydot, the 27 holes nearby, as well as the many sunny days throughout the year. Visit the intriguing Bishop's Castle, historic Robbers Roost, Graneros Gorge, drive the Frontier Pathway Byway, and visit the breath-taking Royal Gorge and Buckskin Joe's. Let your hosts arrange a rafting trip down the Arkansas River for you. Fish in nearby Lake Isabel and Lake Beckwith. In the winter, come for the snowmobiling and cross-country skiing and visit when the campground turns into a Winter Wonderland Christmas Village.

Large, grassy pull-through RV and tent sites are also available. Children ages 10 and under are free.

Location: 20 miles south of Pueblo, on I-25 at exit 74.

3 Camper Cabins
Central Campfire Area

Pay Phone(s)
Non-Smoking Units Available
Recreation Room
Elevation: 6000
Credit Cards: VMD
2 people a night: $29
Open: All Year

Tim & Elena Johnson, Owners
9040 I-25 South
Pueblo CO 81004
719/676-3376 CG
800/562-8646

At the resort:

At resort or within 15 minutes:

Royal Gorge Area

Including Cañon City, Coaldale, Cotopaxi & Texas Creek — Map: K-16 & K-14

Considered the climate capital of Colorado, **Cañon City**'s natural setting protects it from harsh weather. Once a favorite camping area of the Ute Indians, both dinosaur bones and oil were discovered here. Five miles north of the city is the Garden Park Monument commemorating the 1877 dinosaur find. The Arkansas River, flows through the city and offers great fishing west of town, formed one of the most spectacular attractions in the state – the Royal Gorge, 8 miles west. The world's highest suspension bridge hangs a dizzying 1,053' above the rushing river, offering unforgettable vistas of the 8 mile canyon in the city's largest park. Next to viewing the bridge, rafting the Arkansas River is the most popular reason for vacationing here. **Cotopaxi** and **Coaldale** are also popular launching pads to rafting the Arkansas River. The Colorado Territorial Prison in Cañon City, built in 1868, is the only prison museum located next to a currently operating prison. Several scenic byways lead out of Cañon City, including one through Phantom Canyon where the road passes granite tunnels and between sheer cliff walls on its way to Cripple Creek. Other activities include hiking and horseback riding.

Fun Things to Do

- American Adventure Expeditions (800)288-0675
- Arkansas Headwaters Recreation Area (719) 539-7289
- Buffalo Joe River Trips (800) 356-7984, (719) 395-8757
- Indian Springs Ranch National Natural Landmark (719) 372-3907
- Lazy J Rafting Company (800) 678-4274, (719) 942-4274
- Raft Masters (800)568-7238, (719)275-6645
- Raven Rafting & Adventure Trips (800) 332-3381
- River Runners Ltd. (800) 525-2081
- Royal Gorge Bridge Park (719) 275-7507
- Shadow Hills Golf Course (719) 275-0603

Arkansas River KOA & Kamping Kabins™ & Loma Linda Motel

Make the Arkansas River KOA & Loma Linda Motel in Cotopaxi your base camp for family reunions. Bounded by scenic Highway 50 and the Arkansas River, you'll find a whole new world to roam and unwind in. Guest motel rooms with kitchenettes and Kamping Kabins along the river are available. The rustic camping cabin has electricity and sleeps up to four. Bring your own sleeping bag. The clean motel rooms have private showers, television, linens and at least two double beds. The kitchenettes have a stove, refrigerator and dishes. All units have close access to the river as well as picnic tables and campfires. Borrow a grill to cook supper outdoors. Sit back and listen to the roar of the raging river while you gaze at the red rocks and snow-tipped peaks of southern Colorado. Every night you'll have starry, starry skies and wide open spaces filled with fresh air.

The KOA also has clean restrooms and a coin laundry on-site. From here you can fish on the beautiful Arkansas or scramble along its picturesque banks, rock hunting. Summer time activities include miniature golf, nightly movies, shuffleboard and hay rides — all for free! Nearby you can pan for gold, hike, hunt, mountain bike, whitewater raft or horseback ride. After it all, take a dip in the heated swimming pool or challenge your family to a video game in recreation room.

Indoor and outdoor group meeting areas, tent and RV sites are available.

Location: Off Highway 50 at milepost 247, between Cañon City and Salida, one mile east of Cotopaxi.

6 Cabins with Kitchens
3 Camper Cabins
3 Motel Rooms
Central Campfire Area

Pay Phone(s)
All Non-Smoking in Units
Recreation Room
Elevation: 6300
Credit Cards: VMD
2 people a night: $40 - $60
Open: 4/1 to 10/31

Jerry & Jeanne Holdren, Owners
PO Box 387
21435 US Hwy 50
Cotopaxi CO 81223-0387
719/275-9308
800/562-2686 Res only

At the resort:

At resort or within 15 minutes:

Buffalo Bill's Royal Gorge Camper Cabins, Lodge & Camp

The camper cabins have a view of the Royal Gorge only 4 miles away. Bring your own bedding and cooking utensils. Hot showers, clean restrooms and a coin laundry are provided. Each camper cabin has a ceiling fan, picnic table and barrel for a campfire and cooking outside. There is no heat. The lodge rooms have a bunk bed and double bed and heat. You can bring your own bedding for the lodge rooms or it is available. Bring a cooler for your food as there are no refrigerators, except for one lodge room which has a full kitchen. Located on 10 acres, Buffalo Bill's Royal Gorge Campground is away from the road.

A heated, 9-foot deep swimming pool, playground, and video game room are at the resort for the young at heart. Within walking distance is a restaurant. The property store sells ice, firewood, limited grocery items, Indian jewelry, T-shirts, and souvenirs. The Royal Gorge Bridge — only a few minutes drive — is the world's highest suspension bridge hanging at an incredible 1,053' above the churning Arkansas River. Rent a horse from the stables across the street and explore the numerous area trails. River rafting and river fishing are minutes away. A scenic railway and old west town are also close.

RV and tent sites, group tenting area, and an indoor group meeting area are available. Buffalo Bill's Royal Gorge Campground was formally known as Royal Gorge Camp Eight Eighty.

Location: Eight miles west of Cañon City on Highway 50 to Royal Gorge Bridge exit, south to County Road 3A, proceed a few hundred feet, turn left at sign.

4 Lodging Rooms
2 Camper Cabins

Pay Phone(s)
Recreation Room
Elevation: 6300
Credit Cards: VMD
2 people a night: $30 - $59
Open: 4/15 to 10/15

Bill & Sheila McCully, Owners
PO Box 1009
0030 CR 3A
Cañon City CO 81215-1009
719/269-3211
800/787-0880

At the resort:

At resort or within 15 minutes:

Deweese Lodge Bed & Breakfast

Spend your vacation in a log house built by Dall Deweese, on 7.5 acres filled with trees, lush grass and sparkling water. A 220-foot wrap-around verandah with 16 rocking chairs and two porch swings surrounds this lodge where Theodore Roosevelt stayed many times. The four guest rooms share baths, or you may choose to stay in the St. John Guest House which sleeps four. The smoke-free lodge features a two story library with hundreds of books and a double decked fireplace. Breakfast is served in the Solarium in winter where plants, a bubbling fountain and singing birds greet the day and on the verandah in summer. The living room has a piano, television and deep couches just right for chatting with other guests. The bunk house has three beds and sleeps five. An equipped exercise room is also available for guests. The resort can accommodate up to 16 people — ideal for an intimate wedding party.

The lodge also offers catered chuckwagon cookouts booked in advance. On the grounds are horseshoe pits, a volleyball court, a jogging path and a croquet set for those who want to enjoy the sunshine. On cloudy days the rec room has board games, a card table, a pool table and a television. Only 1.5 miles from downtown Cañon City, the lodge is near all the city's amenities. Fish the Arkansas River or visit the spectacular Royal Gorge. Explore for dinosaur bones, take a hike, play golf or horseback ride. There's plenty to do in Colorado's climate capital.

An indoor group meeting area is available.Large meadow and stable for your horse, arrange ahead of time, there is an additional fee. Ask host about half day and full day itineraries for the area. No children are allowed in the lodge however in the cabin and bunk house children are welcome.

Location: 1.5 miles south of Cañon City on Highway 115, from Highway 50, south on 9th, turns into Elm.

1 Cabin with Kitchen
4 Lodging Rooms
3 Beds in Bunk House or Dorm
Central Fireplace
Central Campfire Area

Lobby Phone
Bed & Breakfast Available
All Non-Smoking in Units
Recreation Room
Elevation: 5300
Credit Cards: VMD
2 people a night: $80 - $120
Open: All Year

Linda Bellah, Innkeeper
1226 Elm
Cañon City CO 81212
719/269-1881

At the resort:

At resort or within 15 minutes:

Hidden Valley Ranch & Campground

Hidden Valley Ranch embraces a splendid natural landscape surrounded by the beautiful Sangre de Cristo Mountains while Cottonwood Creek flows through the property filling five stocked trout ponds. The log camper cabins, which sleep two to eight people, have exceptional views of the snowcapped mountains. Bring your own bedding and cooking supplies. Clean restrooms, hot showers and a coin laundry are on-site. All facilities are wheelchair friendly and accessible.

Fish for trophy trout in the private, stocked ponds with no license, you only pay by the inch caught. If you reel in one over five pounds, it's half price! Try one of the on-site mountain bike trails or play horseshoes, basketball, volleyball, badminton and tether ball. Enjoy a guided horseback ride into the mountains. Whitewater raft trips and four-wheel drive trails are minutes away and can be arranged through the hosts. A hot tub and weight room are available. For your convenience, a game room, camp store, gift shop and snack bar are all on the property.

RV sites and tent sites are also available. Ask about their special group rates for four or more families and a special group rate for handicapable and corporate and church groups. Be sure to call ahead for these rates and any special requests.

Location: 0.25miles south of Highway 50 near milepost 242-243, near Coaldale, take either County Road 39 or 40 both lead to Ranch. The property is not visible from the highway.

5 Camper Cabins

Pay Phone(s)
Non-Smoking Units Available
Recreation Room
Elevation: 6900
Credit Cards: VM
2 people a night: Call for Rates
Open: All Year

Chuck Sedmak, Owner
Chuck Greenwood, Manager
0340 City Rd 40, PO Box 233
Coaldale CO 81222
719/942-4171
800/320-4171
E mail: cwsmac@aol.com

At the resort:

At resort or within 15 minutes:

Lazy J Resort & Rafting Company

Vacation in the valley solitude of the Lazy J Resort which sits on the banks of the Arkansas River. With beautiful views of the Sangre de Cristo mountains, the resort offers modern cabins, camper cabins and motel rooms in one- and two-bedroom units. Bring your own bedding and cooking utensils for the camper cabins. Some of the modern log cabins and motel rooms have kitchenettes; and one unit has a fireplace. Nearby are large, grassy lawns for children to play on and families to relax on. Enjoy cool mountain breezes, fresh air and unforgettable scenery daily.

A full-service restaurant specializing in American and Mexican foods, a playground, a volleyball court, horse shoe pits and a heated swimming pool are other amenities. The gift shop features Colorado specialty items, T-shirts, snacks, souvenirs and rafting supplies. Whitewater raft trips for every level, run by the resort, are Lazy J's specialty. They proudly boast an excellent safety record. Take a wild and wet half- or full-day trip. Overnight or custom journeys can be arranged. "Saddle and Paddle" combination trips includes both horses and rafts. If you prefer river fishing, cast your line from near your cabin, or hike to one of the many nearby fishing areas.

Indoor and outdoor group meeting areas, and shady RV sites are also available.

Location: 30 miles west of the Royal Gorge on Highway 50, near milepost 242.

3 Cabins with Kitchens
8 Camper Cabins
4 Motel Rooms
1 Fireplace
Central Campfire Area

Pay Phone(s)
Elevation: 6200
Credit Cards: VMD
2 people a night: $30 - $70
Open: 5/15 to 12/5

Jeff Jeffries, Owner
PO Box 109
16373 Hwy 50
Coaldale CO 81222-0109
719/942-4274
800/678-4274
719/942-4310 Fax
719/269-7725 cellular

At the resort:

At resort or within 15 minutes:

Whispering Pines Resort

The roaring Arkansas River runs for a mile right through Whispering Pines Resort in Texas Creek. On the south side of the river, the newly remodeled motel rooms and rustic camper cabins have a breathtaking view of the Rocky Mountains from the river's banks. If you stay in the camper cabins, bring your own bedding and cooking supplies. Hot showers and clean restrooms are provided. Kick back in the shade and watch the rafters paddle past.

It almost goes without saying that the trout fishing is excellent and the whitewater rafting is great — all right from Whispering Pines. Nearby, you can horseback ride, golf, visit tourist attractions, and get all your groceries, camping supplies and fishing tackle in the nearby shops.

RV and tent sites are also available.

Location: On Highway 50, milepost 250, near Texas Creek.

2 Camper Cabins
4 Motel Rooms

Pay Phone(s)
Recreation Room
Elevation: 7200
Credit Cards: VM
2 people a night: $30 - $45
Open: 4/1 to 10/30

Hal & Mary Davenport, Owners
24871 HWY 50 W
Texas Creek CO 81223
719/275-3827

At the resort:

At resort or within 15 minutes:

Yogi Bear's Jellystone Park Camp Resort

A true family resort, Yogi Bear's Jellystone Park is among 17-acres of shady pine trees with a view of the Royal Gorge Bridge. The cabins have kitchenettes and are a comfortable and inexpensive way to enjoy the Royal Gorge area. Clean showers are on-site for your convenience. You'll have plenty of elbow room and piñon pine, cedar and elm trees to relax under here. Yogi Bear may even visit your cabin.

On-site entertainment includes nightly movies, morning cartoons, weekend campfire programs and hayrides with Yogi and Ranger Smith. The kids will like the video game room, playground, volleyball and basketball courts. Snacks and pancake breakfasts prepare you for a day of fishing, horseback riding, and white-water rafting nearby. Enjoy theme weekends and special meals throughout the year. The camp store sells supplies, firewood, assorted groceries and Yogi and Colorado souvenirs. After a day of Royal Gorge adventures, relax in the heated, 9-foot deep swimming pool or soak in the hot tub and rest on the large sun deck.

Ask about theme weekends, RV sites and RV storage. Enclosed pavilion for group meetings.

Location: 9 miles west of Cañon City, on Highway 50, near milepost 269, at the junction of Highway 9.

3 Cabins with Kitchens
Central Campfire Area

Pay Phone(s)
Recreation Room
Elevation: 6350
Credit Cards: VMD
2 people a night: $37 - $48
Open: 3/1 to 10/31

Jan & Lee Massey, Owners
PO Box 1025
43595 Hwy 50
Cañon City CO 81215-1025
719/275-2128
800/558-2954

At the resort:

At resort or within 15 minutes:

Silverton

Map: M-6

A trip to **Silverton** is a trip back in time. Designated a National Historic Landmark, the town seems frozen in the last century with its luxurious, many-windowed Grand Imperial Hotel (built in 1882), picturesque Victorian homes and restored miners' cabins. In its heyday, Silverton had as many as 32 gambling halls, saloons and "sporting houses" on Blair Street. Granted exclusively to the Utes in 1868, the treaty was ignored when gold and silver strikes brought miners in by the wagonload. Because of the atmosphere, several western movies have been filmed here, not only to take advantage of the historic look, but to capture the splendorous mountain magic as well. At 9,303', Silverton is surrounded by four towering peaks and hundreds of miles of the San Juan, Uncompahgre and Rio Grande National Forests. No matter which direction you go, you'll find hikes through the high mountains, past raging rivers to abandoned ghost towns. The area is also filled with four-wheel drive trails and roads; including the Alpine Scenic Loop Backcountry Byway, to other mountain towns like Ouray, Telluride and Lake City — this area has some of the best jeeping in the world. For a truly memorable vacation, ride the Durango-Silverton Narrow Gauge Railroad starting in Durango, then spend some time in Silverton where history lives.

Fun Things to Do

- Durango-Silverton Narrow Gauge Railroad (970) 247-2733
- Old Hundred Gold Mine Tour (800) 872-3009
- San Juan County Historical Society Museum (970) 387-5838
- Silver Summit Jeep Rentals (800) 352-1637, (970) 387-0240
- Silverton Lakes Jeep Rentals (970) 387-5721

Bowman House

Enjoy the atmosphere of the 1880s in the historic Silverton Bowman House, built in 1895. The vacation home has been remodeled, modernized and furnished with antiques. It offers four bedrooms with double beds, two bathrooms and a complete 1940s kitchen that is updated with modern appliances and conveniences. Other appliances include a washer and dryer. One bathroom features a large, claw foot, cast iron tub for a real old fashioned experience. The entire vacation home, which sleeps up to eight, is yours to share with family and friends while you vacation in the quiet heart of the San Juan Mountains. A furnished, housekeeping, one bedroom apartment that sleeps two is also available and can be rented separately from the house.

The Bowman House was built by Clint Bowman whose Merchants Biscuit Company was the foundation of the present Keebler Company. It's in the heart of picturesque Silverton, walking distance to all the downtown attractions and restaurants. Ride the steam train to Durango and spend the day there exploring another mountain community. Other attractions include taking a four wheel drive tour, horseback rides and exploring museums. A short drive away, you can swim, fish, whitewater raft, golf, boat and mountain bike.

Rentals are weekly only and begin on Sundays. Smoking and pets are not permitted. Well behaved children are welcomed at the Bowman House.

Location: In Silverton on Reese Street.

1 Vacation Home
1 Lodging Room or Apartment

Room Phones
All Non-Smoking in Units
Recreation Room
Elevation: 9318
No credit cards
2 people a night: $50 - $133
Open: 5/23 to 9/15

D.T Van Buren
2148A 47th St
Los Alamos NM 87544
505/662-6419

At the resort:

At resort or within 15 minutes:

Molas Lake Park, Camper Cabins & Campground

In 1996 AAA named Molas Lake "The most scenic campground in Colorado." On the banks of trout-stocked Molas Lake, these "tent cabins" or the 22 foot teepee have the most spectacular views in all of Colorado. This alpine setting is on the Molas Lake Trailhead portion of The Colorado Trail. After several nights on the trail stop here and stay in a "cabin". Bring your own bedding and cooking gear to this excellent, economical place to stay while reveling in the San Juan Mountains scenery. Hot showers, toilets, water, and a laundromat are available for your convenience.

The on-site store carries groceries, fishing licenses, firewood and sandwiches. Molas Lake Park sponsors breakfast horseback and steak cookout rides. They also offer fish cleaning services, rent canoes and provide other entertainment. The area abounds with hiking and four-wheel drive trails in the San Juan Mountains. A nature trail and a hiking trail begin right at the park. Try gold panning and explore ghost towns. Molas Lake is truly the "land of happy campers."

Numerous RV and tent sites are also available.

Location: 5 miles south of Silverton on Highway 550, near milepost 66.

4 Camper Cabins
Central Campfire Area

No Phones Available
Elevation: 10515
No credit cards
2 people a night: $25
Open: 5/25 to 9/30

Shelia Baker & Bob Haisler, Owners
PO Box 776
5 miles S of Silverton
Silverton CO 81433-0776
970/387-5848
800/846-2177

At the resort:

At resort or within 15 minutes:

South Fork Area

Including Wagon Wheel Gap — Map: N-10 & N-9

South Fork is situated at the western edge of the San Luis Valley, one of the biggest intermountain valleys in the world. Since the late 1880s, South Fork, at 8,250', has been a logging and lumbering community. The Rio Grande River between South Fork and Del Norte has been designated Gold Medal trout water which means it offers the greatest potential for trophy trout fishing success in Colorado. The town, at the foot of Wolf Creek Pass with its deep-power ski resort, is near numerous, year-round recreational possibilities. Whether you hike it or drive it, the surrounding mountains have deer, elk, grouse, ptarmigan, bighorn sheep, snowshoe rabbits, and even an occasional bear, bobcat or cougar! The nearby town of **Wagon Wheel Gap** was the scene of several early Indian battles and it's said Kit Carson's brother-in-law farmed here in 1840. The town's railroad station is listed on the National Register of Historical Places. The Silver Thread Scenic Byway begins at South Fork, continues through Wagon Wheel Gap and Creede and ends at Lake City.

Fun Things to Do

- Chinook Smokehouse (800) 238-6837, (719) 873-9993
- Spruce Lodge Rafting (800) 228-5605, (719) 873-5605
- Wolf Creek Ski Area (970) 264-5629

Aspenridge Cabins & RV Park

The boundless quiet is calming at Aspenridge which sits on the picturesque Silver Thread Scenic Byway. The modern cabins have kitchens, bathrooms and cable television. All linens, pots and pans are furnished. Cabins have one or two bedrooms all with double beds. The town of South Fork is surrounded on three sides by the Rio Grande National Forest and some of the largest, undisturbed wilderness areas in the country — the outdoor activities here are countless.

The game room and the indoor and outdoor group meeting areas are great for family reunions and kids. A coin laundry is on-site for your convenience. Nearby, the Rio Grande River boasts excellent, open and gold medal trout fishing. If you prefer, your hosts can supply you with a map to the many local lakes whose deep, calm waters await your expert casting. Hike into the unusual Wheeler Geologic Area, a haunting landscape of pinnacles, canyons and arches accessible only by foot. Rent a horse nearby and take an unforgettable trail ride into nature at its finest. You'll find plenty of old logging and mining roads which make for exhilarating four-wheel drive or mountain bike trips. Make Aspenridge your vacationing and fishing headquarters in southern Colorado. Their hot tub is only open in winter.

RV sties are also available.

Location: Off of Highway 149, near milepost 1, one half mile northwest of the junction at Highway 160.

6 Cabins with Kitchens
1 Vacation Home
1 Woodstove
Central Woodstove
Central Campfire Area

Pay Phone(s)
Non-Smoking Units Available
Recreation Room
Elevation: 8180
Credit Cards: VMD
2 people a night: $35 - $45
Open: All Year

Charles & Brenda Murray, Owners
0710 W Hwy 149
South Fork CO 81154
719/873-5921 & Fax

At the resort:

At resort or within 15 minutes:

Blue Creek Lodge, Cabins, RV Park & Restaurant

This is a vacationer's paradise — a haven for fishing enthusiasts, hunters, skiers, hikers and photographers. Blue Creek Lodge features modern housekeeping cabins, dormitory beds and lodge rooms with a private bath. All cabins have a stove, refrigerator, dishes, pots and pans, linens and carpeting. Three cabins have one room with double beds and private baths, one has a deck. The three bedroom cabin has a fireplace and one and half baths for large families. The efficiency has a king size bed and bath.

The lodge offers hospitality with home-cooked meals in its full-service restaurant. Treat yourself at the soda fountain, carouse in the game room and stock up on curios from the gift shop. Have your hair styled at Thressia's Beauty Salon right on the property. In the winter, try inner tubing, ice skating, snowmobiling and cross-country or alpine skiing at the Wolf Creek Ski Area. In the spring and summer months, enjoy the high rivers in a raft — you can participate in the yearly raft races during the second weekend in June. If you're planning a tamer vacation, go hiking, rock hounding or fly fishing in the Rio Grande River across the road, or in the many mountain lakes nearby. Bring your own horse or rent one nearby for trips into the back country. In the fall, come hunt in some of the finest elk and deer country in the Rocky Mountains!

RV sites and trailers are also available. Children age 5 and under stay free. Ask about their weekly rates. Pets are allowed in the cabins for a fee. No pets are allowed in the lodge. One night deposit is required with reservation.

Location: Off of Highway 149, near milepost 11-12, halfway between South Fork and Creede.

12 Cabins with Kitchens
8 Lodging Rooms
28 Beds in Bunk House or Dorm
1 Fireplace
Central Fireplace
Central Campfire Area

Pay Phone(s)
Non-Smoking Units Available
Recreation Room
Elevation: 8735
Credit Cards: VM
2 people a night: $32 - $64
Open: All Year

Bill & Thressia Philbern, Owners
HC 33
Wagon Wheel Gap Hwy 149
South Fork CO 81154
719/658-2479
800/326-6408
719/658-2915 & Fax call 1st

At the resort:

At resort or within 15 minutes:

Chinook Lodge & Smokehouse

Vacation beneath tall pine trees in the heart of the Rocky Mountains at Chinook Lodge's rustic modern log cabins. The one- and two-bedroom housekeeping cabins feature kitchens and native rock fireplaces. All have antique furniture.

The small artesian shop contains snacks, hunting and fishing licenses. To whet your appetite, the smokehouse makes tasty smoked ham, turkey, fish and old-fashioned beef jerky. The South Fork area is ideal for fishing and hunting. The Wolf Creek ski area is a short 25 minutes touting the best down hill and cross-country skiing in South Fork area.The nearby Gold Medal waters of the Rio Grande River and numerous mountain lakes are an angler's dream come true. The roaring Rio Grande is also fun for "blue-water" rafting trips during the summer.

RV sites are also available. Reservations are encouraged.

Location: At the east edge of South Fork on Highway 160, near milepost 186.

7 Cabins with Kitchens
1 cabin without Kitchen
7 Fireplaces

Pay Phone(s)
Elevation: 8300
Credit Cards: VM
2 people a night: $28 - $38
Open: All Year

Roy & Barb Pruett, Owners
PO Box 530
29666 Hwy 160 W
South Fork CO 81154-0530
719/873-9993
800/238-6837
E-mail: ardee@rmi.net

At the resort:

At resort or within 15 minutes:

Cottonwood Cove Lodge, Cabins & Restaurant

Nestled in thousands of acres of untouched mountains, near the clear, icy waters of the Rio Grande River, Cottonwood Cove has housekeeping cabins with one to three bedrooms, fireplaces, linens and kitchens with supplies. Several of the cabins are along the Rio Grande, or choose a lodge room. An authentic, 1940s guest ranch, Cottonwood Cove is in a picture perfect setting, ideal for a refreshing escape from everyday life. Relax in the cool shade of cottonwood, aspen and pine trees while admiring the view of the surrounding mountains across the way.

The lodge, built in 1945, has a cozy family room, a cafe specializing in homemade pies, a recreational room and gift shop. The restaurant is open for breakfast, lunch and dinner. Cottonwood Cove provides excursions on horseback to nearby scenic areas. You're sure to catch many gold medal trout in newly stocked fish ponds, in the Rio Grande as well as in the surrounding mountain lakes. Mountain bikers will delight in the close proximity of the Wolf Creek Ski Area, Wheeler Geological Area and hundreds of miles of national forests roads here.

Advanced reservations are required for horseback rides. Between November and April, cabin availability is limited. Full hookup RV sites are also available.

Location: On Highway 149, near milepost 13.

24 Cabins with Kitchens
6 Lodging Rooms
9 Fireplaces
Central Fireplace
Central Woodstove

Pay Phone(s)
Bed & Breakfast Available
Recreation Room
Elevation: 8448
Credit Cards: VMD
2 people a night: $39 - $125
Open: All Year

Robert & Carolyn Eubank, Managers
HC 33 Wagon Wheel Gap
Hwy 149 mp 13
South Fork CO 81154
719/658-2242

At the resort:

At resort or within 15 minutes:

Foothills Lodge

At the beginning of the Silver Thread Scenic Byway sits Foothills Lodge and your vacation destination. Choose between modern log cabins with aspen paneling, kitchens and woodburning fireplaces or uniquely decorated lodge apartments with kitchens. Your vacation home can range from one to two bedrooms and have anywhere from one queen size bed to four double beds depending on the accommodation. All but one cabin have kitchens and many can sleep up to eight people. You will enjoy hot showers, carpeting, fresh towels daily, gas heat, Colorado cable television and direct dial telephones. Weekly cleaning is available for stays two weeks or longer.

The indoor hot tub is a popular place to gather after a day of hunting, fishing, skiing, snowmobiling, sightseeing or loosing yourself in a good book. Small children will enjoy the playground, while children-at-heart will enjoy Gold Medal fishing in the Rio Grande just minutes away. South Fork, at the edge the San Luis Valley, is a convenient jumping off point to a variety of nearby recreation activities: Wolf Creek Ski Area, hiking, trout fishing and sightseeing in the beautiful countryside. Adjacent to the lodge you can enjoy a meal at the Hungry Logger Restaurant or Croaker's Saloon. Open all year round, Foothills Lodge is a great escape from it all — and is relaxing!

If traveling with a toddler cribs are available. Pets are not allowed at the lodge.

Location: On Highway 160 at milepost 160. At the south end of South Fork.

6 Cabins with Kitchens
1 Motel Room
5 Fireplaces

Room Phones
Elevation: 8200
Credit Cards: VMD
2 people a night: $35 - $75
Open: All Year

Sid & Priscilla Ham, Owners
PO Box 264
35 Silver Thread Lane
South Fork CO 81154-0264
719/873-5969 wp & Fax
800/510-3897
E-mail: fhlodge@rmii.com

At the resort:

At resort or within 15 minutes:

Goodnight's Lonesome Dove Cabins & Campground

Surrounded by the San Juan Range of the Rocky Mountains and 2 million acres of Rio Grande National Forest, Goodnight's offers six housekeeping cabins. The completely furnished, log cabins are delightfully cozy. All cabins are non-smoking with central heat and have double beds, equipped kitchens, private baths and satellite cable television. Five of the cabins have two rooms, and can sleep up to four people. The other cabin can sleep up to seven. RV sites are also available through the fall.

A country store on site will meet all your basic grocery needs, including fishing tackle, fishing and hunting licenses. The gift shop features handmade gifts, shirts and Colorado souvenirs. The year-round family activities will appeal to the sports enthusiast and nature lover alike. Try hiking, fishing, horseback riding, rafting, mountain biking or simply relaxing in the cool mountain air. Area attractions include exploring the old mining town of Creede, Chimney Rock, Great Sand Dunes National Monument and Mesa Verde. Visit Pagosa Springs and soak in the natural hot springs. Take a narrow-gauge train trip or a four-wheel drive tour through the back country. Hunters can come here year-round to enjoy nature's bounty. In the winter, ski Wolf Creek Ski area, noted to have the most snow in Colorado. Other winter activities include snowmobiling, cross-country skiing, ice fishing, ice skating and sleigh rides. No matter how you spend your day, be sure to save time for a relaxing break in the hot tub at Goodnight's Cabins.

Pets are allowed.

Location: About 6 miles southwest of South Fork. On Highway 160 at mile-post 180.

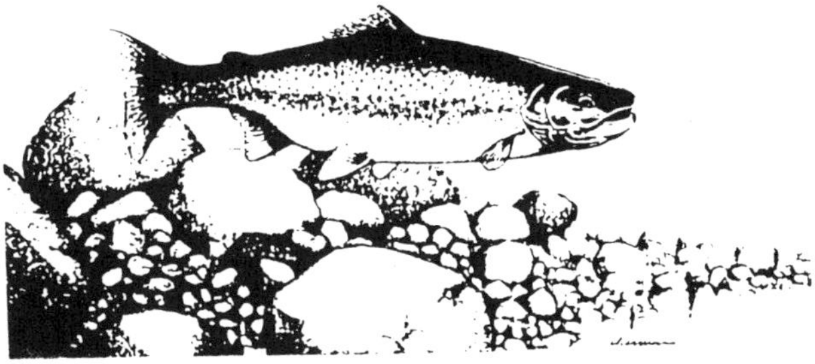

6 Cabins with Kitchens
Central Woodstove
Central Campfire Area

Pay Phone(s)
All Non-Smoking in Units
Recreation Room
Elevation: 8500
Credit Cards: VM
2 people a night: $55 - $65
Open: All Year

Robert & Connie Goodnight, Owners
PO Box 157
6.2mi SW of South Fork Hwy 160
South Fork CO 81154
719/873-1072
800/551-DOVE (3683)

At the resort:

At resort or within 15 minutes:

Rainbow Lodge, Cabins & RV Park

At Rainbow Lodge, choose among 16 modern housekeeping cabins or 13 lodge rooms. 'Rough it' in the spacious, one or two-bedroom log cabins with fireplaces, cable television, and fully equipped kitchens. The one or two-bedroom lodge rooms have queen beds, cable television and telephones.

The lodge is within walking distance of both the South Fork of the Rio Grande and the Rio Grande rivers, which are great for beginning river rafters and anglers. In fact, the entire area is a fishing haven with numerous mountain lakes nearby, all easily accessible in a two-wheel-drive car (four-wheel-drive vehicles are not needed). The mountains surrounding South Fork are home to a variety of wildlife, for hikers, sightseers and hunters alike to appreciate. Take any of the numerous hiking trails to explore nature's wonders here. In the winter, visit nearby Wolf Creek Ski Area, known as much for its pristine snow as its lack of crowds. Ask about the sleigh rides and snowmobile tours as well. Restaurants and evening entertainment are a short drive away.

RV sites are also available from May through October. Pets are welcomed at Rainbow Lodge.

Location: On Highway 160, at milepost 186.

16 Cabins with Kitchens
13 Motel Rooms
14 Fireplaces
Central Woodstove
Central Campfire Area

Room Phones
Recreation Room
Elevation: 8250
Credit Cards: VMAD
2 people a night: $30 - $60
Open: All Year

Teri & Robert Byrd, Managers
PO Box 224
South Fork CO 81154-0224
719/873-5571
719/873-5125 Fax

At the resort:

At resort or within 15 minutes:

Riverbend Resort Cabins & RV Park

In a mountain setting on the South Fork of the Rio Grande River, Riverbend Resort has one-mile river frontage, modern, well-heated cabins with fully equipped kitchens and fireplaces. Three cabins — Aspen, Ponderosa and the Columbine — feature an upstairs loft that sleeps 4 to 8 people. The larger cabins can accommodate up to 15 people each. All cabins have bed and bath linens, color television, decks and breath-taking views of the river. Ponderosa, spruce and aspen trees dot the resort. In 1983, Riverbend was transformed into Kamp Komfort for the movie National Lampoon's Vacation. Visit part of the movie set that still remains.

Riverbend sports horseshoes, a playground and planned group activities. Fish on the trout-stocked river or in many of the nearby mountain lakes. Riverbend is bordered on two sides by national forest and is in the heart of the San Juan Mountains, which offer fantastic hiking, mountain biking, horseback riding, and hunting for trophy elk, deer and bear. While the kids play in the recreation hall, you can relax in the hot tub after a day of view-filled hiking. Darlene is a fiber artist and has added a weaving studio and gallery. In winter, enjoy Wolf Creek ski area only a 20 minute drive away. Cross country ski or snowmobile the many groomed trails in the area.

Grassy RV sites overlooking the river are available. Children under 4 stay free. Ask about their off season rates. The resort has room for your horse. Well behaved pets are allowed in the cabins for a small fee.

Location: 3 miles southwest of South Fork on Highway 160, near milepost 183.

11 Cabins with Kitchens
27 Beds in Bunk House or Dorm
11 Fireplaces
Central Fireplace
Central Campfire Area

Pay Phone(s)
Non-Smoking Units Available
Recreation Room
Elevation: 8350
Credit Cards: VMAD
2 people a night: $40 - $65
Open: All Year

Martin & Darlene Danko, Owners
Box 129
33846 West Hwy 160
South Fork CO 81154-0728
719/873-5344
800/621-6512

At the resort:

At resort or within 15 minutes:

South Fork Lodge & RV Park

Amid some of the deepest powder a Rocky Mountain winter has to offer, South Fork Lodge & RV Park offers thirteen housekeeping cabins. Two cabins have fireplaces and all others have central heating. All units have televisions, kitchenettes and access to the recreation and laundry rooms. The kids can work off their extra energy, while you relax in the hot tub and watch the sun set. With a restaurant and evening entertainment just minutes away, your vacation is sure to have it all.

The South Fork Lodge is open all year, so you can enjoy activities every season, no matter when you visit. In the summers, fish streams, rivers and lakes in the nearby National Forest. Bring your horse to vacation with you, or visit the stables just down the road for wilderness horseback riding. Other summer activities include hiking, river rafting, golfing, mountain biking, and renting boats to cruise the mountain lakes. In the fall, go big game hunting. When the snow arrives, come to visit with your skis, snowmobiles and ice fishing gear. The Rio Grande National Forest offers abundant cross-country trails while the nearby Wolf Creek Ski Area has plenty of slopes to satisfy every skill level. For the romantically inclined, ask about the sleigh rides through a true winter wonderland.

RV and tent sites are also available. Ask about the indoor, group meeting area for your family reunion.

Location: 1 mile from South Fork on Highway 149, at milepost 1.

13 Cabins with Kitchens
2 Fireplaces
Central Woodstove
Central Campfire Area

Pay Phone(s)
Recreation Room
Elevation: 8250
Credit Cards: VMD
2 people a night: $40 - $65
Open: All Year

Don & Faye McGregor, Owners
PO Box 43
0364 W Hwy 149
South Fork CO 81154-0043
719/873-5303
800/457-9156

At the resort:

At resort or within 15 minutes:

Spruce Lodge, Cabins, B&B, Rafting and RV Park

If you're an outdoor sports enthusiast, Spruce Lodge is the place to stay. The resort is at the foot of the San Juan Mountains near the Rio Grande River and only 17 miles from Wolf Creek Ski Area. Built in the 1920s, the Lodge is a quaint, historic log building that blends modern conveniences with turn-of-the-century charm. Choose between comfortable, rustic guest rooms in the main lodge or modern motel rooms, including television and telephone with or without a fully equipped kitchenette, in the adjacent chalet. Smoking or non-smoking units are available and all room rates include a delicious breakfast.

A gift shop with local, handmade crafts and souvenirs is right on the property. Play miniature golf on-site. Ask your hosts about unguided rafting on the Rio Grande — there are mild, fun family trips for beginners. After a day of rafting, soothe your tired muscles in the spacious, indoor hot tub or relax in front of the large river rock fireplace in the main lobby. Other area activities include trout fishing, horseback riding, hiking, hunting and four-wheel driving. Rent a mountain bike and ride the back country trails. Winter sports abound as well, from cross-country and downhill skiing to snowmobiling. Several fine restaurants and a variety of shops are located close by.

Ask about the large meeting area in the lodge for your family reunion. Full hookup RV sites are also available.

Location: North side of Highway 160, at the east end of South Fork, near milepost 187.

2 Vacation Homes
8 Lodging Rooms
9 Motel Rooms
Central Fireplace
Central Campfire Area

Room Phones
Bed & Breakfast Available
Non-Smoking Units Available
Recreation Room
Elevation: 8180
Credit Cards: VMA
2 people a night: $28 - $45
Open: All Year

Josef & Daniela Schroeck, Owners
PO Box 156
29431 US 160
South Fork CO 81154-0156
719/873-5605 & Fax
800/228-5605

At the resort:

At resort or within 15 minutes:

South Park Area

Including Bailey & Fairplay — Map: G-15 & H-13

South Park is a broad valley covering over 900 square miles and is surrounded by the Mosquito and Park ranges. The South Park county seat, tiny **Fairplay**, is on the east side of the Continental Divide and was once a major setting during the gold fever days of the 1860s. That history is kept alive by the South Park City Museum, a careful restoration of life here at the height of the Gold Rush. Discover how the pioneers and prospectors lived, worked and played at this outdoor museum of 32 authentic buildings and wide variety of artifacts. The Old Courthouse, still in use, is one of the oldest in the United States. Prior to gold, the Fairplay area was known for its salt; early French trappers called it "Bayou Salado" ("Salt Creek"). Today adventure abounds, via hiking, mountain climbing, camping, gold medal fishing, gold panning, road or mountain biking, cross-country skiing, snowmobiling, horseback riding and hunting. July brings the World's Championship Pack Burro Race, an annual event the last weekend of the month honoring the contributions of the lowly burro to the area's mining industry. **Bailey**, just 45 miles southwest of Denver, is surrounded by the Pike National Forest. It is an undiscovered mountain hideaway, yet near the big city of Denver. At an altitude of 7,750', it is an excellent area for hunting and fishing. If you love the great outdoors, you'll love South Park area year round!

Fun Things to Do

- McGraw Historical Park, Bailey (303) 838-9511
- South Park Historical City Museum, Fairplay (719) 836-2387

Glen Isle Resort Lodge & Cabins

This national historic site on the Platte River offers activities year round has been under the same family ownership since 1923. You will be "roughing it" in well-insulated, well-furnished cabins that sleep up to 10 people. All cabins contain fully equipped kitchens, private baths, easy chairs, bedding and linens, fireplaces (wood provided) and gas heat. The lodge, built in 1900, is listed on the National Register of Historic Sites and has been owned by the same family for more than 70 years. You may rent lodge rooms with or without breakfast. Glen Isle Resort offers a restful, informal and reasonably-priced family retreat.

Decorated with antiques, the lodge serves breakfast and has gift and antique shops. Resort amenities include a children's playground, games, picnics, cookouts, sing-a-longs, square dancing, movies, Saturday chuckwagon dinners and a library to browse in. Spend the days fishing, hiking, horseback riding, bird watching and hunting. In the winter, try sledding, ice skating and skiing. Centrally located in Colorado, you can reach practically any point of interest by car.

Pets may accompany you to Glen Isle Resort for a fee. A deposit is required with advance reservations. The resort offers an European plan (special rates for children under 10) and Bed & Breakfast to suit your needs. Ask about their off season rates.

Location: 50 minutes southwest of Denver on Highway 285, near milepost 221.

13 Cabins with Kitchens
6 Cabins without Kitchens
14 Lodging Rooms
14 Fireplaces
Central Fireplace
Central Campfire Area

Pay Phone(s)
Bed & Breakfast Available
Non-Smoking Units Available
Recreation Room
Elevation: 7830
No credit cards
2 people a night: $48 - $75
Open: All Year

Gordon & Barbara Tripp, Owners
PO Box 128
573 Old Stage Coach Rd
Bailey CO 80421-0128
303/838-5461

At the resort:

At resort or within 15 minutes:

Mooredale Ranch Resort

Enjoy a relaxing vacation among the pines in a scenic, uncrowded setting at Mooredale Ranch Resort. Pick between distinctive rooms and suites or spacious cottages which can accommodate two to ten people. Each cottage comes with a fully equipped kitchen and dinette. All units have bathrooms, attractive furnishings, fireplaces and firewood. Cottages are made log and rock brick with white trim and many windows to enjoy the views. A few cottages side along the ranch's pond. Adjacent to the pine trees of Pike National Forest, these all offer a picturesque place to unwind.

The full service restaurant serves meals throughout the day and the generous Sunday Brunch is just the treat your weekend needs. The north fork of the South Platte River, which borders the ranch, and the private pond (no fishing license required) will meet the needs of all anglers, young and old, who can't wait to catch a mountain trout! Activities include hiking, horseback riding, swimming in the heated pool and relaxing in the hot tub. Play tennis, take a hayride and send the kids to the playground. Mooredale makes a perfect home base for many area activities, including biking, hiking, skiing, hunting, whitewater rafting, exploring ghost towns and taking scenic drives.

Mooredale Ranch can host weddings, family reunions and company meetings for up to 150 people.

Location: On Highway 285 at milepost 219, two and a half miles southwest of Bailey.

5 Cabins with Kitchens
12 Lodging Rooms
18 Fireplaces
Central Fireplace
Central Campfire Area

Room Phones
Recreation Room
Elevation: 7993
Credit Cards: VMAD
2 people a night: $60 - $100
Open: All Year

Katie & Rinse de Koning, Owners
PO Box 845
Bailey CO 80421-0845
303/838-2775
303/838-1938 Fax

At the resort:

At resort or within 15 minutes:

Steamboat Springs & North Park Areas

Including Clark, Cowdrey, Hahns Peak, Rand & Walden—
Map: C-9, B-9, A-11B-9, C-12 & B-12

A famous ski center, **Steamboat Springs** in the Yampa Valley offers much more than just winter sports. Fish Creek Falls is a breathtaking 283' waterfall and historic bridge. From the falls you have access to hiking and mountain biking trails that lead to the Continental Divide. From town, drive northeast to the Mount Zirkel Wilderness Area where the elevation ranges from 7,000' to 13,000' in a 141,000-acre undeveloped area, ideal for hiking, fishing and hunting. The Yampa River Trail System runs adjacent to downtown. Steamboat Springs was supposedly named in 1865 when French trappers riding through thought they heard the chugging of a steamboat. But it was a hot springs that chugged until 1908 when the railroad blasted out the rock chamber over the springs. Northern Utes (the Yampsatika) summered in the area as early as the 1300s. Whites first settled here in 1875 and although they used skis to get around in the winter, it wasn't until 1913 that they started skiing for fun and the rest is history. Be forewarned, however, according to local legend, the "Yampa Valley Curse" means visitors are cast under a spell that compels them to return again and again.

[Even though the towns of Rand and Cowdrey are east of Steamboat and rightly in the North Park area, we have taken the liberty of including each of them in this book's Steamboat Springs Area chapter. These are diverse areas from Steamboat. But then also are Clark, Columbine, Hahns Peak and Yampa. Such is the independent character of the people and towns in this rugged and independent northwest part of Colorado. Yet for you, dear reader, we have contained them into this chapter.]

Fun Things to Do

- Hahn's Peak Area Historical Society (970) 879-3825, Winter 824-5176
- Mount Zirkel Wilderness Area (970) 879-1870
- North Park Ranger District(970) 723-8204
- Stagecoach State Park (970) 736-2436
- Steamboat Springs Golf Course (970) 879-4295
- Steamboat Springs Ski Area (800) 922-2722
- Tread of Pioneers Museum (970) 879-2214

Country Inn at Steamboat Lake

The Country Inn offers a serene setting in the Rockies at Steamboat Lake. Located in historic Hahns Peak Village, where miners once panned for gold, this roomy log bed and breakfast has warm, welcoming rooms decorated in a country style. All eight guest rooms feature colorful quilts on the bed, charming antiques and private bathrooms. The second floor has a gathering room perfect for lounging and relaxing with its television, stereo, games, books and comfortable collection of recliners. Settle down in the loft for a game of cards or curl up with a favorite book.

The inn's outdoor deck has a hot tub and offers a view of nearby Steamboat Lake and majestic Hahns Peak rising to 11,000'. The restaurant on-site that serves breakfast, included in your room rate, also serves three meals a day, seven days a week. Steamboat Lake is a 1,550-acre playground to explore. Cast for rainbow trout in the morning, picnic under the warm midday sun, and boat in the afternoon. Explore Hahns Peak Village with its historic buildings, gift shops and museum. Other summer activities include hiking, horseback riding, mountain biking and riding A.T.Vs. In the winter, take an old-fashioned moonlit sleigh ride with a team of draft horses. Snowmobile, dogsled, cross-country ski, downhill ski, and ice fish during the snowy months. At the end of the day, slip into the outdoor hot tub and watch the sun set across the lake behind Sand Mountain.

The first floor of the inn has a bedroom equipped for handicap persons. There are two sets of adjoining rooms for families.

Location: 30 miles north of Steamboat Springs, on County Road 129, between milepost 24-25.

8 Lodging Rooms
Central Woodstove

Pay Phone(s)
Bed & Breakfast Available
Non-Smoking Units Available
Recreation Room
Elevation: 8600
Credit Cards: VM
2 people a night: $75 - $95
Open: All Year

Tom & Stephanie Berry, Owners
PO Box 876
61276 CR 129
Clark CO 80428
970/879-3906
800/934-STAY (7829) & Fax Call 1st

At the resort:

At resort or within 15 minutes:

Elk Mountain Ranch

A working private elk ranch, Elk Mountain Guest Ranch borders Medicine Bow National Forest with over 2400 scenic acres. This modern lodge has bed & breakfast two bedrooms with private bathrooms. A housekeeping cabin with a woodburning stove is planned to open the summer of 1997. The ranch is a smoke free environment and there are no phones or televisions in the rooms or cabin.

The Ranch's game room includes board games and a television for relaxing after a long day of frolicking in the great outdoors. Enjoy the pristine mountain setting of the national park with its pine and aspen tree forests, high mountain meadows and beaver ponds. Wildlife watching and photography is a delight with the abundant elk, antelope, deer, bear, and moose. The area boasts blue ribbon fishing. Other area activities include hiking, panning for gold, mine tours, searching for Native American Indian artifacts and guided float trips on the North Platte River. If fall plan a guided hunting trip. In a winter vacation is in your plans enjoy snowshoeing, snowmobile and cross-country skiing.

If you would prefer three meals a day make sure to mention it when you make your reservation.

Location: Seven and a half miles north of junction Highways 125 and 127, then four miles west on Highway 125 to County Road 4.

1 Cabin with Kitchen
2 Lodging Rooms
Central Woodstove
Central Campfire Area

Lobby Phone
Bed & Breakfast Available
Non-Smoking Units Available
Recreation Room
Elevation: 8300
No credit cards
2 people a night: $90 - $130
Open: All Year

Margaret H & Mark Mitchell, Owners
PO Box 124
3000 Jackson Cty Rd 4
Cowdrey CO 80434-0124
970/723-4000 & Fax call 1st

At the resort:

At resort or within 15 minutes:

Elk River Guest Ranch

On the banks of the upper Elk River, surrounded by Routt National Forest and near the pristine Mount Zirkel Wilderness area, Elk River Guest Ranch is an excellent place to get away from it all. Enjoy a private cabin encircled by the outstanding scenery of the Elk River Valley. These cabins offer wood stoves, private baths and full kitchens with comfortable furnishings. The cabins, with daily maid service, have one or two bedrooms and can sleep six to eight people. Bring along your camera to capture wildlife, wild flowers, rushing rivers, billowing high country meadows and, in the fall, aspen in all their colorful, golden glory.

For those who truly want a luxury, no-hassles vacation, ask about the three meals a day delivered to your own cabin! The ranch will prepare you for hunting season or fishing all summer long on Steamboat and Pearl Lakes or on the more than 100 mountain lakes and 900 miles of nearby streams. Elk River Guest Ranch also offers horseback rides of varying lengths, including a lunch trip to Pearl Lake. In the winter, try cross-country skiing or snowmobiling on the 25 miles of groomed trails or downhill ski in Steamboat Springs. Unwind in the large hot tub and join your hosts around the nightly, summer campfires after a day of high country adventures.

RV Sites are available. Reservations must be made in advance with 50% deposit.

Location: 20 miles north of Steamboat Springs. Off County Road 129, on County Road 64 (Seed House Road)

4 Cabins with Kitchens
1 Fireplace
1 Woodstove
Central Campfire Area

Lobby Phone
Bed & Breakfast Available
Recreation Room
Elevation: 7300
Credit Cards: VM
2 people a night: $125 - $175
Open: All Year

Bill & Kathy Hinder, Owners
29840 CR 64
Clark CO 80428
970/879-6220
800/750-6220
E-mail: ergr@cmn.net

At the resort:

At resort or within 15 minutes:

Glen Eden Resort

In the heart of ranch and recreation country, Glen Eden has "contempo-rustic" townhomes (duplexes) along the Elk River, combining natural, rustic materials with contemporary interior design. This is an upscale resort. All accommodations are completely furnished, from firewood to forks. There are TVs in all of the cabins and VCRs in some of the cabins for your viewing pleasure. The townhomes have moss rock fireplaces, two bathrooms, two bedrooms, a fully-equipped kitchen, covered sun porch and views of spectacular Mount Zirkel and Sand Mountain.

The AAA-rated, log-styled pine lodge has a dining room, tavern, saloon and a conference room. For those nippier days, swim in the heated pool or soak in one of two hot tubs. Many activities available at the resort — playing tennis, mountain biking and private trout fishing on the Elk River and in high-country lakes. Fly fishing instruction is also available. Additional activities include rafting and extensive trails for snowmobiling. Your hosts can arrange horseback hunting trips to Colorado's largest elk populations minutes away. You can also go horseback riding around the town of Clark and go boating on nearby Steamboat Lake. The Mount Zirkel Wilderness area, 12 miles away, and Routt National Forest, three miles away, are perfect for summer hiking and winter cross-country skiing. Take a picnic in historical Hahn's Peak or ask your hosts about the many sightseeing opportunities.

The resort is closed for one week each April. Call ahead for more information. Kids under 12 stay free.

Location: In Clark on County Road 129, near milepost 17, 18 miles north of Steamboat Springs.

24 Cabins with Kitchens
Central Campfire Area

Pay Phone(s)
Recreation Room
Elevation: 7200
Credit Cards: VMAD
2 people a night: $85 - $135
Open: 5/01 to 5/20

Rich Landon, GM & Paulette Derstine
PO Box 908
54737 Routt CR 129
Clark CO 80428-0908
970/879-3907
800/882-0854
970/870-0858 Fax
E mail: eden@rmi.net

At the resort:

At resort or within 15 minutes:

Hahn's Peak Guest Ranch

At the foot of Hahn's Peak, Hahn's Peak Guest Ranch has four furnished, unique log housekeeping cabins. The loft units sleep up to six people. Each cabin has a kitchen, a full bathroom with a shower-tub and a deck with a barbecue grill. All linens and towels are furnished.

The general store is well-stocked with groceries, hunting and fishing licenses, tackle, gifts and a little bit of "this and that." Be sure to try the home cooked specials and sub-sandwiches in the deli. Gasoline and propane are also available. Fish on the three large lakes or miles of mountain brooks and alpine streams.Nearby there are guided horseback trips up Hahn's Peak for breathtaking views. Ride your mountain bike or hike on the nearby trails during the milder months, while in the winter, take Routt County's best snowmobile tours. The Hahn's Peak area specializes in scenic snowmobile tours in the winter with 2 hour to full day tours. The downhill skiing at Steamboat Springs is some of the best in the country.

The Ranch does allow pets for a fee of $10.00 per night.

Location: 25 miles north of Steamboat Springs and 7 miles from Clark; on County Road 129, near milepost 24, across from Steamboat Lake.

4 Cabins with Kitchens

Pay Phone(s)
Elevation: 8200
Credit Cards: VMD
2 people a night: $85 - $85
Open: All Year

Bonnie McCullough & Dave&
Donna Papini
PO Box 839
60880 RCR 129
Clark CO 80428-0839
970/879-5878

At the resort:

At resort or within 15 minutes:

Mended Wing Guest House

Hidden away from the business of life, among a grove of pine and aspen trees, is Mended Wing Guest House. Experience a mending of the spirit, mind and soul as you drink in the panoramic views of Mt. Zirkel, Steamboat Lake and Hahn's Peak. Accommodations include king and queen sized beds with down comforters, wool blankets and thick terry robes that stand ready for a trip to the Jacuzzi. The unit also includes a fully equipped kitchen. The loft, accessible by ladder, has a full bathroom all its own and a queen bed with all the same luxury of the master suite. The master suite features a raised sleeping area. A full bath serves both the living room and bedroom. The living room has a queen sofa bed, wood stove and dining area all with views of Mt. Zirkel wilderness. The main level of the master bedroom includes a sitting area, an extra sink, vanity and a cozy library to wile away the hours reading, sketching or relaxing.

The winter season here is a wonderland of activities from snowmobiling to cross-country skiing. Want to try something different? How about a dog sled tour where you'll glide along charted trails with a master guiding his team of dogs. Try ice fishing in the winter and warm weather casting in the summer at Steamboat Lake.

Ask about the expanded continental menus weekdays and the American style weekends.

Location: 25 miles north of Steamboat Springs. On County Road 129, at milepost 24.

1 Cabin with Kitchen
3 Beds in Bunk House or Dorm
1 Woodstove

Room Phones
Bed & Breakfast Available
Elevation: 8150
Credit Cards: VM
2 people a night: $95 - $250
Open: All Year

Andy & Paula Maneotis, Owners
PO Box 773267
60860 RCR 129
Steamboat Springs CO 80477
970/870-1522

At the resort:

At resort or within 15 minutes:

Sky Valley Lodge

Vacation in the warm and inviting elegance of an English country manor at Sky Valley Lodge. Adjacent to Lake Catamount on the edge of Rabbit Ears Pass and tucked into the side of a mountain, you'll appreciate the stunning, sweeping view of the valley below. The twenty-four rooms are divided twelve each between an upper and lower lodge. The lodges have been recently updated with a new kitchenette and new furnishings in almost all rooms. During the winter, snuggle down on feather beds for a cozy treat.

Contemporary gourmet continental breakfast is served daily in the dining room where full breakfast and lighter fare luncheon/dinner menus are available. Family-style dinners with selected entrees may be reserved each morning. Kids can play in the special nook near the dining room while you relax in the bar/lounge. Just seven minutes from Steamboat, the lodge has daily shuttles to take guests downtown for dining and shopping, and to a ski-in, ski-out slopeside hotel where you can store your equipment in the lockers while taking a break from the runs. Warm weather activities includes hiking, biking, hot air ballooning and rodeo watching. In the winter, after enjoying downhill or cross-country skiing, be sure to relax in the sauna or take a dip in the outdoor hot tub. Soak in the soothing water and view the Milky Way in all its splendor.

Sky Valley Lodge is great for family reunions, weddings and private parties.

Location: On Highway 40 1.5 miles up from base of Rabbit Ears Pass, at mile-post 141, looking over Steamboat Springs.

24 Lodging Rooms
Central Fireplace
Central Woodstove

Lobby Phone
Bed & Breakfast Available
All Non-Smoking in Units
Recreation Room
Elevation: 7600
Credit Cards: VMAD
2 people a night: $68 - $178
Open: All Year

Steve Myler, Manager
PO Box 773132
31490 Hwy 40 East
Steamboat Springs CO 80477
970/879-7749
800/538-7519
970/879-7752 Fax
E-mail: steamboat-lodging@toski.com

At the resort:

At resort or within 15 minutes:

Steamboat Log Cabins at Perry-Mansfield

Perry-Mansfield is truly a unique vacation spot: it is both the oldest performing arts camp in the country and a cabin resort. The modern log cabins are in secluded and wooded Strawberry Park, one of the more beautiful areas in the region. The snug cabins, which sleep up to 10 people, contain electric baseboard heat, wood-burning fireplaces, full kitchens and bathrooms, and include all linens and firewood.

Perry-Mansfield was a focal point for American modern dance in the 1930s. Dance pioneer Agnes de Mille was inspired to choreograph her famous ballet "Rodeo" after attending a local square dance at a county schoolhouse not far from Perry-Mansfield. The performing arts tradition continues — in the summer, be sure to attend their lovely theater and dance productions put on by the camp's students. The area is ripe for hiking, fishing or swimming in the nearby natural hot springs pool. In the winter, enjoy snowshoeing, cross-country skiing, sledding and downhill skiing at Steamboat Springs.

The rustic conference facility is ideal for business meetings and family reunions.

Location: In Steamboat Springs, go north on 7th from Lincoln, turn right on Missouri and continue to North Park. Follow North Park for 1.5 miles. Perry-Mansfield is on the left.

6 Cabins with Kitchens
1 Woodstove

No Phones Available
Elevation: 7000
Credit Cards: VM
2 people a night: $95 - $325
Open: All Year

Tonya Baker & Phil Gerdel, Mgrs
40755 RCR 36
Steamboat Springs CO 80487-9298
970/879-1060
800/538-7519
970/870-9436 resort & fax
E-mail: steamboat-lodging@toski.com

At the resort:

At resort or within 15 minutes:

Whistling Elk Ranch

Get a chance to be "city slickers" for a day on this working cattle ranch in North Park where you can help with cattle drives and branding when they occur. Whistling Elk's deluxe, modern cabins feature full kitchens and bathrooms, wood-burning fireplaces, electric heat and two bedrooms. Towels, linens, firewood, cooking utensils and coffee makers are provided. All cabins are non-smoking. Located at the base of Owl Mountain, days here are sunny and warm while the nights are cool and comfortable.

Daily activities at the ranch can include working up an appetite being a real ranch hand helping with the chores or relaxing and taking in the wonderful scenery. The ranch also sponsors a "backcountry camp," where you ride in by horseback or mountain bike and spend the night under a blanket of dazzling stars. Morning greets you with a breathtaking view of Parkview Mountain and the smell of a delicious western breakfast. Fish on the trail or back at the ranch in the 3 miles of private stream or the stocked pond on the ranch's 1,600 acres of private land open to guests. Explore the ranch's many trails, either on a gentle horse, on foot, your mountain bike, or by cross-country skis. Photograph wildlife, including elk, mule deer, black bear, moose, coyotes and eagles. Ask about guided big-game hunts in season. In the evening, gaze at stars from the secluded outdoor hot tub after "working" all day. Whistling Elk offers a vacation far from crowds in the beauty and solitude of the Rocky Mountains.

Location: 90 miles west of Fort Collins on Jackson County Road 27, 9.5 miles southwest of Highway 14; or 4.3 miles northeast of Highway 125.

3 Cabins with Kitchens
3 Woodstoves
Central Campfire Area

Lobby Phone
All Non-Smoking in Units
Elevation: 8700
No credit cards
2 people a night: $79 - $95
Open: All Year

John Ziegman, Owner
PO Box 2
4164 JCR 27
Rand CO 80473-002
970/723-8311 & Fax

At the resort:

At resort or within 15 minutes:

Winding River Guest Ranch

Winding River Guest Ranch is a working cattle ranch bordering Arapahoe National Refuge. Nestled in the heart of North Park, Winding River features five rooms in the 1898 ranch house and four beds in a bunk house. The beautifully appointed rooms are decorated with different themes and have full maid service. Guests share bathrooms in this non-smoking facility. The delicious country breakfast will start your day off right. The ranch is surrounded by hay meadows, wildflowers, cattle, a resident moose, whitetail deer, the winding Michigan River and the wonders of nature. Enjoy spectacular, panoramic views of the majestic mountains, and the western pleasures of an authentic working cattle and hay ranch.

The North Park area offers big game hunting and viewing of moose, bear, bluegrouse, antelope, mountain lion, sagegrouse, deer, big horn sheep, game birds, elk, eagles and other abundant wildlife. The ranch has 2 miles of catch & release private fishing and 8 miles of private access state fishing. Ask about the horse-drawn sleigh and wagon rides the whole family will enjoy. Other activities include bird watching, taking scenic nature walks and fly fishing on the Michigan River. In the colder months, go snow shoeing, cross-country skiing and lake ice fishing. While staying at the ranch, take the opportunity to experience pioneer chores, checking and feeding the cattle with the ranch's Belgian draft horses, Jiggs and Buster. Nearby things to do include touring the Arapahoe National Refuge, bird and wildlife sanctuaries, fishing the Illinois River, taking self-guided auto tours, and visiting the Pioneer Museum and the Sand Dunes Recreation Area.

Location: About 90 miles east of Steamboat Springs. Two and a half miles east of Walden on 4th Street.

5 Lodging Rooms
4 Beds in Bunk House or Dorm

Lobby Phone
Bed & Breakfast Available
All Non-Smoking in Units
Recreation Room
Elevation: 9000
Credit Cards: VMA
2 people a night: $95
Open: 5/15 to 11/15

Debbie & Kent Holsinger & Darleen West
PO Box 37
715 4th St
Walden CO 80480
970/723-4587
970/723-4771 Fax

At the resort:

At resort or within 15 minutes:

Summit County

Including Breckenridge, Dillon, Frisco, Green Mountain Reservoir, Heeney, Keystone, Montezuma & Silverthorne — Map: G-13, F-12, E-11 & F-13

It almost goes without saying that Summit County offers the best in downhill and cross-country skiing as well as snowboarding at its many ski resorts. There's more than just countless opportunities for winter adventures here, though. Charmingly restored, gingerbread Victorian houses lining its streets earned **Breckenridge** a National Historic District designation. Set amidst mountain splendor and the Continental Divide for a backdrop, this former mining town was established in an 1859 gold rush — the first permanent settlement on Colorado's Western Slope. Named in honor of Vice President John C. Breckenridge (in order to get a post office more easily), the town, when the Civil War broke out and the vice president supported the Confederacy, was re-named Breckenridge. In addition to the diverse terrain on the ski resort's three mountains, Breckenridge, at an elevation of 9,603', has the only Jack Nicklaus-designed municipal golf course, renown musical organizations, and miles of hiking trails. Be sure and check out the human maze at Peak 8 — a fun place to get lost! Surrounded by Arapaho National Forest, the city has fishing on the Upper Blue River or the nearby Mohawk Lakes. Go sailing on Lake **Dillon** or shop in more than fifty **Silverthorne** Factory Outlet Stores. Rent a mountain bike in **Frisco** and enjoy extensive **Summit County** bike path system of 47 trails! Four 14ers (mountain peaks 14,000' and higher in elevation) can be climbed nearby. Boating and fishing are popular at **Green Mountain Reservoir** by **Heeney,** 20 miles north of I-70. **Montezuma**, above Keystone, is the only town (we know of) where the pavement *ends* when it reaches town. Locals describe it as "6 miles and 100 years from Keystone" and will tell you why "winters are why we come, summers are why we stay."

Fun Things To Do

- Alpine Slide, Breckenridge (970) 453-5000
- Breckenridge Activity Center (970) 453-5579
- Breckenridge Golf Club (970) 453-9104
- Breckenridge National Historic District (970) 453-9022
- Breckenridge Ski Area (970) 453-5000
- Dillon Ranger District Office, Silverthorne (970) 468-5400
- Frisco Historical Park, Frisco (970) 668-3428
- Pa & Ma's Guest Ranch (719)486-3900
- Peak 8 Human Maze (970) 724-3490
- Summit Historical Society Tours (970) 453-9022

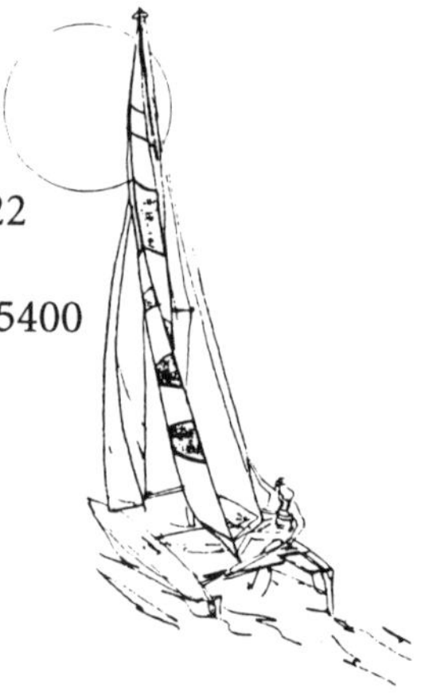

Granny's Inn Montezuma Bed & Breakfast and Cabins

A year-round, high mountain hideaway, Granny's offers charming mountain hospitality. This bed and breakfast inn, surrounded by grand mountain peaks and towering pines, is filled with history and charm. Enjoy the warmth of a country fireplace and postcard views of historic Montezuma from your private, cozy room. A private cabin with back country trails starting right at the door is also available.

Join your hosts for "apres ski" or savor the delights of Granny's hot soups and sourdough bread. The sourdough is made with a starter over 100 years old — a taste of the past baked fresh daily! This is also home to Alpine Adventures. In the winter, bundle up in elk robes and take a romantic, scenic sleigh ride. On the summer rides, visit historic mining areas such as the Silver King, Argentine and Sts. Johns mines with panoramic views. Only six miles and 100 years away from the ski resort town of Keystone, Granny's offers a refreshing change of pace.

Granny's can cater to weddings, banquets, family reunions, or any special occasion you have

Location: From I-70 take Highway 6 east past Keystone to County Road 5 (Montezuma Road). Turn right, follow Montezuma Road to town of Montezuma (about 6 miles).

1 Cabin with Kitchen
4 Lodging Rooms
1 Fireplace
Central Woodstove
Central Campfire Area

Lobby Phone
Bed & Breakfast Available
All Non-Smoking in Units
Recreation Room
Elevation: 10400
Credit Cards: VM
2 people a night: $60 - $85
Open: All Year

Donna Hellyer, Owner
5435 CR 5 - Montezuma Rd
Montezuma CO 80435
970/468-9297

At the resort:

At resort or within 15 minutes:

Green Mountain Cabins & Boat Rentals

Tucked away between the Gore and Williams Fork mountain ranges, Green Mountain Cabins offers accommodations on pretty Green Mountain Reservoir. The log cabins have cooking facilities, however bring your own dishes and utensils.

The marina rents 14-foot fishing boats and canoes by the hour or by the day. Hike and watch the birds on the several nearby trails in the Eagle's Nest Wilderness area, with its pristine lakes and streams teeming with brook trout. For the more adventurous, this area is great for windsurfing, hang gliding, water-skiing and backpacking.

Location: 17.3 miles north of the I-70 Silverthorne exit (exit 205), on Highway 9, near milepost 126. Turn west at the north end of the reservoir on County Road 30, 7.3 miles to Heeney.

3 Cabins with Kitchens

Pay Phone(s)
Elevation: 8000
Credit Cards: VM
2 people a night: $40
Open: All Year

Dick & Maggie Philips, Owners
Blue River Route
0255 CR 1782
Silverthorne CO 80498-0082
970/724-9748
E-mail: rphillips@csn.net

At the resort:

At resort or within 15 minutes:

Green Mountain Inn and Cabins

Green Mountain Inn built in the late 1940s is located in the small town of Heeney with a year round population of seventy people. The old-style mountain cabins still have its original local charm. The inn has an old fashioned county store, rooms, log cabins, a tavern and continental dining. This small mountain resort has 2 cabins and 2 rooms which are ideal for your vacation or weekend plans.

Either let them do the cooking — their restaurant prepares wonderful meals and fresh, homemade pies — or, for those with a gourmet flair, purchase supplies at the grocery store and cook your own on your cabin stove. Enjoy great views from the restaurant's new outdoor deck overlooking Green Mountain Reservoir. After supper, join the tavern crowd for relaxing in this small, peaceful mountain town. Weekend entertainment abounds all summer long. The surrounding wilderness areas offer many activities, including fishing, biking, climbing, boating, water-skiing, windsurfing, hiking, hunting and hang gliding. For a quiet evening rent a television, VCR and movies on site.

Ask about the meeting facilities for groups. Bed & Breakfast is available only on weekends.

Location: Go 17.3 miles north of I-70 at Silverthorne (exit 205) on Highway 9. Near milepost 126, turn west at the north end of the reservoir and go 7.3 miles on County Road 30 to Heeney.

2 Cabins with Kitchens
2 Lodging Rooms
Central Woodstove

Pay Phone(s)
Recreation Room
Elevation: 8050
Credit Cards: VMD
2 people a night: $35 - $45
Open: All Year

Scott & Jeanette Astaldi, Owners
7101 SCR 30
Silverthorne CO 80498
970/724-3812

At the resort:

At resort or within 15 minutes:

MarDei's Mountain Retreat Bed & Breakfast

MarDei's chalet architecture is influenced by and features a European design interior. Guest rooms have king, queen, full or twin beds with down comforters. Choose between a dorm room with four single beds and shared bath, rooms with a double bed and shared bath, a room with a queen sized bed and private bath or a large room with a king and single beds, private bath, balcony and fireplace. Breakfast is served daily and is included in the price.

Cross-country or downhill ski the Summit by purchasing a pass to all four close by resorts. Other winter activities include going on a sleigh ride, snowmobiling, ice skating and heli-skiing. During the summer try fishing, sailing, biking, golfing, rafting, four-wheel driving, horseback riding, hiking, playing tennis, hot air ballooning and even llama trekking! Fishermen, sailors, hikers and backpackers will like nearby Lake Dillon's miles of shoreline and hiking trails. After it all, relax in the outdoor hot tub or unwind by the fireside and take in a movie.

Location: From I-70 take Frisco (exit 203), south to Main Street (4th stop light), right on Main Street to first stop sign (4th Avenue), turn left, go two blocks, on the right side of road of corner of 4th and Teller.

6 Lodging Rooms
2 Beds in Bunk House or Dorm
1 Fireplace
Central Fireplace

Lobby Phone
Bed & Breakfast Available
All Non-Smoking in Units
Recreation Room
Elevation: 9000
No credit cards
2 people a night: $40 - $120
Open: All Year

Amy & Michael Wolach, Owners
PO Box 1767
221 S 4th Ave
Frisco CO 80443-1767
970/668-5337

At the resort:

At resort or within 15 minutes:

Melody Lodge

Built around 1940, Melody Lodge was originally a dance hall and bar with several "fishing cabins" during the construction of the Green Mountain Reservoir. On the way to Heeney, look for the cabins with the red roofs, where the Blue River meets Green Mountain Reservoir. The newly remodeled two-room cabin, with a shower-bath, is fully furnished. The front room has a full bed plus a sofa bed. The second room is a fully equipped kitchen/dining area with all the necessary utensils. The two bedroom suite, in the upstairs of the lodge features a full bath, kitchenette, and private entrance. The one bedroom cabin has a woodburning fireplace with rustic charm. Linens, pillows, towels, dishes, pots and pans are provided in both cabins and the suite. Television is available in the suite and one bedroom cabin.

Being located in the valley between the magnificent Gore Range and the Williams Fork Mountains, Melody Lodge has a wealth of activities available for the outdoor enthusiast. View wildlife and country flora while walking to nearby Green Mountain Reservoir or take your boat or jet ski for a spin there! Try fly fishing the Gold Medal trout waters of the Blue River or enjoy a peaceful canoe or paddleboat ride, only 100 yards from the lodge. The nearby Eagle's Nest Wilderness area is great for hiking; or for the more adventuresome, raft the nearby Colorado and Blue Rivers. Hunt in Arapahoe National Forest in season. Or just relax and enjoy peace and quiet and the beautiful views.

Location: From I-70 take Highway 9 north for 17 miles out of Silverthorne. At Green Mountain Reservoir/Heeney sign, turn left on Heeney Road and go one and a half miles, on the right.

2 Cabins with Kitchens
2 Lodging Rooms
1 Fireplace
Central Campfire Area

Lobby Phone
Bed & Breakfast Available
Elevation: 8100
Credit Cards: VM
2 people a night: $60 - $100
Open: 5/20 to 11/20

Debra Gregory-Mitchener & Dale Mitchener, Ownrs
1534 Heeney Rd 30
Silverthorne CO 80498
970/468-8497 & Fax
888/8MELODY (865-5639)
800/468-8495

At the resort:

At resort or within 15 minutes:

Paradox Lodge

If you crave peace and quiet where the air is always clean and fresh, this is the place. Paradox Lodge overlooks the Snake River and is surrounded by the Arapaho National Forest on a 37-acre secluded alpine location. The completely furnished deluxe cabins have kitchens and sleep up to four (five with a roll-away). The four home-stay rooms are non-smoking and pet-free. Watch the clear, bright night stars from the wood-fired, community hot tub. All accommodations include breakfast to start your day right. Be sure to try a cinnamon roll for breakfast — they are quite delicious. Connie adds a bowlful of healthy ingredients (hidden from your taste buds).

Hike or cross-country ski right from your cabin door, or traverse the mountain bike and four-wheel drive trails. Paradox Lodge is just a few miles from Keystone and many other Summit County ski areas. In Montezuma Valley, explore the historic mining district, including the numerous old gold and silver mines and ghost town sites. Summer brings a profusion of wildflowers, wildlife and music and balloon festivals, among other activities, to the area.

Location: Between Keystone and Montezuma on Montezuma Road (County Road 5) 5 miles east of Keystone, 13 miles from I-70 exit 205.

3 Cabins with Kitchens
4 Lodging Rooms
3 Woodstoves
Central Woodstove
Central Campfire Area

Lobby Phone
Bed & Breakfast Available
Non-Smoking Units Available
Recreation Room
Elevation: 10050
Credit Cards: VMAD
2 people a night: $55 - $120
Open: All Year

George & Connie O'Bleness, Owners
5040 Montezuma Road
Dillon CO 80435
970/468-9445
970/262-6466 Fax
E-mail: 71501.530@compuserve.com

At the resort:

At resort or within 15 minutes:

Tiger Run Resort Chalets

Snug in a scenic fork of the pristine Blue and Swan Rivers, Tiger Run has fully furnished and modern chalets featuring landscaped yards, cable television, patios, paved roads and parking. All chalets are non-smoking.

A laundromat and convenience store are on-site. In the summertime, sail on Lake Dillon, river-raft, hike, horseback ride, bike and fish for trout on nearby streams and the private lake at Tiger Run. Play tennis and golf, or ride a train and a hot air balloon! Local jeep tours will take you to deserted mining camps, through breath-taking fields of high alpine wildflowers above timberline at 13,000'. In the winter, downhill and cross country ski at Breckenridge and Vail, ice skate, sleigh ride, and ice fish. Snowmobile groomed trails to high meadows with fantastic, scenic vistas. After a day of activity, relax in the indoor, heated pool and hot tub in the luxurious clubhouse.

RV enthusiasts may rent one of 175 paved sites by the night, week, or month. Indoor and outdoor meeting areas are also available.

Location: Three miles north of Breckenridge on Highway 9.

25 Cabins with Kitchens
Central Campfire Area

Lobby Phone
All Non-Smoking in Units
Recreation Room
Elevation: 9300
Credit Cards: VMD
2 people a night: $70 - $150
Open: All Year

Russell, Lisa, & Jack, Jeannette Whitt
85 Tiger Run Rd (CR 315)
Breckenridge CO 80424
970/453-9690
800/895-9594
970/453-6782 Fax

At the resort:

At resort or within 15 minutes:

Telluride Area

Including Norwood — Map: M-5 & L-3

Snug in a box canyon along the San Miguel River, **Telluride** offers both superb downhill skiing and many outdoor adventures in a pristine wilderness. The first thing you'll notice when arriving in town are the lofty, jagged peaks, some reaching to nearly 14,000' in elevation, towering over the quaint Victorian town. Like many other small mountain towns, Telluride came into existence because of gold and silver strikes in 1875. In the 1880s, Telluride got its name when a rare sulfurous element, tellurium, appeared in local gold deposits. From the early days, this tiny town had a reputation for "hell-raising" with its gambling and a red light district, prompting the nickname "to-hell-u-ride." Though those wild days are in the past, adventures still abound here. Nowadays, you can downhill and cross-country ski, snowmobile and trek into the back country in the winter. In the summer, explore nature on foot, horseback or mountain bike. You'll find great fishing on the Dolores and San Miguel Rivers as well as at Trout and Woods Lakes. Those who love to four-wheel drive will find plenty of scenic, high mountain passes to traverse, including the stunning trip over Ophir Pass into Silverton. Telluride is the town of festivals, including the Bluegrass Festival in late June, the Jazz Celebration in early August, the Film Festival in early September and the Hang Gliding Festival in late September. The small town of **Norwood**, 30 miles northwest of Telluride, is much more rural and laid back.

Fun Things To Do

- Telluride Golf Club (970) 728-6366
- Telluride Historical Museum (970) 728-3344

Annie's Country Bed & Breakfast

The house specialties at Annie's are peace, quiet and sourdough bread and pastries! Built during the lean years following the First World War, this working ranch has seen only a few changes for the sake of convenience such as electricity, indoor plumbing and central heat, thus retaining it's historic and true country feel. The outhouse and fireplace are still in place and working, but the outhouse is used only for reading per county rules. Choose a room with either a private or shared bath. Beds in the guest rooms feature linens dried in the high country sun and pure mountain air; flannel and down for the cool nights, cotton during the warmer season. King, queen, double or single beds are available. Experience true Colorado hospitality on this "Currier & Ives" style working ranch.

Wake to the mouth-watering aroma of a full cowboy breakfast with sourdough specialties. Lunch and dinner are served on request. The common room has games and reading material available. You won't find a TV here! Fish at the property or drink in the beauty of nature from the gentle hiking trails nearby. Other activities include big game hunting, arrowhead hunting and four-wheeling. Enjoy the thousands of acres of Federal Lands from 14,000' peaks to desert terrain, either within a fifteen minute drive. The B&B is a pleasant alternative to the pricey condos of Telluride any time of the year. Take some time to visit nearby Telluride, Silverton and Ouray — each is a unique mountain town with something different to offer, from downhill and cross-country skiing to shopping to natural hot springs. Visit their Web site at http://www.telluridemm.com/norwood/annies.html.

Location: Take Highway 145 to 44ZN Road, between milepost 99-100, the take 44ZN a half a mile north. Make a right turn onto ranch lane, then .25 miles.

3 Lodging Rooms
Central Fireplace

Lobby Phone
Bed & Breakfast Available
All Non-Smoking in Units
Recreation Room
Elevation: 7014
No credit cards
2 people a night: $40
Open: All Year

Anne Shaffer, Owner
PO Box 495
551 CR 44ZN
Norwood CO 81423-0495
970/327-4331

At the resort:

At resort or within 15 minutes:

Dream Catcher /Buckhorn Lodge & Cabins

Originally named Buckhorn Lodge this historic hunting and fishing lodge, in the heart of deer and elk country, has been expanded into an outdoor enthusiast dream come true with a full range of activities. A dream catcher is a symbol of love among Native Americans, who believe the catcher filters the bad dreams & spirits so only the good ones remain. The entire resort is non-smoking. There are 2 log sided housekeeping cabins with full kitchens, private baths, gas heat and sleep up to six people; and five non-housekeeping cabins with wood-burning stove and a bathhouse nearby, these also sleep up to six people. The main lodge (Buckhorn) has 3 sleeping rooms with shared baths down the hall.

Snacks and breakfast are served daily. The Great room in the two-story main lodge has two fireplaces. The solar room is a cozy sitting room perfect for catching up on your reading. The Recreation building has board games and a television for relaxing and dreaming, with a hot tub — a comfortable place to end the day. There are four ponds for water play - enjoy swimming, fishing and row boating. There is also a small animal petting farm the children will enjoy. Horseback riding trail rides start from there. Next to the Lodge are Lone Cone State Wildlife Area and San Juan National Forest with mountain walking, hiking, mountain biking and four-wheel driving.

RV and tent sites are available. Pets are allowed for an extra fee. They have an indoor meeting area for group gatherings.

Location: Twenty-two miles south of Norwood, and 35 miles north of Dolores on Route 526.

2 Cabins with Kitchens
5 cabins without Kitchens
4 Lodging Rooms
5 Woodstoves
Central Fireplace
Central Campfire Area

Lobby Phone
Bed & Breakfast Available
All Non-Smoking in Units
Recreation Room
Elevation: 8000
Credit Cards: VM
2 people a night: $44 - $100
Open: 4/15 to 11/15

Debra Coliins, Owner
Star Route 256
Norwood CO 81423
970/749-7493

At the resort:

At resort or within 15 minutes:

Lone Cone Elk Ranch Bed & Breakfast

A bed and breakfast guest ranch, Lone Cone Elk Ranch is open year round. The ranch is located in the small agricultural town of Norwood where cattle ranches and farms dot the landscape. The complete downstairs of the two-story home is yours during your stay. It includes two bedrooms, a bathroom with a shower, a spacious living area with a fireplace and a private entrance. There is a television in the common area family room for your convenience.

Choose between two options: the bed and breakfast plan which includes accommodations and breakfast, but no ranch activities; or the guest ranch plan which includes home-cooked meals, accommodations and ranch activities. A hot tub is planned for 1997. Listen to our bull elk bugle in the fall and watch the baby calves in the spring. Other ranch activities center on fishing, hiking, wildlife watching, taking photos and relaxing in some of the most beautiful areas the San Juan Mountains have to offer. Inquire about their pack trips for a real wilderness experience. In the fall, Lone Cone Elk Ranch specializes in trophy deer and elk hunting on both private and national forest hunting grounds. This is a wonderful chance to experience first-hand what life is like on a working ranch.

Lone Cone Elk Ranch likes to custom plan activities to your interests, so you can try it all or just plain relax.

Location: One mile west of Norwood, take Grand Avenue in town which turns into Z42 Road at the west edge of Norwood.

4 Lodging Rooms
Central Fireplace

Lobby Phone
Bed & Breakfast Available
All Non-Smoking in Units
Recreation Room
Elevation: 7000
No credit cards
2 people a night: $40
Open: All Year

Sharon & Bob Hardman, Owners
PO Box 220
4200 Z Rd
Norwood CO 81423-0220
970/327-4300

At the resort:

At resort or within 15 minutes:

Winter Park

Map: E-14

Located in the beautiful Fraser Valley and enclosed by the Arapaho National Forest, **Winter Park** is home to numerous activities. Don't be fooled by the name because Winter Park is also a summer playground. You'll discover an exhilarating alpine slide, excellent fishing, breath-taking hiking, fun white-water rafting and dazzling scenery. There is also an extensive mountain bike trail system covering some 500 miles of mapped trails and 200 miles of marked trails using old logging and ranching roads sure to delight two-wheeler beginners or experts. Drive over the spectacular Berthoud Pass which crosses the Continental Divide at 11,301'. Or take the Rollins Pass Road in a four-wheel drive, following the original railway over the Divide which was used for 24 years until the Moffat Tunnel was completed in 1927. Anglers will be drawn to both the beautiful settings and the rainbow, brook, mackinaw and cutthroat trout and kokanee salmon in the lakes and rivers of the Arapaho National Forest.

Fun Things to Do

- Alpine Slide (970) 726-5514
- Grand County Historical Museum (970) 725-3939
- Pole Creek Golf Course (970) 726-8847

Sitzmark Lodge Chalets/Cabins & RV Park

Open year round, Sitzmark offers plenty of outdoor fun. The secluded, housekeeping chalet-cabins sleep six and have fully equipped kitchenettes, fireplaces and cable television. Cabins have two double beds, refrigerator, microwave, and cable television. Linens are provided for both the chalets and cabins. Maid service is available upon request.

Fish on the private, stocked trout lake and along the Frasier River during the summer. Rent a horse from the nearby stables or bring your own to ride in Arapahoe National Forest's natural wonders. Hike on the many trails as well. Nearby, enjoy cookouts under the pines, the heated swimming pool, the playground and the full service restaurant. Try the Alpine Slide in Winter Park for downhill summer fun, whitewater rafting, mountain biking, four-wheel driving, playing miniature golf and exploring local museums are all part of the Winter Park experience. Of course, in the winter, the downhill skiing at Winter Park and Mary Jane ski areas is a major attraction. Other activities include snow-cat tours, inner tubing and horse-drawn sleigh rides.

Pets are allowed. A rustic RV and camping park is planned.

Location: On Highway 40, at milepost 228.

2 Cabins with Kitchens
4 cabins without Kitchens

Pay Phone(s)
Elevation: 9000
Credit Cards: VMAD
2 people a night: Call for Rates
Open: All Year

Harold L Baker, Owner
PO Box 65
78253 Hwy 40
Winter Park CO 80482-0065
970/726-5453

Athe resort:

At resort or within 15 minutes:

Snow Mountain Ranch®/YMCA of the Rockies

On a vast 4,950 forested acres near the western entrance to Rocky Mountain National Park, Snow Mountain Ranch has large, private modern housekeeping cabins equipped with bedding, linens, towels, cooking utensils and dishes. The cabins include two to five bedrooms and fireplaces, while the lodge rooms sleep up to six people. Ask about the new 79-room Indian Peaks Lodge and the new 8-bedroom Heritage Reunion Cabin. From summer youth programs with craft classes, talent shows and archery lessons, to winter sleigh rides and ice fishing, Snow Mountain is designed for family fun.

For your convenience, the ranch has a gift shop, restaurant/snack bar and library. Stay on site to swim in the large indoor pool, relax in the sauna, practice on the climbing wall, play tennis and miniature golf or roller skate in the skating rink. Snow Mountain Ranch sponsors numerous activities, such as family and youth programs, hiking, horseback riding and cross-country skiing. Rent skis at the complete Nordic ski center in the winter for trips to nearby Winter Park and SilverCreek ski areas.

The ranch can accommodate groups of 1,500 people at its conference facilities — ideal for either a small seminar or a huge family reunion. Full hookup RV sites are also available. Pets are allowed to accompany cabin guests only.

Location: Between Winter Park and Granby on Highway 40, near milepost 219.

39 Cabins with Kitchens
7 Vacation Homes
260 Lodging Rooms
46 Fireplaces
Central Fireplace
Central Campfire Area

Pay Phone(s)
All Non-Smokingin Units
Recreation Room
Elevation: 8800
No credit cards
2 people a night: $20 - $253
Open: All Year

Kent Meyer, Managing Dir.
PO Box 169
Winter Park CO 80482-0169
303/443-4743 Denver local
970/726-4628
303/449-6781 Fax

At the resort:

At resort or within 15 minutes:

For definitions of glyphs, see page 2. Numbers in table indicate driving time in minutes to activities near the resort.

For definitions of glyphs, see page 2. Numbers in table indicate driving time in minutes to activities near the resort.

Resort	Town/Area	Page																				
Fireside Cabins & RV Park	Estes Park Area	81	•						•	•	10	1	5	10		10	•					
Fireside Inn	Pagosa Springs	178	•			•		•			5	•	10	10	10	10	10				10	5
Five Branches Camper Cabins & Camper Park	Durango & Vallecito Lake	56		•			io	•	•	•		•	•			•	•					•
Foothills Lodge	South Fork Area	236	•					•				5	5		5	10	10			15	•	15
Forest Creek Cabins	Collegiate Peaks Area	25									15	5	15	3	3	15	5	15		15		5
Forest Lakes Chalets	Durango & Vallecito Lake	57	•			$	i					•	10			1	•			•	•	•
G & M Cabins	Lake City	149				$					10	2	10		3	15	•	2				15
G R Bar Ranch Cabins	Grand Mesa Area	126										•	•			•	•	•				•
Gingerbread Estate Cottages	Central City to Georgetown	22										15	15			15						
Glen Echo Resort	Poudre River Canyon Area	207		•	•	•	io		•	•		•	15			15	15					15
Glen Eden Resort	Steamboat Springs Area	249	•		•		io	•			•	•	5		•	15	•	10		1	15	15
Glen Isle Resort Lodge & Cabins	South Park Area	243			•	$	i				5	•	1				•			•		15
Golden Eagle Ranch	Eagle County	69				•		•				•				•	•					•
Goldminer Hotel, Rocky Ledge Cabin	Peak-to-Peak Scenic Highway	188	•		•		i					1	5			5	•	•	5	•		
Goodnight's Lonesome Dove Cabins & Campground	South Fork Area	237	•	•		•	io	•	•	•		1	1		10	10	5		15	•	•	5
Grand Mesa Lodge	Grand Mesa Area	127		•		•						•	5			•	•					15
Granny's Inn Montezuma Bed & Breakfast	Summit County	257			•		i					15		15			•	15	15	•		
Green Mountain Cabins & Boat Rentals	Summit County	258				•						•				•	•			•	•	10
Green Mountain Inn	Summit County	259		•	•	$	i					1				1	•			•	•	10
Green Snow Oasis Cabins & Shop	Mesa Verde Area	166				$						•	10				•					•
Green Willow Motel Cottages	Pikes Peak Area	194									1	•	5				5					
Groundhog Fishing Camp & Outfitter	Mesa Verde Area	167		•				•	•	•		•	•			•	•					•
Gypsy Terrace Bed & Breakfast	Poudre River Canyon Area	208	•		•			•				•	15		•	15	10					15
Hahn's Peak Guest Ranch	Steamboat Springs Area	250		•	•	$		•			7	1	1			1	•	1		•	•	1
Hidden Valley Ranch & Campground	Royal Gorge Area	224	•	•	•	•	io	•	•	•		•	•				•					•
Highland Haven Creekside Inn	Evergreen	101	•	•	•		i				15	•	15	5		5	15					15
Historic El Colorado Lodge	Pikes Peak Area	195					o				•	10	3				5					
Historic Ute Pass Cabins & Motel	Pikes Peak Area	196	•				io				5	15	10				5			15		
Idlewilde Cottages by the River	Estes Park Area	82	•									•	2	15		15						
Indian Meadows Lodge	Poudre River Canyon Area	209		•	•	$	io	•	•	•		•	5		•		1					•
Inn at Boxer Ranch	Poudre River Canyon Area	210	•	•	•		io	•				•					•			•		10
Inn of Glen Haven	Estes Park Area	83			•		i				15	•	•	15		15	•					15
Island Acres Motel & Log Lodges	Gunnison Area	135						•				•	15	5	5	15		2				
Josey's Mogote Meadow	Conejos River Canyon	40				$	io		•	•		•					15					15
Kelly Place B&B and Archælogical Preserve	Mesa Verde Area	168		•	•		io	•					•				•	•				•
Kickapoo Lodge	Grand Lake & Granby Area	113				•						•	5	15	5	•	10					

For definitions of glyphs, see page 2. Numbers in table indicate driving time in minutes to activities near the resort.

Resort	Town/Area	Page																				
Knotty Pine Lodge	Glenwood Springs Area	103					i				3	1	15	10	10		•	5	10	5	10	
Lake Fork Resort	Gunnison Area	136		•	•	$	io	•				5	10			5				•		15
Lake Haven Resort	Durango & Vallecito Lake	58		•		$						•	5			•	15				15	15
Lakeview Resort Cabins, Suites, Lodge Rooms	Lake City	150				$	i		•			•	•		15	•	•	•				•
Last Frontier Lodge	Black Canyon Area	14	•	•	•	•	o	•				5	•			•	•			10		15
Lazy J Resort & Rafting Company	Royal Gorge Area	225		•	•	•	io		•	•	•	•	•		•		•					•
Lazy R Cottages	Estes Park Area	84	•									1	5	10	10	10				5	15	
Lazy Ranch Bed & Breakfast	Eagle County	70		•	•	$	i	•			10	•	•	10	10		•	10	5	•	5	•
Ley-Z-B at Sapinero	Gunnison Area	137		•	•	•	io		•	•		•	15			•	•					•
Limon KOA & Kamping Kabins™	I-70 East	146		•		•			•	•	•	2		5								15
Lodge at San Isabel	Pueblo, Colo. City, Westcliffe	217			•	$	i	•			15	•	15			•	•			•	•	•
Logwood Lodge B&B, The Verheyden Inn	Durango & Vallecito Lake	59			•		i				5	•	2	5	15		3	5	15	10	15	10
Lone Cone Elk Ranch Bed & Breakfast	Telluride Area	267			•	•	i	•				10	5							•	•	•
Lone Wolf Lodge	Durango & Vallecito Lake	60				$						5	5			5	15			•	10	15
Lonesome Dove Cottages	Grand Lake & Granby Area	114	•			$						5	1	10	1	5	10			•	•	15
Lost Canyon Lake Lodge	Mesa Verde Area	169	•	•	•		io					3				15	•			7		5
Lost Canyon Resort	Gunnison Area	138				•	o					•	5	15	5		•	5		15	15	15
Love Ranch	Collegiate Peaks Area	26				•					5	•	5		10		15					15
Machin's Cottages in the Pines	Estes Park Area	85				•						5	5	15		15						
MarDei's Mountain Retreat Bed & Breakfast	Summit County	260	•		•		i				15	5	10	10	5	5	5	5	10	10	5	15
Matterhorn Cabins, Motel & Tours	Lake City	151				•						2	10		4	15	•	•				15
Melody Lodge	Summit County	261				•		•				2			15	5	•			10	10	10
Mended Wing Guest House	Steamboat Springs Area	251	•		•						7	2	2			2	2	2		•	2	•
Molas Lake Park, Camper Cabins & Campground	Silverton	230		•		•		•	•	•		•	•			•	•	15				•
Moncrief Mountain Ranch & Lodge	Lake City	152	•		•		io	•				•	•		15	5	•	5		•	•	5
Mooredale Ranch Resort	South Park Area	244	•		•	$	io	•			•	•	•				•					•
Mount Elbert Lodge & Cabins	Collegiate Peaks Area	27			•	$	i					•			10	15	•			•		
Mountain Cabin Rentals	Collegiate Peaks Area	28					i					•	7		15		•		5	3	1	1
Mountain Greenery Resort	Poudre River Canyon Area	211		•	•	$	i		•			•					15	5		15		15
Mountain Haven Inn & Cottages	Estes Park Area	86	•				i				10	•	5	10	10	10				10		
Mountain Home Lodge	Conejos River Canyon	41	•	•	•		i	•				•	10				•			•	•	•
Mountain Lakes Lodge	Grand Lake & Granby Area	115				$	o					•	5	15	15	3	•			•	•	15
Mule Creek Outfitters & M Lazy C Ranch	Pikes Peak Area	197			•		io	•	•	•		15	•			15	•			•	•	•
National Park Resort Cabins & Campground	Estes Park Area	87	•			$			•	•	10	2	1	12	10	12	15					15
New Castle/Glenwood Springs KOA	Glenwood Springs Area	104		•	•	•	o		•	•		•	15		15	5	•					
Nonehshe Cabins	Grand Lake & Granby Area	116										1	1	10		1	•			•	•	15

For definitions of glyphs, see page 2. Numbers in table indicate driving time in minutes to activities near the resort.

For definitions of glyphs, see page 2. Numbers in table indicate driving time in minutes to activities near the resort.

For definitions of glyphs, see page 2. Numbers in table indicate driving time in minutes to activities near the resort.

Resort	Town/Area	Page																				
Ute Trail River Ranch	Pikes Peak Area	203				$	i	•				•				10	•					
Valhalla Resort	Estes Park Area	95	•								•	5	2	10		10				5		
Vallecito Resort	Durango & Vallecito Lake	65		•		•	io		•	•		•	10			3	5					15
Van Eden Ranch Retreat, B&B, Mountain Cabin	Central City to Georgetown	23	•		•		io	•			15		•		15		•	15		•		•
Western Recreation Ranch	Black Canyon Area	17				•	i	•	•			•	•			•	•					•
Western Riviera Cabins & Motel	Grand Lake & Granby Area	120	•									•	1	5	1	•	3			3	•	15
Whispering Pines Resort	Royal Gorge Area	226		•		$			•	•		•	15		•		•					15
Whistling Elk Ranch	Steamboat Springs Area	254	•					•				•	•			15	•			•	5	•
Wildhorn Inn & RV Park	Pikes Peak Area	204				•		•	•			10	10			10	5			15		5
Willowtail Springs	Mesa Verde Area	174					i					•	10			15				•		10
Winding River Guest Ranch	Steamboat Springs Area	255			•		o	•			5	•	10				5			•	10	
Win-Mar Cabins	Collegiate Peaks Area	35										1	15		3	1	1	15		15	15	3
Wit's End Guest Ranch	Durango & Vallecito Lake	66	•		•		i				•	•	•			5	•	•		•	•	•
Woodlake Park Cabins & Campground	Lake City	156				•	o		•	•		•	3		5	3	•	5				15
Woodlands on Fall River	Estes Park Area	96	•								10	•	4	7	5	7				15		
Yogi Bear's Jellystone Park at Estes	Estes Park Area	97					o		•	•	•	15	15	15	15	15	•					
Yogi Bear's Jellystone Park Camp-Resort	Royal Gorge Area	227	•	•	•		i		•	•	•	2	2	15	•		5					5
Yolande Placer Cabins	Aspen & Crystal River Valley	11						•	•			•	1			5	•					

For definitions of glyphs, see page 2. Numbers in table indicate driving time in minutes to activities near the resort.

About The Authors

Hilton and Jenny Fitt-Peaster spend the entire summer visiting almost every cabin, cottage, lodge and country bed & breakfast resort in Colorado. They have been doing this for 9 years and are acknowledged as the foremost experts on this subject.

In 1988, the authors founded the Colorado Cabin*Resort* and Lodge Associations, which merged with the Colorado Campground Association in 1991 to become the Colorado Association of Campgrounds, Cabins & Lodges. The Fitt-Peaster's served as the association's executive directors for nearly 20 years.

For 18 years Jenny and Hilton with their daughter Rebekah have published annually *THE COLORADO DIRECTORY of Camping, Cabins, Lodges, Fun Things To Do.* They also own and operate Colorado Cabin Resort & Campground Realty, Inc. — the only real estate brokerage in Colorado specializing exclusively in these types of properties statewide since 1983.

By an industry-wide vote in 1995, Jenny was elected as an inaugural director-at-large of the new Colorado Travel & Tourism Authority. She was re-elected in 1996 and in 1997 and continues to serve on its board and executive committee.

In 1992 the authors established Rocky Mountain Vacation Publishing, Inc. to publish the first edition of this unique book.